LEARNING:
ANALYSIS AND APPLICATION

LEARNING:
Analysis and Application

by

JOHN F. TRAVERS

SCHOOL OF EDUCATION
BOSTON COLLEGE GRADUATE SCHOOL

DAVID McKAY COMPANY, INC.

NEW YORK

To my wife,
Barbara

Preface

No PROBLEM HAS PLAGUED educators and psychologists in recent years more than the process by which the human being learns. Recognition that learning is one of the basic operations of the human has stimulated educators and psychologists to initiate extensive and detailed examinations of the learning process.

Ironically, in spite of man's concern with his own nature, learning as the subject of analysis and research is a relatively modern development. In 1890, William James's *Principles of Psychology* was published. This text, which quickly became a classic, had no chapter devoted to a consideration of learning. But a growing appreciation of the value of studies of learning has led to a mutually rewarding relationship between educator and psychologist.

The educator follows closely the findings and interpretations of psychology and so hopes to improve curriculum, materials, methods of instruction, human relations, and guidance. The psychologist sees the school as an obvious laboratory to test his ideas. It is a common interest in the learning process that links both disciplines.

Yet this interest, as theoretical and sophisticated as it might occasionally appear, is no abstract exercise in futility. Consider the American public school system. The organization of the school, the methods of instruction, and the materials utilized, are, to the average person, strictly routine determinations. Yet underlying each of these decisions is a definite commitment to a particular psychology of learning.

Perhaps the staff, both teaching and administrative, is unaware of any psychological orientation. Certainly parents are ignorant of any such commitment. Nevertheless, it cannot be overemphasized that someone, at some time, has adopted a specific psychology of learning for the entire school system. A value judgment was made. *This* psychology of learning was thought superior to *that*.

Consequently, materials and methods of instruction are chosen that reflect the learning theory that is most appealing. Such materials and techniques, if selected by an adherent of one school of psychology, may seem equally as attractive to the adherent of some conflicting psychology. But, certain materials, and the like, are preferred because they seem to facilitate the attainment of goals that are psychologically sound. So a psychology of learning is instrumental in decisions about essential elements of the school system.

To be effective in such practical decisions, the results of learning research must be clearly applicable to human beings in a social setting. Otherwise, research and practice will travel dual highways, never meeting. It is only when research and practice meet and complement each other that the benefits are mutually rewarding to both education and psychology.

Yet, the very ease with which the results of research into the learning process may be put into educational use poses a serious problem. Most investigations of learning have been with animals, and it is quite simple to apply the findings of animal research to human learning without adequate acknowledgment of the great gap that separates man from animal. Avoiding such a danger is a necessity, and still one sympathizes with the researcher.

In his endeavor to adhere rigidly to scientific data, he is reluctant to insert his own interpretations into his findings before they are applied to human learning. Such a procedure is controversial at best, dangerous almost always. Conant (*The Education of American Teachers,* 1963, p. 134) comments on this problem when he discusses the professional preparation of teachers.

If those who write and read books in psychology were not always concerned with finding the "key to the mystery every man faces" and keen to use it, a good introduction to the establishment of a new science might be presented with little or no reference to human beings. As it is, most authors make the extrapolation from animal experimentation to human behavior seem so self-evident as to blur some important philosophic and methodological issues.

Experiments that are designed to observe animal reaction in tension-reduction circumstances have a severely limited applicability to the educational milieu. Food deprivation is a means of motivation far different from conscious goal-seeking by students. Although animal experimentation will continue to yield valuable information about learning, the time has come to concentrate research upon the school and study human beings—who are able to communicate with each other—in a social environment.

While animal experimentation has aided in the growth of knowledge about learning, the assumption that humans function in exactly the same manner as animals is invalid. That there is a degree of similarity is indisputable, but to transfer experimental conclusions from animal to human with no admission of difference is misleading and unscientific. Properly used, animal experiments offer interesting possibilities for explaining the more mechanical aspects of learning.

Yet any analysis of the human learning process offers many additional obstacles. For example, the human being is capable of several different types of learning. He may exhibit behavior which indicates that motor learning has occurred, or rote learning, or comprehension, or problem-solving. Each of these behavioral patterns seems to represent a distinct kind of learning. The learning process may, or may not, be identical for each category. But the modification of behavior that results is totally distinct for each category. There are also many subdivisions possible for each category.

As an illustration, comprehension, at first glance, seems to imply an assimilation and understanding of verbal materials. Students should do more than acquire and retain knowledge, however; they should also apply it to solve problems, transfer it to related disciplines, and, perhaps most important, they should recombine the parts of previously learned material into new, creative forms.

These various types of learning within the single cognitive category show the wide range of learning of which the human is capable. Much the same is true for each of the above learning categories. Even motor learning, which the average person considers to be a relatively simple process, exhibits many discrete subdivisions.

Usually, a motor skill is learned by mastering each part of which it is composed. Once the separate elements are learned, they are then reunited into a meaningful whole in order to aid precision, speed, and mastery. Consider a figure skater or a golfer in action. An inner coordination that far exceeds that needed to master each act involved is required. And, to add to the difficulty of analyzing motor learning, some mental commitment is unquestionably involved since the learner not only manipulates muscles, but he must *understand* the relationship of parts to whole, and he must also comprehend the goal he is striving to attain.

Inherent in these examples of both comprehension and motor learning are many unanswered questions about how the human being learns even the most rudimentary kind of skill. This book will attempt to grapple with these questions and help the reader to discern the complexity of learning at a level above that of the animal.

Perhaps the most decisive of the various methods by which the human adjusts to his environment is learning. Given the controlled learning atmosphere of the school, there is every indication that the time has come for increased research within the school environment. Here, every sort of human learning occurs; the hierarchical arrangement of the learning process is evident even to the most untrained eye.

Therefore, this book is intended to alert the future teacher to the intricacies of learning, and to caution the experienced teacher against the dangers of complacency. The more that teachers know about the psychology of learning, the better can they strive for excellence in their teaching.

Although the purpose of this text is to assist teachers, it is not a book directed mainly at practice. Rather, it focuses on research and theory, and *suggests* application to practice. If teachers are acquainted with the results of research, and can grasp the significance of theory, their teaching should escape the ruts and pitfalls of unexamined methodology.

From everything that is now known, human learning appears to operate in essentially the same manner for all types of learning, and for all ages. The characteristics of the learning process remain basically the same. What does change is the activity that accompanies the various kinds of learning. By proceeding from learning product to learning process, it is hoped that the reader will imitate the professor who "can never better distinguish himself in his work than by encouraging a clever pupil, for the true discoverers are among them, as comets amongst the stars."

JOHN F. TRAVERS

Contents

LEARNING:
ANALYSIS AND APPLICATION

CHAPTER 1

The Nature of Learning

THE DEFINITION OF LEARNING

HOW TO DEFINE learning is a question that has frustrated educators and psychologists for as long as they have recognized its importance. For the layman, the problem is not so acute. The average person sees learning as the acquisition of a tangible skill or body of knowledge. Although appealing, such simplicity disturbs teachers and researchers. If the definition of learning is to be confined to knowledge and skills, there is the implication that learning *products* are the sole outcome.

Some Key Questions

On the other hand, most educators and psychologists visualize learning as a *process* and not a product. The learning product is a result of the learning process and it is the *how* of human learning that most interests investigators. What are the reasons that a particular environmental pattern of stimuli results in different products in individuals who are apparently similar in native capacity and goal-orientation? What happens within these persons—what is the learning process? Do individuals organize the learning situation in a radically different manner? Do they react to certain key elements of the learning field, and, if so, how and why? How do they organize their behavior in their reaction to pressures from the environment? These are some of the questions that learning as a process raises. And it is these questions that must eventually be answered if knowledge of learning is to advance beyond the present primitive stages.

In their efforts to define learning both as a process and a product, psychologists have reflected their personal philosophy of the nature of man. As Allport (1961, p. 84) says:

> Theories of learning (like much else in psychology) rest on the investigator's conception of the nature of man. In other words, every learning theorist is a philosopher, though he may not know it. To put the matter more concretely, psychologists who investigate (and theorize about) learning start with some preconceived view of the nature of human motivation.

As the psychologist sees man, so does he define his process of learning. But, because his endeavors seem inadequate, one wonders how seriously he regards his definition. One believes that the psychologist often formulates a definition merely because it is expected of him. Perhaps it is unreasonable to anticipate more. After all, he is attempting to define a field of study, to indicate the core, and to delimit the boundaries of a subject about which his information is very limited.

Some Representative Definitions

Nevertheless, the trials continue. And it is worthwhile to appraise the definitions offered by several leading authorities in the field. The following excerpts are representative of the search for a common denominator that would be universally acceptable:

Kingsley and Garry (1957, p. 12)—Learning is the process by which behavior (in the broader sense) is originated or changed through practice or training.

Bugelski (1956, p. 120)—According to the present line of speculation, then, learning is the process of the formation of relatively permanent neural circuits through the simultaneous activity of the elements of the circuits—to-be; such activity is of the nature of change in cell structures through growth in such a manner as to facilitate the arousal of the entire circuit when a component element is aroused or activated.

Blair et al. (1962, p. 103)—What is learning? Any change of behavior which is a result of experience, and which causes people to face later situations differently may be called learning.

Handbook of Research on Teaching (1963, p. 386)—Learning may be conceived of as a change, due to experience, in the students' ways of thinking, feeling, and acting.

Kolesnik (1963, p. 215)—Learning may be defined in nontechnical terms as the acquisition, retention, and application of knowledge, skills, attitudes, ways of thinking, or some other type of new response.

Encyclopedia of Educational Research (1960, p. 752)—Learning, in the context of education, refers to the growth and decay of interests, knowledge, and skills, and to the transfer of these to new situations.

Mouly (1960, p. 227)—Learning refers to those changes which take place as a result of special stimulation and does not take into consideration the changes associated with the maturation of inherited structure and predispositions, nor does it apply to such changes in the effectiveness of the individual's reactions to stimulation as might be associated with fatigue or drugs.

McGeoch and Irion (1952, p. 7)—Learning, as we measure it, is a change in performance which occurs under the conditions of practice.

Travers (1963, p. 29)—Learning is said to have occurred when a response undergoes modification on its recurrence as a result of conditions in the environment which have produced relatively permanent changes in the central nervous system.

Commins and Fagin (1954, p. 39)—In this sense, the learning process is a modification of functional tendencies.

Anderson and Gates (1950, p. 16)—Learning may be considered in its broadest sense as a process of adaptation. Through the process of learning, men acquire new ways of behaving or performing in order that they can make better adjustment to the demands of life.

Cronbach (1963, p. 71)—More precisely, learning is shown by a change in behavior as a result of experience.

Woodruff (1951, p. 59)—The process of learning is the vehicle by which the individual is changed from a bundle of potentialities to an acting organism with ideas, habits, skills, preferences, and other distinguishing personality characteristics.

All of these definitions attempt to achieve an explanation of learning that recognizes it as something that occurs within the individual and, as a result, changes the learner's behavior. Thus, we must admit that there is no common, universally accepted definition. The psychologist realizes that definitions which concentrate upon the product do not help to explain the nature of the learning process.

Recall, for a moment, a typical dictionary definition of learning (Webster's Collegiate Dictionary, 1941, p. 571):

> learning, n. 1. Acquisition of knowledge or skill. 2. Knowledge or skill received by instruction or study.

Does this definition help, in any way, the analysis of learning? If a person is able to manifest many bits of information, learning has occurred. But, is this what we mean by learning? Is this the goal of education? Can the students who "learn" in this way transfer their knowledge and techniques to the social and technical problems of the twentieth century? These questions are germane because the rapidity with which knowledge grows in both the social and scientific fields demands, not mastery of facts from students, but techniques of problem solving and the ability to transfer proven methods of attack to novel material and situations.

The Problem of Terminology

Unhappily, until quite recently, educators and psychologists overlooked a fundamental fact that was at the center of every teaching-learning situation. Few of those concerned with education agreed about the terms that were used to discuss teaching-learning problems. For example, when investigators analyze learning as a product, what exactly do they mean by knowledge? For some, it means a mastery of subject matter, but for others it is a more inclusive term that denotes complicated phenomena such as knowledge of relationships.

To aid communication within the field of education, Bloom et al. (1956) have formulated a taxonomy of educational objectives which tries to classify student behavior by carefully defining several categories into which all intended student behavior can be placed. The complete taxonomy has three parts: cognitive, affective, and psychomotor. In the cognitive domain there are six major classes:

1.00 Knowledge
2.00 Comprehension
3.00 Application
4.00 Analysis
5.00 Synthesis
6.00 Evaluation

Each class except "Application" has several subdivisions.

Here, the question may be repeated—what exactly do educators and psychologists mean by knowledge? In their effort to make the definition of knowledge more meaningful, Bloom and his associates have devised the following classifications (Bloom *et al.*, 1956, pp. 201–204):

KNOWLEDGE

1.00 *Knowledge*
Knowledge, as defined here, involves the recall of specifics and universals, the recall of methods and processes, or the recall of a pattern, structure, or setting.

1.10 *Knowledge of Specifics*
The recall of specific and isolated bits of information. The emphasis is on symbols with concrete referents.

1.11 *Knowledge of Terminology*
Knowledge of the referents for specific symbols (verbal and non-verbal).

1.12 *Knowledge of Specific Facts*
Knowledge of dates, events, persons, places, etc.

1.20 *Knowledge of Ways and Means of Dealing with Specifics*
Knowledge of the ways of organizing, studying, judging, and criticizing.

1.21 *Knowledge of Conventions*
Knowledge of characteristic ways of treating and presenting ideas and phenomena.

1.22 *Knowledge of Trends and Sequences*
Knowledge of the processes, directions, and movements of phenomena with respect to time.

1.23 *Knowledge of Classifications and Categories*
Knowledge of the classes, sets, divisions, and arrangements which are regarded as fundamental for a given subject field, purpose, argument, or problem.

1.24 *Knowledge of Criteria*
Knowledge of the criteria by which facts, principles, opinions, and conduct are tested or judged.

1.25 *Knowledge of Methodology*
Knowledge of the methods of inquiry, techniques, and procedures employed in a particular subject field as well as those employed in investigating particular problems and phenomena.

1.30 *Knowledge of the Universals and Abstractions in a Field*
Knowledge of the major schemes and patterns by which phenomena
and ideas are organized.

1.31 *Knowledge of Principles and Generalizations*
Knowledge of particular abstractions which summarize observations of phenomena.

1.32 *Knowledge of Theories and Structures*
Knowledge of the body of principles and generalizations together
with their interrelations which present a clear, rounded, and systematic view of a complex phenomenon, problem, or field.

This is, unquestionably, the most thorough and detailed venture
in the search for accuracy and precision that educators have yet undertaken. So, when anyone casually refers to "knowledge," there is
a range of classifications into which their term may be placed and
which aids in clarity. However, consider the time and effort required to organize this one aspect of the classification—the thousands
and thousands of educational objectives that must have been considered, analyzed, and classified. Consider, also, the tremendous
task of evaluating objectives to ascertain if each could be legitimately placed in one of the categories. Were there sufficient categories to encompass all of the educational objectives?

The reader's attention is drawn to these questions so that the
difficulty of defining learning may be more fully appreciated. Recall
the distinction that was made between learning as a process and
learning as a product. To define learning as a process is far more
difficult than to define learning as a product. Yet the pitfalls in defining learning as a product are apparent. The extensive divisions
and subdivisions of the *knowledge* taxonomy testify to the predicament of definition, even with the more tangible products of learning.

Despite its difficulty, attempts at definition of learning as a process
must continue. Future efforts will reflect increasingly sophisticated
methods of educational and psychological research which will test
not only the definitions of learning but also the assumptions upon
which they are based. As the investigator compares definitions with
his increasing cognizance of man himself and the products of learning, he will tend to make definitions of learning more educationally, logically, and psychologically sound than has thus far been
possible.

The Importance of Definition

We have talked about the obstacles that lie in the path of acceptable and accurate definition. However, it is important that the reader realize the difficulties, the divergent opinions, and the persisting efforts that are being made to resolve an exceedingly complex issue. For, as Allport said, learning will be defined as man is viewed. As important as this is to the philosophy of education, it is equally as important to the psychology of learning, curriculum construction, and instructional materials and methods. As the educator defines learning, so will he build his curriculum, select materials, and choose particular instructional techniques. His interpretations of learning will decide which learning products are most desirable. So, again, the significance of process is clear—it dictates the type of product that the school prefers. Definition as a process is primary; definition as a product is secondary.

Although definition is critical, many psychologists are unhappy, not only with existing definitions, but also with the attitude of those who try to explain what they mean by learning. Bugelski (1956, p. 9), in particular, criticizes this disposition by some:

Perhaps the psychologists who make light of the need for a definition of learning have made a real point. It would be better if they carried their lightness a little further and openly refused to try. To pass off the question with a semiserious definition may be more harmful than humorous since it implies that either one does know what learning is or that progress can be made without a definition.

Perhaps the uncertainty or reluctance that Bugelski mentions is characteristic of anyone who claims expertise in a subject which he cannot define.

A Working Definition

What definition does this book adopt? Basically, that learning is a process, and that the learning process must be what is meant by true learning. The acquisitions of learning are merely the outer manifestations of what has occurred within. Admittedly, our knowledge of the "within" is scanty, but to ignore, or refuse to recognize, the inner workings of the human is as foolish as it is pointless. Thus, a beginning is made by stating that learning is a process.

We can fashion assumptions about what goes on in man when he learns only by careful scrutiny of *what he has learned*. Therefore, our definition must include the *what* of learning—the learning product. From inspection of the learning product, postulates may be made about the learning process. The researcher can observe a certain behavioral pattern, compare it with radically different behavior, and then speculate about the nature of the learning that caused such different behavioral patterns. For example, recall what was said earlier in this chapter about the types of learning. A scientific appraisal of problem solving must answer the question: were these two distinctive learning outcomes the result of an identical learning process? Or were there two or more totally different learning operations functioning in these examples? By reasoning from the product, much information can be obtained about the process.

Our definition, however, is incomplete. Learning of any kind implies a change. If behavior remains unchanged, was there any learning? The question will be raised immediately: does the sheer acquisition of knowledge, particularly of a factual nature, produce behavioral changes? But does not the possession of this kind of knowledge (Bloom's knowledge of specifics) change the student's behavior in his knowledge of reality? The student who parrots the multiplication tables with little, if any, comprehension, nevertheless has changed his behavior with respect to combinations of numbers. Thus, the use of the term "learning" connotes change.

A word of caution is urged. Change, of itself, *does not imply improvement*. It is quite easy to mistake the two, especially when we think of learning solely under the direction of the school. This is what the average person does when he gives meaning to learning, that is, he pictures students sitting in a classroom and working toward desirable, worthwhile objectives that have been determined by the school and society. This is a narrow, restricted definition of learning to which no educator or psychologist could subscribe. For example, when the child learns that a tantrum will force his parents to give him what he wants, most people do not classify this behavior as learning. It is usually dismissed as outrageous, uncontrollable behavior. But let us place the identical behavioral pattern in different circumstances and attempt to predict the average person's reaction. Occasionally, a three or four year old youngster will play with friends who frighten parents with their tantrums. Our three year old comes home and decides that it might work with his parents. Thus, at the first hint of denial, he goes into his act—time for the tantrum! Much to his surprise, however, his parents not only are unfrightened, but also they take violent exception to his behavior and a swift spanking is forthcoming.

One can sense the reaction of the average observer. "Good. That will teach him." Or, "He learned his lesson that time." Such a reaction is almost certain, and the implication is clear. Behavior that manifested improvement was called learning; behavior that lacked improvement was not so designated. Yet, behavior was learned in both cases, and, as a result, behavior was changed. Therefore, it is clear that learning involves change, and the changed behavior need not necessarily be improved behavior.

Consequently, this book rests upon a definition of learning as a process that results in the modification of behavior. The resultant modification of behavior must be attributed to learning and not to changes brought about by maturation of the organism, or such agents of change as drugs, fatigue, and the like. In this definition all of the limitations that have been brought to the reader's attention are recognized and accepted. Nevertheless, it is not restricted to the nervous system for explanation, nor does it reject the place and function of the physiological processes of man. It is not bound by terms such as insight, nor does it reject them. And, most importantly, it tries to reconcile learning as a process with learning as a product. From secondary characteristics it enables investigators to probe for primary elements.

The reader should now understand the magnitude of the problem of definition and should realize that a book on learning can be categorized rather quickly by its definition of learning. This is as it should be, particularly at a time of scanty knowledge about the process itself.

Different definitions will broaden the scope of inquiry and aid in the acquisition of essential information.

CHARACTERISTICS OF THE LEARNING PROCESS

The definition of learning will determine, quite accurately, what the observer hopes to find in his analysis of a learning activity. Since it is impossible to remove ourselves from our observation, our conclusion unavoidably will be prejudiced.

Identity of Characteristics

Nonetheless, there are certain characteristics which appear in a learning situation with sufficient frequency to warrant further examination.

Thus, a person wants a particular object, or thing, that is, he is goal-oriented. As he moves toward the goal, he is frustrated—he must do something, perhaps something novel, to achieve his objective. He must learn what is needed to remove any obstacles that are in his path. Therefore, he changes his behavioral pattern and tests to determine if his modified behavior will attain the goal. If so, he is satisfied; if not, he reevaluates his behavior and modifies his reactions until he succeeds.

Frustration and reinforcement are both essential for true learning. If a person's path to a goal is not blocked, there is no learning. When a drive arises within the individual, he merely selects a response pattern that has succeeded on previous occasions. No learning is involved. The person falls into a habit system which has satisfied and will continue to satisfy a need.

The consequence of the learning sequence must also have a central position in the modified activities that lead to goal attainment. If there is no reinforcement, or reward, either extrinsic or intrinsic, the learner will react in a negative way. Either the good no longer becomes desirable to him, or the sequence of activities that lead to goal acquisition will be lost.

Both of these concepts illustrate what was meant by the earlier statement that school objectives should be educationally, logically, and psychologically sound. Why should the school system force students to achieve goals which could be easily attained under quite different circumstances? This is the danger that the concept of life-adjustment failed to avoid. The students were placed in artificial

learning situations about which most of them had definite, precon-
ceived ideas. As a result, they scarcely modified their behavior to
achieve unsound objectives.

This is also true of university teaching. Often students, in counseling sessions, complain that instructors spend class hours simply
repeating material that is contained in an assigned class text. Thus,
for two, three, or four hours a week, precious opportunities for
meaningful learning are lost for these students. They are not widen-
ing and deepening their behavioral patterns; rather, they are rely-
ing upon previous learning that was undoubtedly more mechanical.

Thus, the risks are identical for both the first-grade teacher and
the university professor. If instructors, at all levels, do not pose real
obstacles for their students, there will be no learning. Once the
obstacle has been removed, and the goal acquired, the student
should appreciate the significance of the goal in relation to his learning activities. There must be some feeling of satisfaction with the
completion of a successful response pattern. Otherwise, if the school
establishes objectives that are meaningless to the students, two reactions are likely to occur. The goal becomes worthless in the eyes of
the students and motivation is lost. Or, the sequence of learning
activities that led to the goal is quickly lost.

Although frustration and effect are basic to the learning process,
there are other characteristics that emerge from *any* learning sequence. The process is the same regardless of the *form* of the acquired learning—the learner is in a position where he must remove
barriers between himself and the goal he desires. This is not an
"accidental" type of behavior under discussion. Commins and Fagin
(1954, p. 456) state:

Learning does not occur by chance. The outcome of any behavior depends on antecedent conditions within the learner, conditions in the
learning situation, and the consequences of what the learner does. When
we talk about the psychology of the learner, we are concentrating on
him! what he brings to the situation, how he interprets the cues, what
he does, and what changes the outcome brings about in his mental organization. From this point of view, the learning process is an active,
purposeful organization of the learner's activities. We are not here concerned with learning as "acquisitions" of information or habits, nor with
connections between stimuli and responses, but with the basic tendency
of the learner to organize activity to satisfy his needs.

An Analysis of the Characteristics

In the organized sequence of activities just described, the characteristics that seem relatively consistent are: a motivated individual, an obstacle in his way, environmental stimuli which aid and prod him toward his goal, the individual's perception of his field, his response pattern, and finally, the goal itself. Many authors identify other elements but actually it is more a semantic rather than a real variation. Examination of the "steps in the learning process," or the "elements of learning," will confirm the opinion that all commentators are concerned with approximately the same features.

If the characteristics of the learning process could be illustrated they would appear as shown in Figure 1-1.

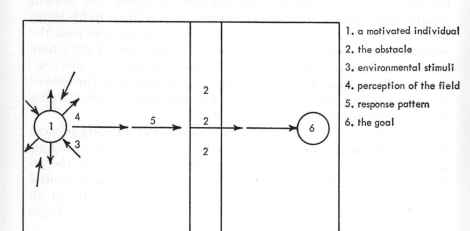

1. a motivated individual
2. the obstacle
3. environmental stimuli
4. perception of the field
5. response pattern
6. the goal

FIGURE 1-1.   *Characteristics of the Learning Process*

1. **A motivated individual.** Learning will not occur without motivation. An individual acts to satisfy a need; therefore, he is prepared to engage in activity which he hopes will reduce his feeling of dissatisfaction. (The relative merits of extrinsic versus intrinsic motivation will be discussed later.) Consequently, this need is within the person and not imposed by external sources. Sometimes the initial impetus must come from outside the person (the teacher) but, unless his need is transferred within, the goal and the activities

that lead to it will quickly be lost. Unless the student feels a need to act, he will not engage in the purposeful activity which educators desire. Educators have had, and will continue to have, great difficulty with this problem because the goals of school and society often are not the goals of youngsters. How to make the goals real and meaningful is one of the most vital chores facing educators in this century. Many appealing environmental stimuli will prod the youngster to satisfy his needs by different, and often undesirable, activity. The school must combat this trend by understanding what are the real goals of youth, and then transferring the needs that gave rise to these goals to school-determined objectives. There must be a happy compromise between the youngster's goals and the school's goals. Otherwise, educational objectives will become sterile and unreal to students.

The fundamental importance of motivation to learning is agreed upon by all psychologists. For example, Kingsley and Garry (1957, p. 197) state that activity is basic to learning and that motivation is basic to activity.

And Mouly (1960, p. 229):

Learning takes place as a result of response to stimulation. Unless the individual has some unsatisfied need or drive which makes him receptive to stimulation and causes him to act in an attempt to reduce the tension associated with this unsatisfied need, no learning will take place. Actually, the individual has many needs and purposes, only a few of which he can attend to and the direction of the learning that will take place will depend on the relative strength of the motives in relation to the nature of the situation in which he finds himself.

2. Some obstacle blocks the person's line to the goal. Learning occurs only when there is a problem frustrating the person. Regardless of the nature of the learning, the learner is blocked from his goal. The golfer wishes to drive his ball 200 yards down the middle of the fairway. This demands a smooth, powerful swing. The problem at this level of learning (motor) is how to acquire the proper swing and how to remove the awkward, unnecessary parts of his crude swing. Thus, the golfer is blocked from his goal.

Or, the student masters the rudimentary facts of a particular discipline. But, in the examination, the teacher does not ask for mere repetition of material. He presents the student with a question that rote memory alone will not answer. Now, the student is forced to examine the question; what information does he possess that will answer this particular question; must he group some parts of his knowledge in his response; if so, which parts should he combine? Thus, there is an obstacle in the path of his answering the question correctly.

In any example that could be selected to represent the characteristics of the learning process, the blocking characteristic will be fundamental. And it is here the school exercises a crucial function. For it is in the selection of obstacles that the youngster learns how to appraise a problem and choose the correct methods of attack; if the barrier is too difficult, frustration may cause the learner to break his pattern of responses and to disregard the goal. If the obstacle chosen by the school does not have the necessary blocking qualities, the student repeats previous behavior that led to a successful conclusion and there is no learning. The problem that is presented to the student must be sufficiently difficult to cause him to seek its solution by using knowledge and techniques of attack, but it should not be so difficult as to discourage him in his efforts.

3. Environmental stimuli are present in the problem situation and serve as a continuous urge to the goal. The learner finds himself in a position in which his customary responses are not satisfactory. Motivation is present since the person has an unfilled need; he discerns a goal which he believes will satisfy his need. But he cannot reach the goal—his path is blocked. He now searches his environment for clues which will help him to find a solution.

These clues, however, cannot be utilized in a one-to-one fashion but, instead, the learner must perceive the relation between stimuli and, also, the relation between the stimuli (clues) that he selects as vital and the goal that he is seeking. The importance of imposing obstacles that must be overcome to reach attainable goals is again evident. The student must be able to reach the goal by using stimuli which he can recognize and which he can combine. If he is not ready to respond to certain clues, that is, if his prior learning and experience are not adequate for this learning experience, *he will not* learn. Unattainable goals and unfit stimuli produce discipline and delinquency troubles in many classrooms.

A final, cautionary word must be mentioned about environmental stimuli. Teachers who recognize that clues are an indispensable part of learning must be alert to the danger of false signals. The examination question that stresses misleading words or the geography unit which overemphasizes motor learning (construction of a mechanical device for irrigation) and neglects the reasons for which these are needed have provided false stimuli. The student has selected, and used, through no fault of his, stimuli which are dominant in his environment and which are not appropriate to the particular goal desired. The teacher must plan so that the necessary stimuli will be sufficiently distinct for the student to grasp their significance in relation to the fixed objective.

4. The individual perceives his field. His perception depends upon his background and what he sees in this particular field. Field means the learning situation—that is, a motivated individual with a goal as well as everything in his environment that acts on the person and influences his drive toward the goal. The interaction of the characteristics is again apparent. The learner needs something; he cannot reach his goal; he examines his environment for clues; now he must decide just what stimuli he can use in the attempt to satisfy his need. Are the stimuli sufficiently clear? Can he distinguish which clues will help him to use his knowledge and techniques? Is he mature enough to recognize the relationship between stimuli and goal? Does he have the background that is necessary to respond correctly to the stimuli?

In this phase of perception, the student shows behavior that may be designated as differentiation. Just as the golfer must separate the parts of the proper swing in order to understand of what it is composed, the learner in a more abstract problem follows exactly the same procedure. He "takes apart" the problem and distinguishes the stimuli which are essential to its solution. He disregards the stimuli which are unnecessary, or false, because, if he responds to these indiscriminately, he will be forced into activity which is not purposeful. The importance of the obstacle is again seen. It must challenge, but not defeat. The environment must provide clues which will enable him to utilize his own store of information; however, these stimuli must not be excessively apparent, nor too obscure.

Still, as the learner reacts to the pressures from his environment, he realizes that this *one* alone, or that *one* alone will not lead to problem solving. He sees that they must be combined for him to succeed. After the vital elements of the situation are recognized, the learner must begin to "put things together." This process is called integration. When the golfer has learned the separate movements that are necessary for a good swing, he must combine them. When the student senses that he must add these figures but then subtract the total from another figure, he also is combining stimuli. Thus, the golfer has the "feel" of the swing, and the student "sees" the necessary steps. Differentiation and integration reflect the individual's perception of his field and will dictate the response pattern that the person uses to achieve his objective.

5. The individual settles on a response pattern. After deciding upon a specific goal, and perceiving the significant stimuli in his field, that is, those that will help him reach his goal, the individual now responds. And *he responds as a whole*. He reacts to the stimuli by utilizing past learning experience and his own unique stage of readiness. He is reacting with a purpose and is not manifesting blind, random behavior.

If his response is unsuccessful, he next reexamines the problem, searching for clues that he overlooked when he first organized his behavior. Did he select the correct stimuli? Were they combined properly? Was his response pattern appropriate for the stimuli? What is most important, however, is that the student *does* reexamine them.

Again, the reader notes the importance of the problem, or barrier. The student must feel qualified to solve the problem or discouragement will lead to surrender. The student's reaction to initial failure is crucial. If the school has fixed objectives that the student thinks he can accomplish, he will make additional readjustments. If, however, the goal seems totally unrealistic, he may not think school achievement is worth the effort. Cronbach (1963, p. 74) discusses this:

Thwarting occurs when the person fails to attain a goal. If his first try is not confirmed, he may make a new interpretation and change his action. Through such adaptive behavior, he will usually hit on some action that brings him closer to the goal. At the same time, his goal may also be modified as he changes his idea of what he can attain.

The learner may instead respond non-adaptively, stubbornly repeating the same unsuccessful act, giving up entirely, or acting erratically and thoughtlessly. To distinguish between adaptive and nonadaptive behavior is difficult, because giving up, for example, is sometimes sensible.

Even if the initial response pattern is successful, learning undoubtedly was awkward if it was a motor skill, or slow and cumbersome, if it was cognitive. Consequently, the learner continues to modify his behavior in future endeavors. He does this by a more perceptive analysis of his field, by constant discrimination of stimuli, and by eliminating superfluous responses. Finally, when he meets a similar problem on future occasions he marshals the correct response pattern in a decisive and exact response pattern.

6. The individual decides upon a particular goal to fulfill his need and initiates activity to attain this goal. Because of his experience and perception of his field, a student decides that a certain goal will satisfy his need. The goal that he settles upon must appear to him as attainable and meaningful. Note the words "must appear to him." If the school does not have the school's objectives become the student's goals, where will be the motivation for learning? Serious consideration must be given to this question, for, with increasing school drop-outs, much of the difficulty may be traced to a lack of mutual understanding of the what and why of goals by students and teachers. The school and student do not initially share the same goal-orientation and, before learning can actually begin, there must be a reconciliation of the two. Forcing youngsters to attain goals that seem totally unrelated to reality is a major cause of the educational 3-Ds: Discipline; Delinquency; and Drop-outs. If the youngster accepts educational objectives as his own, he is willing to undertake the activities that will result in the modification of behavior. Learning is purposeful; it is not random and it is not blind. But to be purposeful, it must be goal-oriented and must involve self-activity which, therefore, demands a conscious pursuit of a discernible goal.

There must also be a feeling of satisfaction attached to the achievement of a goal. This is frequently referred to as reinforcement. That is, the behavioral pattern that leads to the attainment of a goal that fulfilled a need will be strengthened and will tend to be repeated on future similar occasions. If the person's response pattern fails to achieve the goal, it will be modified until it does. Even if the goal selected by the individual is acquired, it may not be suitable for a satisfactory solution to a problem. Consequently, the person must reevaluate his entire process—the goal, proper stimuli, responses, and the like. For it is the individual who ultimately determines if the goal satisfies, if it actually fulfills his need. What satisfies person A may not satisfy person B. One student's B may be as unsatisfactory to him as another's D. But if the goal is gratifying, the entire sequence of activities is retained and is assimilated into the individual's repertoire of response capacities. This is known as the process of generalization.

Thus far the characteristics of the learning process have been differentiated and now we wish to review and integrate them so that the components of learning can be reassembled and viewed as a whole.

THE LEARNING SEQUENCE

How the Characteristics Function

An individual will modify his behavior because of a drive toward a goal which he thinks will satisfy a need. Motivation within the person causes him to seek an appropriate outlet for his energy. He now begins to direct his energy into a more organized type of activity. His restlessness leads him to search for an object, a thing, or even an idea, that serves his requirement. He chooses a particular goal from many possible goals.

Here, the individual either begins learning activity, or reverts to habit. If it is a goal that he has repeatedly acquired, there will be no opportunity to engage in learning. Repetition of past response patterns will be sufficient. If he cannot reach his goal by his usual activity, however, he must modify his behavior. This he does by examining his field—what lies between him and his objective. He critically inspects the obstacle and decides if it is within his capacity to surmount it.

Assuming that it is possible (an assumption not always warranted), he decides upon the *most* appropriate line of action. This requires an analysis and interpretation of his field. He utilizes the stimuli that are present, which he views according to his own experience and needs of the moment. He next starts to arrange the stimuli in an organized manner. He perceives a relationship among certain of the stimuli which he thinks will lead to the realization of his goal. His response design follows the arrangement that he has made of the stimuli. Thus, some stimuli seem more pertinent and important than others, and it is these which he tries to harmonize as a guide for his activity.

Next, he actually starts his movement toward the goal. Perhaps he is successful; perhaps he is not. If not, he repeats the sequence that was just described. If, however, the accomplishment of his goal satisfies the need, the learner will repeat his performance under later, similar circumstances. Eventually he will refine and fix his response pattern, and, by the process of generalization, he will merge this response sequence with his total behavioral responses.

The Learning Sequence in Operation

As an example of the learning sequence, consider the child learning to read. He observes older members of the family enjoying books, magazines, and newspapers. They can read names and titles on television. Gradually, there develops within the youngster a desire to read. But he is blocked. There is an obstacle—he does not know the sound and combinations of letters, nor the meaning of words and their combination into sentences, paragraphs, and stories.

Motivation drives him to seek a goal to satisfy his need. His goal is to learn to read. But how can he satisfy this want? When youngsters first manifest this need, they are about four years old. A family that is aware of this interest will surround a youngster with colorful, appealing children's books. They will not force these books on the child, but will let them act as environmental stimuli. The child, in a year, probably is ready for kindergarten or the first grade. Here he sees an attainable goal—learning to read under the direction of the teacher.

Now he begins to work toward his goal. The teacher will insure that the pupils have a sight vocabulary of approximately 250 words before she initiates formal instruction. This background of sight words will enable all of the class to have had experience with whole words before differentiation occurs. The teacher broadens the perceptual field of her class by steadily adding to their sight vocabulary.

She presents pictures of objects to the class and identifies each one. This is usually done on a flannelboard. Then the word that symbolizes the object is printed beneath it. The boys and girls study the word and associate it with the picture of the object. They pronounce the word. Finally, the word alone is shown to the class, and, if a firm association has been made, the class will pronounce the word with no visual aid. This can be shown as follows:

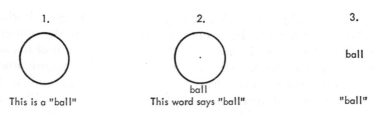

This presentation is oversimplified. But the attempt to aid the pupils' perception and the use of controlled environmental stimuli are psychologically sound.

Next, the teacher begins the process of differentiation. The child's attention is drawn to parts of the stimuli, that is, the individual letters of which the word is composed. Since the goal of the teacher's instruction is rapid, meaningful reading, she makes sure that the children undertake analysis of words they know and understand (there is a difference between knowing a word and understanding its meaning).

Children usually begin phonetic analysis with initial consonants. For example—this letter goes below the line and curls—g. There are two sounds to this—gem and get. (This is a good example of the need to combine analysis with meaning.) The same procedure holds true for middle and final consonants, and long and short vowels. These are built into syllables and then into words.

During the process the child is steadily refining his response pattern. He starts the process of integration by putting the letters together to make words. He will make many mistakes. For example, he might confuse a and o, or b and d, but then his immediate goal —correct pronunciation of a given word—will elude him and he must again modify his behavior. But he is slowly reaching his ultimate goal—learning to read. He is combining letters into words, words into sentences, and sentences into paragraphs until, at last, he can read a complete story. His learning is now made permanent by generalization.

The youngster who learns to read resembles the child who is try-ing to build with blocks. Both must proceed through a series of steps to accomplish a finished product. Figure 1-2 illustrates the "building blocks" of the learning sequence.

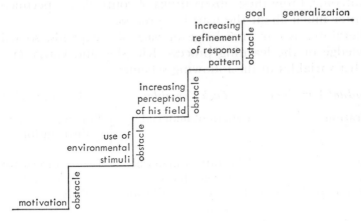

FIGURE 1-2. *Stages in the Learning Sequence*

CONCLUSION

What is learning? The question asked at the beginning of the chapter is not answered but the reader should have a more exact impression of the problem. The difficulty of definition and lack of common meaning of terms illustrate basic obstacles which must be overcome before productive research can be initiated. At our present stage of knowledge, the scanty information of what occurs within man severely handicaps investigations into the process of learning. We can observe definite phases of the learning process, and this, coupled with animal experimentation and increased studies of human learning, will progressively sharpen our insight into the way in which the human being forms concepts, solves problems, creates new music and literature, as well as the manner in which he acquires motor skills, and the like.

Observation, analysis, and research will be assisted by a continued study of the impact upon learning of variables, some of which may be controlled by the investigator. Individuals differ, situations differ, and different individuals' reaction to the same situation differ, not to mention the same individual's reaction to similar situations at different times. For example, if the length of time given to solve a problem varies from one trial to another, an observer can determine if varying the length of time permitted for the task changes the outcome. From these observations of controlled experiments, he can infer much about the learning process.

Therefore, as our knowledge of variables expands, so will our knowledge of the learning process. Kingsley and Garry (1957, p. 130) list variables in the following scheme:

Individual Variables	Task Variables	Method Variables
Maturation	Length of material	Practice, amount and distribution
Age	Difficulty of material	Degree of learning
Sex	Meaningfulness	overlearning
Previous experience	Retroactive inhibition and interference	drill
Capacity		
mental age		
intelligence		
aptitude		
Physical handicaps		Recitation
Motivation		Knowledge of results
		Whole versus part method
		Sensory modality used
		Temporal relations
		Set
		Guidance
		Incentives

Variables will be treated in more detail later; however, when we insert them into the already complicated picture of learning that has been drawn in this chapter, the immensity of the task confronting the learning investigator becomes apparent. Following the characteristics of the learning process that we discerned, we also shall begin the process of differentiation before we strive for integration. Therefore, in the next chapter, let us examine the human being, in whom the learning process functions in such an unexcelled, but obscure fashion.

CHAPTER II

The Physical Basis of Learning

INTRODUCTION

One of the most fundamental problems of physiological psychology concerns the nature of changes in the nervous system that accompany learning. It is a fundamental postulate—almost, but not quite, self-evident—that the changes in behavior called learning are in the last analysis reflections of changes in the nervous system. It is not surprising, then, that there has been a great deal of experimental work on the relationship between the nervous system and learning. That work, however, has not solved the basic problem. As a matter of fact, it has done little more than show us how complicated the problem is. The reader, however, should find this chapter one of the most rewarding and interesting in the whole of learning (Deese, 1952, p. 324).

WHERE DOES LEARNING occur? As educators and psychologists probe the mysteries of the learning process, their interest varies from observation of behavior to analysis of the nervous system. At different times in the history of psychology, particularly since the nineteenth century, the nervous system has played a more or less prominent role in the consideration of behavior. Presently, recognition of the role of the nervous system in learning is dominant in both educational and psychological thought. All of those concerned with psychology realize that learning does not occur in a vacuum. Man must have material that he can both comprehend and utilize in order to change his behavior. Man cannot react to, nor affect changes in, either himself or the world until stimuli arrive at the prediction areas of his brain.

The Importance of the Body

These stimuli, which also will ultimately affect the changes in his behavior, are sent to the brain by receptor organs and nerve pathways. Man's body, therefore, is acting as a medium; however, the implication is clear. The environment in which we place a student has been structured into further stimuli which will aid the student to attain certain, preselected objectives. Much planning and thought have gone into the materials and arrangement of the educational milieu. Nevertheless, if anything is faulty in the pathways which carry these predetermined stimuli, the desired educational objective is immediately lost. Such deductions led to the inevitable conclusion that whatever affects the nervous system affects learning.

Investigations into the place and function of the nervous system in behavior have occurred intermittently through the history of both psychology and education. This is one of the reasons why animal experimentation has been so influential in the analysis of behavior. Investigators are attracted by the apparent simplicity of animal learning in addition to the more readily controlled methods of experimentation which may be utilized. Such ease of experimentation has paralleled psychology's historical endeavors to achieve scientific status. When it broke with philosophy, psychology looked to physiology as its model.

If psychological studies could be forced into the confines of the laboratory, they could erase the stigma of "consciousness" that subjected psychology to ridicule. This could not be accomplished while psychology continued to concern itself with mind, concept, reason, and the like. It must deal with observable phenomena which could be subjected to empirical investigation. What was there in the human that satisfied such criteria? Obviously, the answer was man's body, and, in particular, man's nervous system. Thus, there is a tradition in both psychology and education for a fairly detailed study of the nervous system in any description and analysis of the learning process.

Many psychologists and educators have been intrigued by the possibilities that study of the nervous system offers. Thorndike turned to the nervous system for his explanation of learning, specifically, to the synaptic junction. But, it is not only the nervous system that must be discussed in any treatment of the physical basis of learning. Muscular and glandular systems play an important, if secondary, role in learning.

Does the Nervous System Belong?

Not all educators, or even psychologists, agree that there is a place for anatomical and physiological descriptions of man's systems in a course or a text that studies the learning process. These conflicting opinions are important and worthy of our attention. Those opposing the study of nerves, muscles, and glands in a learning text or course ask these significant questions: How does it help teachers in their daily classroom activities? What does knowledge of the manner in which the nerve impulse travels through the neural pathways mean for a teacher who is confronted with twenty-five to fifty pupils each morning? How does it help him solve the disciplinary problem presented by a surly, unruly teenager? Or, how does it help the first-grade teacher with a youngster who cannot distinguish the use of hard g and soft g in his reading? Those who oppose the study of man's nervous system, for example, argue that such effort is wasted.

Is it? If the teacher understands the environmental stimuli which are causing such turmoil in his teenager, he realizes that the youth's endocrine system is undoubtedly extremely active. Therefore, to offset this, the teacher can consider certain activities which will enable the student to free himself of inner conflicts and frustrations, within the guide lines of a particular curriculum and which also will be consistent with educational objectives. Admittedly, this is an idealistic pattern, but it is better to treat causes than symptoms and this can be done if a teacher possesses the necessary knowledge.

Much the same can be said about the reading problem. Why does a youngster mispronounce the sound of g? Could there be a visual problem which does not enable him to perceive differences in the letters following g and which determine its sound? Could he be omitting vital letters, and if so, why? If the correct stimulus is not derived from the printed word, the pronunciation and meaning will be hopelessly confused.

Despite these considerations, those who oppose such detailed study of the human being do so with conviction and persuasiveness. For example, Blair, *et al.* (1962, p. 8) say:

Traditional textbooks and courses in educational psychology have frequently failed to make the contribution they should to teacher education. Teachers have been known to have taken one or more courses in the field of educational psychology and yet have been unable to apply effectively the knowledge gained to their teaching. Too often, they have seen but slight connection between what is discussed in the textbook or the educational psychology course and what goes on in the classrooms where they work. To them, educational psychology has appeared to be just another academic subject whose facts must be learned for test purposes and just as quickly forgotten. There are probably several reasons for this. In the first place, the topics chosen for treatment in some textbooks in educational psychology have been only remotely related to the actual on-the-job behavior of teaching. Certain fairly recent books, for example, discuss at length such topics as microscopic features of the nervous system, visceral processes, the synapse theory of learning, the neural basis of imagination, the Muller-Lyer Illusion, and the ergograph test. In these books, actual children or teaching situations seldom, if ever, make their appearance. For the course in educational psychology to function in the work of the teacher, only that content should be selected and emphasized which has maximal educational applicability.

Certainly Blair leaves no doubt as to his position. If the subject matter, or the material, cannot be put to practical use in the classroom, they are worthless.

But there are others, equally as persuasive and articulate, who feel that such studies are of value to the teacher and will ultimately benefit the child. Travers (1963, p. 255) states:

Concepts of learning related to neurology have acquired considerable significance during the last ten years and have represented an approach productive of knowledge. For this reason the student of education can no longer ignore the anatomical structure and physiological functioning of the child if he is to acquire some understanding of the learning process as it takes place in schools. Since the teacher-educational curriculum typically ignores the fact the child has a body, the workings of which determine what he can and cannot learn, this chapter begins by attempting to provide a sketchy outline of knowledge in this area. Later in the chapter, some discussion is provided to solve the important concepts related to learning which have been built on this knowledge.

No one can deny that there is a serious cleavage among psychologists and educators as to the place and function of anatomy and physiology in the study of learning. No one would deny, either, that these studies have been historically important in both psychology and education or that they likewise have been extremely productive.

THE BODY IN LEARNING:
A PERSPECTIVE

From what has been said, it is clear that a knowledge of man's body is necessary for an adequate appraisal of the learning process. What does man's biological inheritance donate to the learning process? How does man know? Can he know reality? How do emotions affect the control and direction of learning by their impact on the nervous system? These are hard, practical questions that demand answers in classrooms at all levels of education. These problems are as old as man himself, but modern methods of research have afforded new insights. Therefore, the student of learning should be aware of the history of these problems so that the mistakes of the past will not be repeated in the present or future.

The Great Issues

Modern man turns, as Western man always has, to the Greeks for original and stimulating thought on the great enigmas that have plagued him. No attempt will be made to examine in depth the problems that are pertinent to learning but the reader should note the inevitable trend from the dependence of psychology on philosophy to a gradual reliance upon experimentation. The reader should also note the tendency to analyze man's body, rather than mind, for the explanation of his behavior.

The Greek thinkers of the fifth century slowly turned their attention from the world around them and began to consider man's nature. Disdaining the superficial endeavors of the Sophists with their attempt to manipulate human action by persuasion, Socrates believed knowledge of the soul was possible and that virtue is the result of this knowledge. To be ignorant is to be evil. Thus the principle that man's rational nature is dominant in his personality can be seen.

Plato, who believed that the world of ideas is more real than that of things, laid the foundation for the mind-matter dichotomy, which has plagued psychology and also education since his time. But today, the opposite is true. If ideas represent the perfect world, they are unattainable and consequently must be unscientific. If any part of man's behavior cannot be observed, many modern educators and psychologists believe it should be disregarded. Science must focus on the observable and the measurable.

Aristotle recognized the mind-matter distinction. But he did not view it as "either-or," as did Plato. He believed that one existed in the other and that it would be impossible to distinguish completely mind from matter. The importance placed on man's mind has had a marked influence on education. Educators have long been fascinated by a disciplinary type of learning. Although this approach to learning was abandoned in the 1920s, cultivation of man's mind, plus a recognition of individual needs, is again the goal of American education.

The more modern period began with the work of Descartes in the seventeenth century. With doubt as his method, he found that he could doubt everything but the fact that he was doubting. Hence, his famous, "I think, therefore, I am." Descartes gave added impetus to the mind-matter controversy. He believed that in each human body there is a reasonable soul. In his theory of dualism the action of the body is purely mechanical, or directed by the soul. The mind-body relationship is one of interrelation.

Another great figure in psychology, John Locke, became convinced that all knowledge comes from a single source—experience. In 1690, he published his famous *Essay Concerning Human Understanding* in which he compared a child's mind to a *tabula rasa* (blank tablet). Experience will write upon this blank tablet and thus the human being forms ideas. If an idea could be traced from experience, it was acceptable; if not, it was false and had no basis in fact.

Following Locke, other philosophers such as Berkeley, Hume, and Kant began to question the existence of objective reality. This school of critical inquiry believed that things can never be known as they are—only as determined by our thoughts. Objective reality is beyond us; we can never know the world as it exists outside of our knowing. Note the importance now placed upon experience. The direction of thought is apparent. Rational psychology is inadequate; what is needed is an empirical psychology which will not concern itself with ultimates.

As the school of critical inquiry was increasing in importance, another more affirmative movement was developing. This was the theory of association. The difference between the two schools was that associationism accepted the world as we perceive it. It was David Hartley who, in 1749, gave the basic principles of associationism—there is a direct connection between sensation and idea (Boring, 1950, p. 197). If sensations have been experienced together, the resulting ideas tend to occur together. If one has been associated with two, three, and four, in sensory experience, sensory experience one occurring alone will arouse ideas two, three, and four, which had previously accompanied it.

In this early period, psychology had moved from the rational to the empirical. For psychology to move into the modern era only one step remained. This step was experimentation.

In the transitional period from introspection to experimentation, one of the first individuals to note is Ernst Weber. Investigating weight discrimination involving muscle sense, in 1846, he discovered that there is no exact correspondence between the physical stimulus and its perception.

Weber never fully realized the significance of his findings. It remained for Gustav Fechner to realize its psychological importance. He was greatly interested in the relationship between stimulus and sensation, since he felt that this was the point of contact between the physical and mental worlds (Heidbreder, 1933, p. 79). However, the work of both Weber and Fechner was as important for the methodology of their investigations as for their results. The attempts at experimental control and quantitative expression of results began the development of experimental psychology with which we are familiar today. The transition to today's classroom is clear. Objectivity in research, and measurement of learning outcomes are indispensable tools to the educator.

Also prominent in the founding of the new science was Hermann von Helmholtz. His experiments on sight and sound are significant because they showed the complicated processes involved in the apparently simple phenomena of seeing and hearing. Today's recognition of the vital role played by sense discrimination in learning reflects the works of the pioneering psychologists. Equally important, perhaps more so from the modern viewpoint, was Helmholtz's demonstration of the possibility of studying psychological data by experimentation and observation.

It was Wundt, however, who crystallized the thought of the new approach. His great work, *Physiological Psychology* (1873), attempted to summarize the psychological data of the time and to illustrate a systematic approach to this data. How? He advocated introspection and experimentation. The psychological experiment should closely imitate the physiological experiment—a controlled environment and as objective data as possible. It is interesting to recall that Wundt never attempted to apply these methods to the higher thought processes. These can be studied only by what Wundt termed "social products," that is, by study of such human characteristics as language, law, mores, and so forth. It was in Leipzig, in 1879, that Wundt founded what is frequently designated as the first psychological laboratory. (Actually William James was conducting informal laboratory experiments of a psychological nature at Harvard as early as 1875.)

There were other influences in the development of the new science, such as Darwin's *Origin of Species* (1859), Galton's work on individual differences and his concomitant statistical methods, and French concentration upon the abnormal by such famous names as Pinel, Charcot, and Janet (Heidbreder, 1933, pp. 105–111).

Nevertheless, the great impetus came from Germany, and, in particular, the Leipzig laboratory. It made a strong impact on American psychological thought, largely because of such Wundtian students as Cattell and Hall. Thus, we see that the break with philosophy was complete and that experimental psychology had its beginnings in experimental physiology.

Boring (1950, pp. 27–31) traces the routes of experimental psychology in much greater detail; he states (p. 27):

There were, if we note only what is obvious and important for psychology between 1800 and 1850 nine important developments, all but two of which belong as much in the history of physiology as in the history of psychology. We may list them here and then go on to discuss four of them, leaving the other five to the separate chapters which follow.

Boring's nine developments are as follows:

(1) Sensory and motor nerves
(2) Specific nerve energies
(3) Sensation
(4) Phrenology
(5) Localization of function in the brain
(6) Reflex action
(7) Electrical nature of the nerve impulse
(8) Velocity of the nerve impulse
(9) The personal equation

Continued investigation and discoveries in these nine categories aided psychology's break with physiology and philosophy.

As psychology has assumed the status of a discipline, it has taken what it needs from its past to maintain steady progress. This brief historical perspective emphasizes the beginnings of modern psychology in both physiology and philosophy. In its development, psychology has constantly used knowledge of man's body in its attempts to understand man's behavior. Thus, the more that was known about sensation, reflex action, nerve excitation, and brain function, the better able was psychology to understand man's reaction to his environment.

As education has utilized the findings of psychology in its efforts to improve the learning process, it too has focused attention upon man's body. How best can the school appeal to students' senses? How can pupils' perceptions be refined? To answer these questions, educators must know and understand the bodily functions of the human. Hence, there is historical justification for discussing the place of nerves, muscles, and glands in a course or book on learning. But, more important, the student and the reader should realize that whatever influences the learning process has an effect upon education, and, therefore, should be within the scope of the teacher's competence.

NERVE ACTIVITY AND LEARNING

Nervous System [1]

The nervous system consists of two parts: the central nervous system and the autonomic nervous system. The structural unit of the nervous system is the neuron or nerve cell. It consists of a body and two types of process, the axon and dendrite. Figure 2-1 shows a typical nerve cell in which there is usually one axon and two or more dendrites associated with any cell body.

The cell body itself varies in size and shape in different parts of the nervous system. It may range from 4 to 125 microns in size, and it may be triangular, multangular, round, spindle, or pear shaped (Best and Taylor, 1944, p. 416). The typical nerve cell has a clearly distinguished nucleus near the center of its protoplasm. The neuron, then, consists of the nerve cell body proper and its attachments, which are designated axon and dendrite. The axon conducts nerve impulses away from the cell body while the dendrites transmit impulses toward the cell body. The neurons are linked together in the central nervous system, axon to dendrite, or to the cell body. Thus, there are formed in the body long, intricate chains which form the conducting parts of the nervous system. The junction between the axon of one neuron with the dendrite or the cell body of another is called the synapse. This junction is not a union of the two but it is a contact between the two. Figure 2-2 illustrates this relationship.

The synaptic junction has long fascinated learning theorists. It is known that the nerve impulse passes from the end of the axon of one neuron to either the dendrite or the cell body of another neuron. Exactly how the transmission of nerve impulse occurs is unclear. The synaptic junction offers resistance to the passage of the impulse from the axon to dendrite. If the nerve impulse successfully travels from axon to dendrite, it makes the task of similar succeeding impulses easier. This led to "The Synaptic Theory of Learning." The reader can see how it would affect classroom instruction. This would suggest that the teacher should drill, drill,

[1] This discussion is based on Charles Best and Norman Taylor, *The Living Body* (New York: Henry Holt and Company, 1944), pp. 328–471. Similar information may be obtained from any standard physiology text available.

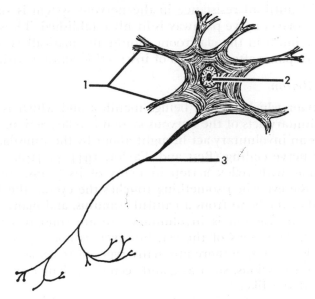

FIGURE 2-1. *The Neuron or Nerve Cell*

1. dendrites   2. nucleus   3. axon

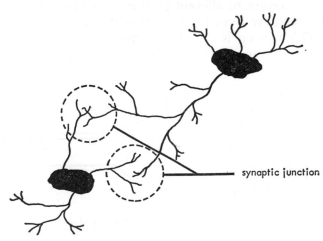

FIGURE 2-2. *The Synaptic Junction*

and drill until all resistance in the nervous system is surmounted and the correct nerve pathway is firmly established. Thus, presentation of stimuli in the classroom should automatically result in the correct response after a period of instruction and repetition.

Reflex Action

Behavior which human beings manifest and which is the result of involuntary acts of the nervous system is reflex action. A nervous reflex is an involuntary act brought about by the stimulation of the sensory nerve ending (Best and Taylor, 1944, p. 419). The reader is familiar with reflex action in many of its forms, for example, closing the eye when something touches the eyelid, the immediate removal of the hand from a painful stimulus, and many others. Although our reaction is involuntary, we are conscious that it has occurred. Awareness of the act, however, is not essential to reflex action. For example there are many types of reflex action of which we are unconscious, such as gland secretion, change in blood pressure, and the like.

The anatomical basis of reflex action is the reflex arc. The reflex arc consists of two neurons joined together in the central nervous system, axon to dendrite. The dendrite receives the stimulus and transmits the impulse to the central nervous system. Thus, it is called the receptor or afferent neuron. The other neuron transmits the impulse away from the central nervous system to a muscle or gland. This neuron is called the effector or efferent neuron. The place where the two neurons join in the central nervous system is

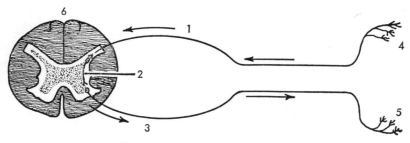

FIGURE 2-3. *The Reflex Arc*

1. receptor neuron   2. connector neuron   3. effector neuron
4. sense organ   5. effector organ   6. spinal cord

called the reflex center. Figure 2-3 illustrates the reflex arc and shows the relationship of neurons to reflex center.

Although the reflex arc, for clarity, was described as consisting of only two neurons, in the human being it is more likely that the reflex arc consists of lengthy, intricate chains of neurons. As Best and Taylor (1944, p. 421) say:

In any reflex action of higher animals, a great number of reflex arcs are involved. For example, should a person's arm be given a sharp and unexpected slap, he would jerk the arm away; associated movements of the shoulder and trunk would probably occur; he would turn his head and eyes to the source of the injury and, most likely, utter an exclamation of some sort. A large number of muscles—those of the arm, shoulders, trunk, neck, eyes, tongue, larynx, and respiration—would therefore take part in the action. Each muscle is supplied in turn by a large number of nerve fibers—effector (motor) neurons—and the stimulus must have excited a large number of afferent nerve endings—receptor neurons in the skin.

The Spinal Cord

The spinal cord and the brain form the central nervous system, which is considered the physiological basis of man's intellectual activity. The spinal cord is similar to an electrical wire which carries electricity. Instead of wire, the spinal cord consists of nerve fibers, and it has a small canal which extends throughout its length and connects with the ventricles of the brain. The human being has thirty-one pairs of spinal nerves.

These nerves have two roots, an anterior and a posterior, which are attached to the spinal cord. As its name implies, the anterior root is attached to the front of the spinal cord and consists of efferent (motor) neurons, which carry the impulse away from the central nervous system and which will cause the individual's reaction. Whereas, the posterior root is attached to the back of the spinal cord and contains only afferent (receptor) neurons. These transmit impulses from the sense organs to the spinal cord. Figure 2-4 shows the various parts of the spinal cord.

The importance of the nervous system in learning cannot be overlooked even from a purely mechanical viewpoint. For example, during the conscious part of a person's day, the voluntary muscles remain in a slight state of contraction, even if they are not being used. This is referred to as muscle tone. All voluntary muscles manifest this characteristic, but it is more noticeable in some than others. The antigravity muscles of the body (lower limbs, trunk, neck) show this tendency because they must maintain the posture of the body against the force of gravity (Best and Taylor, 1944, p. 429). Any damage to the controlling section of the brain (medulla oblongata) affects muscle tone. Therefore, the spinal reflex arc which directly controls muscle tone must be in a normal, healthy state if learning activity is to function. Although this is not at all a common occurrence, it is a good example of the vital role played by the nervous system.

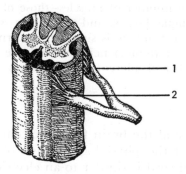

FIGURE 2-4. *The Spinal Cord*

1. anterior root   2. posterior root

The Brain

The brain is the section of the nervous system found in the skull. The parts of the brain are the cerebrum, the midbrain, the pons, the medulla oblongata, and the cerebellum. Figure 2-5 illustrates the sections of the brain.

Of particular interest to the student of learning is the cerebrum. It is the largest section of the human brain and is the basis of highly developed activities of the nervous system, such as memory and intelligence. The cerebrum also possesses the centers for sight, hearing, smell, taste, and general body sensations (Best and Taylor, 1944, p. 438). The cerebrum is separated by a type of groove running from front to back. This groove is called a fissure and divides the cerebrum into halves called cerebral hemispheres. These hemi-

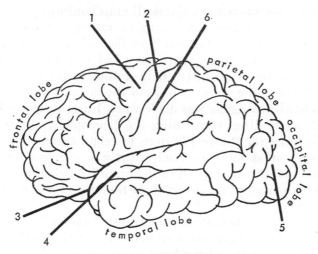

FIGURE 2-5. *The Brain*

1. motor area   2. fissure of Rolando   3. fissure of Sylvius
4. auditory area   5. visual area   6. sensory area

spheres consist of an outer layer of grey matter called the cerebral cortex and an inner mass of white matter. The inner part of the cerebrum, or white matter, consists mainly of nerve fibers.

It is the cerebral cortex (grey matter) which most interests the student of learning. For it is here that the control of certain functions of the human being have been located. Recall that the cerebrum is divided by a longitudinal fissure. Each cerebral hemisphere, in turn, is divided into four parts, called lobes, by two additional fissures, the fissure of Rolando and the fissure of Sylvius. The frontal lobe is in front of the fissure of Rolando; the parietal lobe is behind the fissure of Rolando; the temporal lobe is beneath the fissure of Sylvius; and, finally, the occipital lobe is located at the back of the cerebrum.

For many years, investigators have been fascinated by attempts to attribute certain functions to definite areas of the cerebral cortex. In the early part of the nineteenth century F. G. Gall and G. Spurzheim were intrigued by the possibilities of localization of function. They stated that there were thirty-seven powers of the mind which corresponded to the same number of organs of the mind. According to this theory, the exterior of the skull must conform to the interior of the brain. Thus, any thickening or enlargement of the skull would indicate an excessive faculty of the mind, and, also, any depression in the skull would represent a lack of a faculty. Although this theory was never accepted, it nevertheless did focus attention upon the brain as the physical basis of the mind.

More scientific progress was made when Luigi Rolando, in 1809, published his findings concerning the hemispheres of the brain. But it remained for Pierre Flourens to relate certain functions to certain brain areas more precisely than was previously done. He determined that the main parts of the brain have definite functions, but he did not attempt to specify these functions for any part of the cerebrum itself.

Continued experimentation concentrated on more exact localization of function. There has been steady research into this problem and many famous names have been associated with it, for example, Goltz, Franz, and Lashley. It was Lashley who formulated the principle of equipotentiality, which holds that the more cortical tissues available, the more vivid will be learning. Particular cortical tissue is relatively unimportant.

Localization of function remains a critical but unsolved problem. However, it is important that the reader, at least, be aware of the background of this question. Today, there is general, but cautious, agreement about localization of function.

The frontal lobe contains the motor area which governs voluntary movement of toes, ankle, knee, hip, trunk, shoulder, elbow, wrist, fingers, neck, face, tongue and larynx.

In front of the motor area of the frontal lobe is a section of the brain about which little is known. At one time it was thought that this particular part of the brain was the center of man's intelligence. Operations on the frontal lobe however, have been followed by little, if any, frontal defect. As Kelly (1956, p. 41) says:

Most of the frontal and large portions of the parietal and temporal lobes are not involved in the immediate reception of impulses nor in the transmission of impulses to the muscles. These areas are as richly supplied with interconnecting neurons as any part of the cortex. Hence, it is assumed, without any positive proof that these areas form the seat of a function which the cerebrum is known to possess, namely, that of association.

The parietal lobe seems to be mainly sensory in function. Frequently, it is referred to as the somesthetic area. Sensations of touch, warmth, coolness, and kinesthesia (sense of muscular movement) are located here. Finally, the temporal lobe seems to be the auditory area of the brain, and the occipital lobe the visual area. The extreme rearward part of the occipital lobe seems to have an associative function. This includes the recognition and intepretation of visual impressions and the integration of these with other sensations (Best and Taylor, 1944, p. 444).

The knowledge that we now have about localization of function might tempt the reader to reach a deceptively simple conclusion. As Travers (1963, p. 262) says:

The areas on the surface of the cerebral hemisphere, which have specialized functions as terminations of the sensory tracts, are known as the "sensory-projection" areas. They are the areas on which the impulses derived from the sense organs are projected. The specialization of function which these areas represent is likely to be misinterpreted by the student who encounters it for the first time, for he is likely to jump to the conclusion that these areas are the ones which produce the phenomena of perception. The student is likely to conclude erroneously that since the occipital lobe of the brain functions mainly in connection with vision, visual perception is a function which occurs in the occipital area alone. Such is not the case. While the occipital lobe plays an essential role in visual perception, there is ample evidence that visual perception is dependent for its functioning on extended areas of the brain and that perceptual functions cannot be completely localized within one particular area of the cerebral cortex.

The most recent experimentation with animals has continued to emphasize this conclusion. Rats, trained in brightness discrimination, lose the brightness habit after visual cortical removal, but are able to learn the brightness again in the absence of a visual cortex. This is a problem that has concerned psychologists and physiologists for the last fifty years. An assumption, which psychologists and physiologists make, although reluctantly, is that these habits are acquired by subcortical structures. This assumption raises different questions: what are the structures and why do they not function when the visual cortex is present? Thompson and his associates, working with rats, have explored performance differences due to cortical and subcortical lesions and have achieved inconclusive, varying outcomes (1960, 1961).

The Autonomic Nervous System

The autonomic, or involuntary, nervous system deals with those functions which are carried out automatically and which ordinarily do not intrude upon consciousness. The autonomic division of the nervous system influences behavior in a very complicated way. It governs the action of the heart, the gastro-intestinal tract, the smooth muscle of the blood vessels, the urinary bladder, and, through its action on the adrenal, it aids the body in times of stress.

Anatomically, the neurons of the autonomic nervous system are basically the same as those of the spinal cord and the brain. The autonomic nervous system is divided into two parts: the sympathetic and parasympathetic divisions. The action of these two divisions of the autonomic nervous system upon any organ (heart, intestines) are antagonistic to each other. The parasympathetic action on the heart is inhibitory while the sympathetic action is excitatory. Many instances of an animal's reaction in time of danger are examples of the predominance of sympathetic action under such conditions. The dilated pupils, rapid heart action, and contraction of the spleen are the result of the sympatho-adrenal system. Thus, there can be no doubt that the autonomic system is a part of man's effector mechanism and produces action (Travers, 1963). But the specific consequences of autonomic nervous activity are too complicated and involved for our present level of knowledge to offer acceptable answers.

The Nerve Impulse

The nerve fiber is the conducting unit of the nervous system, and the message that the fiber transmits is designated as the nerve impulse. Necessary and outstanding properties of the nerve fiber are excitability and conductivity. These properties are very highly developed in the nervous system. When a nerve fiber is stimulated (electrically, mechanically, thermally, or chemically), a disturbance is caused at the point of excitation. If strong enough, this disturbance spreads along the nerve, and the wave of excitation is the nerve impulse.

The nerve fiber itself consists of an inner layer of protoplasm, called the axis cylinder, which is enveloped in a coat of fat called the myelin sheath. The myelin sheath, in turn, is enclosed by a thin, transparent membrane called the neurilemma. At various points, the nerve fiber seems to be pinched so that the neurilemma moves to the center of the fiber and almost touches the axis cylinder. These points of constriction are called the nodes of Ranvier.

It is interesting to consider the circumstances which cause a nerve impulse to pass along a nerve fiber. A difference in electrical potential in the nerve fiber arises simultaneously with the nerve impulse. The part of the nerve that is excited is electrically negative compared to other parts of the nerve. This difference in electrical potential has enabled investigators to discover that the "all or none" principle applies to nerves. Thus, a stimulus barely strong enough to excite the nerve fiber causes the transmission of an impulse which is of the same magnitude and velocity as one caused by a stimulus of much greater strength. That is, a stimulus that is capable of arousing any reaction at all causes the greatest response possible. But the more powerful stimulus produces greater frequency of impulses than does the weaker.

Encouraging clues are affording man a better comprehension of the mechanics of nervous activity than was previously possible. It has long been known that there is a chemical reaction involved in the transmission of the nerve impulse. In 1933, Sir Henry Dale, an English neurophysiologist, discovered that a chemical, acetylcholine (acetic acid plus choline), functioned in the passage of a nerve impulse across the synapse. Dale and his associates believed that acetylcholine was found only in nerve endings and in the involuntary nervous system. However, experimentation with the electric eel showed that a large amount of the enzyme cholinesterase was present. Its function is to split acetylcholine and prevent its accumulation throughout the nervous system.

Consequently, researchers have concluded that acetylcholine is responsible for the nervous activity of both the central nervous system and the autonomic nervous system. It also appears to be responsible for the actual transmission of the nerve impulse (electrical in nature) along the nerve fiber; it is the material which gives the nerve impulse its energy as it passes along the nerve fiber.

Exactly how does this chemical function in the transmission of the electrical nerve impulse? The electricity has its source in the positively charged sodium ions present in body fluids, whose entry into the fiber is blocked by a barrier of fatty material. This barrier is made permeable by the acetylcholine after it combines with a protein receptor. The combination of acetylcholine and sodium changes the permeability of the nerve fiber to the movements of the positively charged sodium ions. The change in permeability then alters the electrical potential of the nerve and thus makes possible the transmission of the impulse throughout the entire nerve fiber.

Once the impulse has passed, the nerve fiber is unable to conduct for a brief time. This is called the refractory phase. The transmission of the nerve impulse has exhausted the ability of the fiber to conduct immediately. Best and Taylor (1944, p. 393) liken the refractory phase of the nerve fiber to the gunpowder fuse after the spark has passed, leaving only a trail of ash. The absolute refractory period during which the nerve cannot conduct has an interval of about 0.001 second. This phase is followed by an interval during which the ability of the nerve to conduct again is gradually replenished. This is called the relative refractory period and encompasses about 0.01 to 0.02 second. The fiber may conduct during this interval but requires a stronger than average stimulus to activate it.

A person's behavior is modified only as his reactions differ from what they were in similar past situations. To a great extent this is determined by the reaction of muscles and glands to the nerve impulse. This is the observable aspect of learning which was discussed earlier. Now, the place and function of muscles and glands in the learning process must also be examined.

Muscles in Learning

The part that muscles play in man's adjustment to his environment makes muscle anatomy and physiology a legitimate topic in any analysis of learning. Several learning theories, as we shall see, depend upon the function of muscles for a partial explanation of the learning process. Here, again, we see the significance of a healthy body in the learning process. If nerves, muscles, or glands are damaged or unhealthy, the individual reacts differently from his healthy neighbor. The methods of adjustment to the environment change in such a person. This is not to say that the learning process itself differs in any way; however, different neural pathways, or different muscular tissue, will be used in the response. With such an individual there is always the distinct possibility that an emotional reaction may influence learning. So, the reader again should realize that the greater the teacher's knowledge of all forces affecting learning, the greater will be his or her chance to aid pupils attain desirable objectives.

Knowledge of muscle action, therefore, is necessary because we recognize the essential role played by the muscles in adjustment to the environment. Muscular tissue is of two types—striped (striated) and unstriped (smooth). The voluntary muscles of the body are striated, for example, the muscles of the limbs. Involuntary muscle is, for the most part, smooth.

The muscle cells are long and slender and are usually called muscle fibers. These fibers are grouped into bundles, and the bundles are linked by connective tissue into larger masses. Consequently, the contractibility of a muscle depends upon the accumulative effect of the fibers of which it is composed.

Muscle, like nerve, responds to any one of four types of stimuli (electrical, mechanical, thermal, and chemical). The muscle may be stimulated directly (a stimulus in contact with its surface) or through its nerve.

In summarizing the characteristics which enable muscles to perform a function of motion, Kelly (1956, p. 45) gives the following classifications:

1. Irritability or excitability, that is, the power to receive and respond to stimuli.
2. Contractibility, that is, the power which enables the muscles to change shape so as to become short and thicker when they receive impulses transmitted to them through the motor nerves. It is the power to contract, involving the shortening of the muscle and its fixation in a new form.
3. Extensibility, that is, the power which enables the muscle to be stretched and/or extend its form.
4. Elasticity, that is, the power which enables the muscle to return to its original form.

The Glands in Learning

There are two types of glands in the body. Those glands that deliver their secretions into the alimentary tract or upon the surface of the body are called glands of external secretion or exocrine glands. The sweat glands and the lachrymal glands of the body are such glands. These are not overly important in a discussion of man's behavioral pattern.

The important glands are those that discharge their secretions directly into the bloodstream. In this way, they are conducted to the tissues of the body and exert their influence. These are the duct-less glands, or as they are more commonly called, the endocrine glands. The secretions of these glands are called hormones. (The term hormone, however, is not restricted to the endocrine glands.) The science of endocrinology has become important both to psychology and physiology in recent years. Damage to, or removal of, any of the endocrine glands results in radical behavior disturbances and, in some cases, rapid death. The major significance of these glands is that they are excitatory in action. They visibly affect growth, development, and the functional activity of the various tissues.

These glands are: the thyroid, parathyroid, adrenal, pituitary, sex glands, thymus, and pineal. The anatomy of these glands should not concern us here. What is important is the malfunction of any of them and the resultant effect on behavior.

For example, trouble with the thyroid can cause retardation of skeletal growth and failure of sexual development. The individual is moody, irritable, and unable to relax.

The individual with a parathyroid deficiency is depressed and nervous. If the deficiency is sufficiently serious, it is followed by twitchings, occasional muscle spasms, and, perhaps ultimately, death.

The function of adrenalin in the human body scarcely needs any mention since we are aware of, and have experienced at some time, the "lift" that carries us through a crisis. In times of stress, adrenalin is poured into the bloodstream, which quickens the heartbeat, thus feeding nourishment to the muscles so that they may work at peak efficiency. This is the explanation for "an individual rising above himself," either by an unusual momentary manifestation of vigor or by an exceptionally prolonged vigorous period.

The pituitary, the "master" gland of the endocrine system, appears to regulate growth and development. It exercises an influence on the functioning of all of the other glands of the system. Over-activity of the pituitary in childhood results in the phenomenon known as gigantism. Conversely, deficiency of the pituitary results in the dwarflike individual.

The effect upon behavior of these glands is readily discernible; many signs of behavioral disturbances may be directly attributed to the endocrine. If bodily and mental functions can be upset by the system, the learning process can also be seriously altered. Normal, effective learning will not occur if any of the endocrine glands is not working in its proper physiological sense.

CONCLUSION

It is hoped that the reader will appreciate the ambivalent attitude toward the consideration of the body in any investigation of the learning process. Although we may freely admit that the teacher will not always be cognizant of the more secretive physical elements of learning, nevertheless, two results are desired from the brief mention that has been made here of learning rooted in man's physical nature.

First, the more known about the learning process, the more effective will be the teacher's instruction. He will make an appeal to sensation, and eventually, perception and concept formation, by more appropriate and discriminating selection of stimuli. Added knowledge of the nervous system will, gradually it is admitted, filter down to the teacher and provide new insights which may be appealed to by novel and exciting materials and methods of instruction.

Second, if a learning problem occurs, a teacher, utilizing similar information to that just discussed, will first examine the physical nature and well-being of the student. The cause of nonlearning may have its roots in a physical disability. Thus, a physical examination should be made before any decision of a psychological character is brought to bear. An understanding of basic human physiology is essential to analyze, interpret, and utilize psychological phenomena which depend, partly at least, on bodily functions.

CHAPTER III

Learning and Motivation

INTRODUCTION

> The psychology of motivation is in its infancy. In fact, it can hardly be said to exist as a separate discipline or field of study within psychology today. It is discussed a little in the elementary course, again in courses in abnormal psychology and personality, and finally in theory courses as it relates to the psychology of learning. The result is that it is difficult for the student and the psychologist to focus on motivation as such, rather than as a topic which serves only to clarify some other problem (McClelland, 1955, p. v).

THIS STATEMENT, written by a respected student of motivational problems in 1955, was true then as well as today, and it will also be true in the foreseeable future. Despite this, the study of motivation continues to attract enormous amounts of time, labor, and research money.

And deservedly so, since all animal and human behavior is activity which receives its energy from the motivational process. Thus, the more knowledge that students can accumulate about motivation, the more knowledge they will acquire about the various types of behavior that animals and humans manifest. This is particularly true for learned behavior. Without motivation, there will be an absence of learning. Recall the characteristics of learning that were presented in an earlier chapter.

The first characteristic was a motivated individual. If the individual did not desire anything, there was no activity; therefore, there was no learning. The desire for something is motivation; it causes a feeling of restlessness in the person which furnishes the energy for the responses needed for goal-achievement. Consequently, the person feels impelled toward an object, thing, or person that will remove his sense of need. From this initial impetus comes the sustaining force that encompasses the other characteristics of learning. His selection of an appropriate goal; his reactions to environmental stimuli; his continuous refinement of his perceptual field; his response patterns; all of these derive their power and direction from the individual's motivation.

A partially motivated student (one who has not fully identified with educational goals) lacks some, if not all, of these learning characteristics. His drive toward the goal is weak, therefore his perception of his field is vague; he overlooks significant clues in his environment; his response pattern is disorganized. A total lack of student motivation (*no* identification with school objectives) will insure that the student pursues different, if not conflicting, goals. Unquestionably, poor or nonexistent motivation is responsible for teachers' disciplinary problems and the schools' drop-out problem.

Motivation or its lack, however, should not be the only concern of teachers. Varieties of motivation are also significant for the teacher. The great majority of students will diligently pursue the same goal but for different, and often unrelated, reasons.

Consider the following example. Students reading this text undoubtedly have one need in common—they wish to pass a particular course. But this supposedly common need has so many individual subtleties of meaning that the postulate of one common need may be seriously questioned. Some students may read the text because it is a course requirement and they may be motivated by no other goal. Others may have developed a genuine interest in the psychology of learning and are studying the text, not only to pass a course, but also because knowledge of the learning process has become a significant objective. Still others may not see how the text relates to the course, or how the course relates to their distant objectives. And, unquestionably, there are others who see this text and course, not as an objective, but as an obstacle to their goal. They may have been forced to enroll in the learning course when they would have much preferred to select a more meaningful (to them) objective.

These are some of the uncertainties that arise when a class or group motivation is analyzed. The scope of the motivational riddle is expanded immensely when individual needs and drives are examined. Exactly what are the motivational thrusts activating the specific and unique personalities who constitute a class? For example, do the following students—the young man of nineteen who is attending school at the insistence of his parents, the senior girl who has just become engaged, the mature veteran who has returned to college after his tour of duty, or finally, the young girl away from home for the first time—have any common purpose? Aside from a general and often ill-defined notion of becoming a teacher, their needs and drives have little similarity.

A male student of nineteen faces many doubts in his choice of a career. Often he is attending a university to which he has been sent by his parents, and, equally as often, he is equipped with inadequate information about his choice of career. His personal needs frequently appear only vaguely related to the university's educational objectives. Certainly he must entertain many doubts about his future when he contemplates military service. This is an immediate, real barrier to any remote goals he might wish to attain, and yet, it is a factor that the average American male must consider. Most likely, he also discusses careers with classmates and faculty and he may acquire new insights which may either strengthen or weaken his original selection. Consequently, the instructor has to associate the fluid needs of the student with the goals that the instructor thinks are indispensable for a thorough comprehension of the learning process. Otherwise, little, if any, learning will occur.

Similarly, a girl, who, as a high school senior, decided upon a teaching career, now becomes engaged in her senior year of college. Is the earlier goal of teaching as meaningful to her as her forthcoming wedding and marriage? Does not the motivational process drive and direct her primarily to thoughts and plans about her marriage? Will course work suffer as a result? Is there any possibility that she will endanger her chances of obtaining her degree? Again, the instructor faces an arduous task. How can he connect the genuine needs of this particular student with the objectives of the course and her own distant objective—teaching? If the instructor fails to accomplish this, the course will become a senseless smattering of facts with little real learning.

Consider the veteran of twenty-five, or twenty-six—is his motivation the same as that of the nineteen year old? He may have traveled to many parts of the world, seen many things, conversed with many different types of people, and undergone many significant experiences. Possibly, he may be married and have a family. Despite this, he is probably fiercely determined to achieve his goal. If it is teaching, he will endure any hardship or suffer any sacrifice to win his degree and begin his career. How can the instructor in the learning course connect the goals of the course to this veteran's needs? Will his rich, experiential background cloud the necessity and value of theoretical considerations? If the student decides that the psychology of learning is too "bookish," the learning sequence will be crushed by the obstacle which must be present if meaningful learning is to occur. Happily, however, this is usually not typical of the more mature student.

Finally, consider the young girl who is away from home for the first time—what are her needs and drives in this new, cold, disinterested environment? It is very likely that she arrived at this novel and disturbing locale with mixed feelings of hope, anticipation, and trepidation. Suddenly, she is in huge classes taught by instructors who apparently know nothing about her, including her name. Perhaps this is true of the learning course—she finds she must take it immediately as a prerequisite for observation and student teaching. Because she is alone, uncertain, and groping for rapport with both roommates and classmates, how real can the objectives of the learning course be to this student, and what can the instructor hope to accomplish?

The examples above are applicable to any level of education, from the first grade to graduate school. The needs of the individual and the educational objectives both change, but the fundamental task remains the same—individual needs must be united with school goals. This remains, and rightly so, the primary concern of the teacher. If there is no union between the student's needs and academic goals, the person's drives will direct him to ends that disrupt learning and considerably alter remote goal-attainment.

Although it is simple to stress the importance of motivation in learning, it is much more formidable to suggest means by which motivation can be recognized and utilized in the learning process. Classes ranging in size from twenty to 200 make identification of individual motivation a herculean, if not impossible, chore. This is especially true of many public school classes. Here the youngsters attend a particular class because the law coerces them to do so, and it also places a similar compulsion upon their parents. Many youngsters may not wish to attend school but they must be taught, and the success of the teaching-learning procedure will depend upon the manner in which the instructor avails himself of the realities of motivation. Specifically, and individually, how can a student's wants aid academic achievement?

This question comprises many intangibles, and any teacher, at any level, must approach them as impartially as possible. Too often, teachers see things in a student's relation to a course which actually are lacking. Again, students' objectives are not necessarily teachers' objectives. What the question does imply is that the teacher recognize the students as persons. This is not a purely academic statement, as any student who sits in large classes, or any instructor who teaches such classes, will quickly realize. Examination of student records and student conferences require extensive time and effort, but the labor will be richly rewarded.

For the more teachers understand student needs and drives, the more effectively they can aid students to appreciate the value of the course. Teachers can direct the energy that needs arouse toward scholastic purposes and thereby increase rapport with students while helping them to attain their more remote goals.

Such potent use of motivation implies thorough comprehension of the motivational process. Today, theories of motivation vary, much as do theories of learning. Yet, teachers should be alert to the new insights that appear with encouraging frequency. Therefore, some acquaintance with motivational theory will aid reflection about the daily classroom application of student stimuli.

Techniques of motivation remain relatively constant although theories differ. As mentioned in the analysis of the learning process, one views learning, and motivation, much as he views the nature of man. As Hilgard (1962, pp. 125–127) says:

The following considerations help to account for the differences in lists that various writers propose:

1. The expression of human motives differs from culture to culture and from person to person within a culture. This difference arises because many motives are learned as a result of specific experiences and in any case are expressed through learned behavior.

2. Similar motives may be manifested through unlike behavior. A motive to assert antagonism to another person may be expressed either by an attack upon him or by withdrawal from his presence.

3. Unlike motives may be expressed through similar behavior. Thus two people may take up oil painting, one to please a parent, the other to annoy a parent.

4. Motives often appear in disguised form. Boys have been known to steal because of sexual conflicts. Here the motive for stealing was not a "motive to acquire" (recognized by some psychologists as one of the basic motives) but a disguised sexual drive.

5. Any single act of behavior may express several motives. A scientist at work in his laboratory may be motivated by a yearning to search for truth, by a desire for fame, by the necessity of increasing his earning power to support his family. All these as well as other motives may be active at the same time. The principle of multiple determination of behavior is an important one, but it makes difficult the description of the motives active at any given time.

These five considerations mean that we cannot arrive at a definitive list of motives simply by classifying the activities in which men engage. Instead, we must infer basic motives underlying these activities. Even though we know a great deal about human motives, and even though inferences are accurate, we still have to decide how detailed our list shall be. Perhaps the desire for status may be treated as a single motive. Or, if we wish, we may treat the various aspects of status—domination, prestige, power, and security—as separate motives. Hence the fact that experts choose lists of different lengths does not necessarily imply contradiction.

Hilgard aptly summarizes the dilemma of motivational research. Anyone concerned with either the practical or theoretical aspects of motivation appreciates the necessity for as much enlightenment as possible about human needs and drives—especially those interested in the behavioral sciences. Unfortunately, some motivational theorists stress man's physiological drives, others emphasize a changing hierarchy of needs in the human, and still others accentuate man's psychological needs. Because students studying for a teaching career require some awareness of motivational theory, the following section briefly presents the speculations of five noted authorities—Murray, Harlow, Maslow, Cronbach, and Allport.

THEORIES OF MOTIVATION

I. Henry A. Murray

When an organism lacks something which it should have to remain in a state of satisfaction, it (the lack) is commonly designated as a need. From observation of the human organism, Murray has formulated a detailed list of needs which has served as a foundation for extensive research. This is not a complete classification of human needs, nor is it intended to be. As Travers (1963, p. 157) says:

Various scientists have suggested ways in which the needs of adult man may be classified. Any classification is more a matter of convenience than the result of theorizing. Also, almost any classification can include only the more common needs. For example, a few individuals have a highly developed need for timepieces—covering their walls with clocks, and generally carrying more than one watch in their pockets. The need for this kind of stimulation is rare, so rare that it is hardly worthwhile including in any classification system that is developed. The same would be true of the need for raising Arabian horses or any of the other fads and fancies which are so commonly encountered among human beings. A classification of needs which is to be of any use must cover the common needs that frequently play a part in the behavior of man. Such a classification will not be complete, and, indeed, a complete classification hardly seems to be possible at this time.

Murray's taxonomy, which appeared in his *Explorations in Personality* (1938) postulated two categories:

1. Primary or viscerogenic needs.
2. Secondary or psychogenic needs.

Man's primary needs are his biological wants—food, water, and the like. Although he treated them as distinct and legitimate divisions of human needs, Murray nevertheless recognized the relationship between the two and suggested that the psychogenic needs probably depend upon satisfaction of the primary needs.

Since the psychogenic needs are more related to the question of learning, they will be weighed more carefully here. They represent the common needs of man, but this does not suggest that all men manifest *all* of these needs to the same degree. Some individuals have no need for dominance, for example. Others have a definite need to exercise control over individuals and groups. Still others have a need for dominance, but it can be satisfied in a relatively simple fashion. For example, exercising the function of the "head of the house" can satisfy, wholly or partially, this need. Consequently, individuals differ, not only in the type of need they evidence, but also in the degree to which the need is satisfied. Therefore, Murray's types of needs are indicative, but are not total.

The psychogenic needs (with abbreviated explanations) are:

1. Acquisition—to gain possessions and property.
2. Conservance—to collect, repair, clean, and preserve things.
3. Order—to arrange, organize, put away objects.
4. Retention—to retain possession of things.
5. Construction—to organize and build.
   (Murray states that these five needs are directed toward inanimate objects.)
6. Superiority (a combination of two needs):
   a. Achievement—will to power over things, people, and ideas.
   b. Recognition—efforts to gain approval and high social status.
7. Achievement—to overcome obstacles (Murray refers to this as an elementary ego need which may act alone or be fused with other needs).
8. Recognition—to excite praise and commendation.
9. Exhibition—to attract attention to one's person.
   (These four needs represent the drive toward prestige and accomplishment).
10. Inviolacy—to prevent a depreciation of self-respect.
11. Infavoidance—to avoid failure, shame, and humiliation.
12. Defendance—to defend oneself against blame or belittlement; to justify one's actions.
13. Counteraction—to overcome defeat by continued action.
    (These four needs portray man's desire for status and his avoidance of humiliation.)
14. Dominance—to influence or control others.
15. Deference—to admire and willingly follow a superior.
16. Similance—to imitate; to identify with another; to agree and believe.
17. Autonomy—to resist influence or coercion; to strive for independence.
18. Contrarience—to act differently from others; to be unique; to take the opposite side.
    (These five needs explain the exertion of, and resistance to, human power.)
19. Aggression—to assault, injure, or harm another.
20. Abasement—to surrender. Surrender. Masochism.
    (Murray calls these two needs an illustration of the sado-masochistic dichotomy.)

21. Blamavoidance—to avoid blame or punishment; to be well-behaved and obey the law.
(Murray distinguishes blamavoidance because it entails inhibition. It is the desire to avoid socially unacceptable conduct.)
22. Affiliation—to form friendships and associations.
23. Rejection—to snub, ignore, or exclude another; to remain aloof and indifferent.
24. Nurturance—to nourish, and, or protect another.
25. Succorance—to seek aid, protection, or sympathy.
(These four needs expound man's utilization of affection—seeking it, exchanging it, giving it, withholding it.)
26. Play—to relax; to amuse oneself; to seek diversion.
27. Cognizance—to explore; to ask questions; to satisfy curiosity.
28. Exposition—to point and demonstrate; to relate facts.

In his discussion about needs, Murray underscores the importance of painstaking observation in order to comprehend man's motivational pattern. For the teacher, the value of such observation is of incalculable worth. Consider this statement (Murray, 1938, pp. 112–113):

In judging an individual it is important to observe which needs are periodically satisfied and which are repeatedly frustrated. Here we have to take account of specific abilities. Frustration may lead to inhibition of a need, to atrophy from hopelessness or to exaggerated re-striving. It is necessary to note the occurrence of gratuitous end situations (unnaturally facile climaxes), common in the lives of the over-privileged. With the latter, needs may be so easily satisfied that they rarely enter consciousness. Hence, these people may appear as if they had none. Here, the conclusion must be that it is hard to judge the strength of needs without knowing which of them are being regularly stilled during times when the subject is not being observed.

If teachers are alert to the conditions which both satisfy and frustrate their students, they can manipulate the classroom to insure the best possible atmosphere for learning. The teacher who recognizes student needs and relates them to educational objectives not only facilitates learning, but also minimizes disciplinary disturbances.

II. Harry Harlow

Since 1953, the Nebraska Symposia on Motivation have contributed to the organization and differentiation of the research and literature on motivation. In the 1953 Symposium, Harry Harlow attacked the drive-reduction theory of motives (based on physiological needs) and challenged the concept of homeostasis (the organism's attempt to maintain a normal, physiological state). In his paper to the 1953 Symposium, he stressed the priority of external stimuli as the origin of activity. Bugelski (1956, p. 221) thus comments on the Harlow paper:

It is easy enough to deny motivation in certain types of learning situations if one restricts the general concept to such commonly used experimental drives as "hunger" for example. Harlow (1953) in the above mentioned Nebraska symposium shows that hungry animals do not necessarily learn better, or at least do not persist in solving certain kinds of manipulative puzzles as well as animals who cannot be said to be hungry and do not receive food for solutions. In a discrimination learning situation, Harlow points out, animals continue to learn correct responses even though they are not hungry and eat after both correct and incorrect responses. Harlow is interested, in this paper, in pointing out that tissue needs are of less significance than other motivation sources such as curiosity, some type of manipulating drive, or simply external stimuli, at least for the kinds of problems his monkeys were exposed to.

During the past decade, increasing scrutiny has been given to the entire topic of exteroceptive stimulation—the organism demands a certain minimum of external stimuli. If external stimulation falls below this minimum, the organism intensifies its activity, which will raise the stimuli level. So, Harlow's work has inspired needed inquiries into the "without" of motivation, as well as the "within."

These drives with which Harlow is concerned are often referred to as "curiosity," "exploratory," or "manipulative" drives. He attributes much of psychology's disregard of external stimuli as motivating forces to Watson's Behaviorism. After a promising inception, external stimuli as motivation fell into disrepute. Harlow is at a loss to give specific explanations for this, but indicates any subjective philosophical implications were discarded. Much of modern motivational theory emanates from an uncritical acceptance of physiological states as the producer of behavior. Learning theorists, searching for an exposition of motivation which would accommodate their personal assumptions about learning, understandably were intrigued by the prevalent "tissue theories."

Harlow vigorously assails systems of drive reduction and questions their contributions to learning, particularly to learning problems on the human level. Psychologists, fascinated by drive reduction, will habitually limit their research to relatively insignificant issues and ignore major questions which might afford notable perceptions into learning as a process. As he says (Harlow, 1953, p. 25):

There are logical reasons why a drive-reduction theory of learning, a theory which emphasizes the role of internal, physiological-state motivation, is entirely untenable as a motivational theory of learning. The internal drives are cyclical and operate, certainly at any effective level of intensity, for only a brief fraction of any organism's waking life. The classical hunger drive physiologically defined ceases almost as soon as food—or nonfood—is ingested. This, as far as we know, is the only case in which a single swallow portends anything of importance. The temporal brevity of operation of the internal drive states obviously offers a minimal opportunity for conditioning and a maximal opportunity for extinction.

Here, Harlow introduces his curiosity drive to exemplify drives other than physiological drives. A purely biological drive, hunger, will completely upset the learning pattern. The organism will initiate a response pattern to obtain food. Harlow presents several questions:

1. If homeostasis is the sole rationalization of behavior, why does not the organism remain passive after he secures food? Both animals and humans continue to explore their environment; they maintain curiosity. Why?

2. In his experiments with rhesus monkeys (Harlow, 1950), continuous availability of food did not diminish learning, as drive reduction would intimate. Why?

From these experiments, Harlow concluded that there was no positive relationship between drive state, drive reduction, and learning in primates.

He affirms that drive reduction has some pertinency to learning, but assigns it a small, unimportant function in the learning process. Therefore, dissatisfaction with the conditioned response as the sole explanation of learning has impelled Harlow to search the environment for more revealing clues to man's behavior. This quest has led him to welcome curiosity—manipulation behavior—as the key to learning. Observations of children, and experiments with rhesus monkeys, have reinforced his belief that motivation aroused by external stimuli is the most fruitful rationalization yet proposed.

The need for stimulation, evidenced in Harlow's work, has momentous overtones for the teacher. Unless students maintain a minimum level of stimulation in the classroom, they themselves will initiate activity to boost the rate of incoming stimuli. Such activity will unquestionably be directed at goals that are noneducational. The result, both for learning and discipline, is obvious. Thus, teachers must provide a meaningful and interesting classroom milieu to insure sufficient stimuli for motivation. The materials of the environment must be regulated according to the level, changed frequently to sustain interest, and, finally, must be clearly connected with current classwork. Manipulation of materials for the sake of manipulation is not enough.

Often, classroom lethargy, disciplinary problems, and lack of learning are caused by an insufficiency of stimuli. Although not directly relevant to the schools, the damage which stimuli deficiency can precipitate is amazing. Every reader is acquainted with the phenomenon of brainwashing, which made such an effective impact during the Korean War. Hebb (1958) describes the astonishing results of the McGill studies which concentrated on the effects on the human when he is isolated from his environment: visual hallucinations, disturbances of self-perception, impairment of intelligence test performance, and the like. Consequently, Hebb has little hesitation in believing that man's motivation is a function of his exteroceptive stimulation.

As extreme as these examples are, they vividly depict man's need for external stimulation, and, to a lesser degree, characterize students' need for external motivation in school. Thus, as our theoretical view of motivation continues, the need for recognizing both its internal and external aspects becomes apparent. Murray's needs focused more on man's inner self; Harlow's curiosity-manipulation drive looks outside man. The remaining theories strive to integrate the internal and external components of motivation.

III. A. H. Maslow

Few theories have had greater acceptance than that of Maslow (1943, 1954). As Travers (1963, p. 165) says:

Maslow (1943) has proposed the following hierarchy of needs which, in the absence of any experimental evidence, is probably as well developed as any:

Physiological needs
Safety needs
Love and belonging needs
Esteem needs, including achievement and recognition needs
Self-actualization needs
Desires to know and understand

But before we determine what Maslow means by each of these, it will be extremely valuable to examine certain propositions which Maslow contends must underlie any theory of motivation. He rejects physiological drives as a model for motivational theory because a theory should focus upon basic goals, rather than temporary needs. This insures a place for unconscious motivation and acknowledges the subtlety and complexity of motivated behavior, that is, any motivated behavior may satisfy many needs, while any one act may have many sources of motivation.

The complexity of motivation is apparent when we understand man's need structure. Human needs are formed in hierarchies of prepotency, that is, one need may not be satisfied until a lower, more prepotent need is gratified. Thus, all of man's drives are related to the satisfaction or dissatisfaction of other drives. So, to scrutinize the nuances of motivation, Maslow challenges theories that rely on lists of drives, and he focuses upon goals, rather than separate drives. Consequently, any advanced speculations about motivation must concentrate upon the human, rather than the animal. It must not investigate man's field alone and neglect the human organism; an interpretation of the environment as man sees it is indispensable for motivational analysis. The uniqueness of the human's world must be the center of motivational study so that psychological, as well as physiological, ingredients may be evaluated.

Maslow then attempts to devise a theory which would satisfy

these requirements. His theory fixes upon what he considers to be man's basic needs: physiological, safety, love and belongingness, esteem, and self-actualization.

A. The Physiological Needs

The physiological drives are usually the foundation of motivational theory. But it is hopeless to construct any list of basic physiological needs since there can be as many needs as one wishes to fashion. Also, the physiological needs may serve as the means for satisfying other, different needs. Surely, these physiological drives are the most prepotent of all needs. If these drives remain unsatisfied, the organism is dominated by them and all other needs recede. The organism can entertain no other interest until the physiological drives are gratified. For example, there are many vivid stories about the effects of starvation upon the human. He can think of nothing but food; he dreams of it; his whole life centers on the attainment of food. Nothing else matters; the hunger drive is supreme.

Maslow feels that this is true, but, how common is it? Such emergency conditions are rare in today's society. Students of motivation often confuse the function of physiological drives in the human because so much experimentation is with animals, and animals exhibit very little other than physiological drives. The human experiences pure physiological drives so seldom that it can almost be discounted. A more pertinent question is: what happens when the human's physiological needs are met? What then motivates him? Now higher needs emerge and these, in turn, predominate in the human. Thus, needs operate in a hierarchy of prepotency, and gratification becomes vital to Maslow's need organization since it is only upon gratification of a lower need that the organism will be released to pursue higher (social) goals.

B. The Safety Needs

Once the physiological needs have been appeased, a new set of needs appears, which Maslow has designated as the safety needs. If conditions become sufficiently extreme, the safety needs may control man's behavior. This is more readily seen in children than in adults because mature humans suppress, if possible, fear reactions. Children, though, startle easily; they quickly develop feelings of insecurity which tend to govern their reaction. Children have an undisguised need for a safe, stable environment. Their behavior becomes disorganized when their ordered world is disrupted, and they strive desperately to preserve whatever balance they can.

The inferences for education are clear. A hostile, unpredictable classroom will compel students to construct their own safety measures in the classrooom. Often this will be done at the expense of learning, or, if the safety need dictates mastery of material, the benefit of such activity may be seriously questioned. Also, the impact of such uncertainty in a child's life is frequently seen in later years with the formation of the neurotic personality. A tense, unhealthy classroom surrounding will not, of course, determine adult neuroses, but it may become part of a child's already inconstant world. Hence, it adds to the confusion and disorder which may be present because of quarreling parents, a broken home, and the like. Even with the normal child, a persistent fear-ridden class produces ill effects on the learning process. Note the use of the adjective "persistent." A swift measure of authority administered in the school becomes steadily more desirable in our society. This is learning as much as mathematics, English, French, psychology, and the like, but if it exceeds permissible limits, students may retreat from preferable educational goals and attempt to establish educational security. Maslow's view of safety needs demands additional attention from educators.

C. Love and Belongingness Needs

As Maslow ascends his need hierarchy, the need for affection, love, and belongingness becomes well defined when physiological and safety needs are assuaged. The individual concerns himself with improving his relations with others. Here, in the hierarchy, he seems to move away from himself and seek fulfillment in others. Today, much of the existing maladjustment is the result of the deprivation of this need. Maslow stresses the ambivalence with which society views love and affection and sees such an attitude as the cause of much personal difficulty. There are many shades of meaning which can be applied to this category of needs, *but* sex is not its entire expression. It is a single constituent in the totality of the love, affection, and belongingness need, and it involves giving, as well as receiving, because, without the aspect of giving, love is restricted to the pure physiological level of drives.

There are many overtones for education in this particular category of needs. Youngsters who feel they are unwanted, who feel they do not belong, who feel no rapport with classmates, instructors, or school, are the core of many of the school's dilemmas. Notice the blending of needs as they operate in children. Most youngsters experience little trouble satisfying their physiological needs since local, state, and national agencies afford at least the necessities of life. But many children, regardless of the degree of satisfaction, lack the safety needs which provide an ordered world, and, when they enter a school environment in which they feel rejected, their insecurity is aggravated and they rapidly intensify their behavioral disorders. The school's comprehension of children's needs is critical in an age when youngsters bring their problems of insecurity into the school, which is the single element of society that contacts all of the youth of a community. Satisfaction of needs is an indispensable phase of education, and, as inspection of the higher grades of Maslow's hierarchy continues, the urgency, as well as the complexity, of need gratification becomes more distinct.

D. *The Esteem Needs*

Each human being has a need for real self-respect, and also a need for the esteem of others. By real self-respect, Maslow means that which is based upon solid achievement. He advocates two subdivisions of this category:

1. The desire for strength, achievement, confidence.
2. The desire for reputation, prestige, importance, attention, appreciation.

When the lower needs are satisfied, man seeks recognition from others. If it is deserving and forthcoming, the individual faces obstacles with a feeling of confidence. A feeling of usefulness and adequacy results. If this recognition is lacking, an inferiority complex may arise; the individual feels helpless when he confronts hardships.

Again, the lessons for education are obvious. Unless the school furnishes some success, some feeling of accomplishment, a youngster will attempt to achieve it in another form—often detrimental to the school's interests. Not that school success or reward should be so routine as to be meaningless—youngsters perceive such false efforts very quickly, and resent them deeply. This is what is meant by real self-respect. Teachers must provide opportunities for genuine success for all of the students. Again, this will be laborious and time-consuming, but it is well worth the effort. For, the better that the lower needs are satisfied, the more effectively will students be able to concentrate upon more complicated problems of learning.

E. The Need for Self-Actualization

Even if all of these needs are satisfied, Maslow states that there may still be a feeling of discontent and restlessness unless the person is doing what he wishes and what he is capable of doing. If he is fulfilling his capacity, he is becoming what he is. How many people ever attain this state is questionable, but, to the extent that individuals at least partially succeed, to that same extent can the human being hope to possess the energy and vision which will enable him to focus upon the higher, more involved issues of life which ultimately bring greater joy and peace of mind.

These, then, are the basic needs as Maslow beholds them. There are, however, definite conditions which encircle these needs, and which are critical to a thorough satisfaction of the basic needs. Restricting the freedom of the individual causes an emergency response pattern because without the necessary freedom, need satisfaction is unachievable. Maslow's freedom is both logically and psychologically sound because it permits need satisfaction and yet it does not infringe upon the rights and needs of others.

Also, Maslow refers to the curiosity drives (recall the work of Harlow) and accepts their importance in any analysis of needs. Since knowledge is so limited about the operation of curiosity or exploration in humans, Maslow tentatively identifies the desire to know and understand and reckons them as much personality needs as the basic needs discussed.

Finally, in his deliberations about the basic needs, Maslow speaks of the flexibility of the hierarchy. It is not rigid, although most people demonstrate needs in the order described, but there are many exceptions. Certain, usually exceptionally creative, persons may strive for self-actualization, regardless of the measure of satisfaction of lower needs.

Many such examples could be given, and they illustrate a most significant concept—partial need satisfaction. The normal human being is partially satisfied and partially dissatisfied in all of the basic needs. As a lower need is partially satisfied according to the individual's discernment, a higher need begins to emerge. Thus, there is a gradual evolution of need, and the complexity of motivation is once more witnessed.

IV. Lee J. Cronbach

Cronbach (1963), a noted educational psychologist, analyzes personality and behavior by needs. Individuals strive for goals which have much in common, that is, they display similar needs. Cronbach identifies a need as a broad motive which makes unique goals attractive and important to the individual. Once they are specified, the school can help to satisfy them by linking educational value to personal needs.

Cronbach acknowledges five needs which influence school behavior: affection, adult approval, peer approval, independence, and competence and self-respect.

A. Need for Affection

All humans evidence a need for affection. To the extent that this need is met, a person develops normally and achieves harmonious relationships with family and friends. The need for affection manifests itself early in life and persists throughout a person's years. If a child feels secure in his home, he usually transfers the security with him as he broadens his contacts with others. If he accomplishes this transfer, he then establishes rewarding relationships with teachers, classmates, and friends, which greatly aid the learning process because of the elimination of emotional tensions from the school atmosphere.

From his analysis of the affection need, Cronbach (1963, pp. 114–115) derives five principles which apply to all social needs:

1. An experience associated with other gratifications comes to be desired for itself.
2. From time to time changes in a person's social surroundings and in the demands upon him make it impossible for him to satisfy his needs by the actions that formerly satisfied them.
3. If a person fails to master the developmental tasks at one age, satisfying the same need at later ages is more difficult.
4. The development of a person is interlocked with the needs and development of others around him.
5. Development continues throughout life. Important adjustments and learning remain to be accomplished in adulthood.

B. Need for Approval by Authority

Children learn, at an early age, that the adult world commands obedience and respect. Often a child is in a quandary because his own drives force him into strife with authority, and it is here, at this critical time, that a youngster forms his response pattern to society. How this pattern unfolds may well reflect the stability of the child's immediate adult world. If there is firmness and reasonableness in a youngster's treatment, and in what is expected of him, there will be a corresponding firmness and reasonableness in the maturing individual's reaction to authority. If this stability of adult expectancy is lacking, the damage done can be extensive, as witnessed in the extremes of rebellion or overdependency.

C. Need for Approval by Peers

Cronbach distinguishes this category from the need for affection because relations with others extend far beyond the boundaries of the family. Friendship with those of one's age group is both enjoyable and gratifying and represents normal personality development, for a person's social pattern must change as the nature of the social group changes with advancing years. If the individual's response pattern does not change, approval by friends and associates is withdrawn, and the person's activities and companions are severely restricted with ensuing personality tangles. Consequently, learning is arrested and the teacher faces the task of consciously, and guardedly, offering support to such a student. The student thereby hopes to enhance his status in the eyes of his classmates.

D. Need for Independence

Cronbach understands the delicate relationship between need for approval by authority and the apparently contradictory need for independence. Society demands obedience to its laws; otherwise chaos would result. And yet, there must be sufficient permissiveness to encourage the creativity which independence of thought and action generates. Today, living in an age of social and political revolution, the homes and schools of the nation are groping to maintain the proper balance between control and independence in its citizens. The responsibility is incumbent upon both home and school. The home must have instilled adequate independence to enable a child of five or six to leave home and remain in school for a full day. The school must sustain discipline but encourage initiative and expression of ideas.

E. Need for Competence and Self-Respect

Here Cronbach appraises the individual's relationship with his world. Does he know his strength and his weaknesses? Is he striving toward realistic goals? Or is he overcome by feelings of hopelessness in his encounters with the world? Man's control and manipulation of his environment produce a tangible sense of fulfillment. Cronbach's use of competence is quite similar to the exploratory drive mentioned earlier as well as the concept of self-actualization. As competence develops, a feeling of adequacy grows and the person is able to confront life's problems with confidence. Such an attitude helps immeasurably in attaining educational goals. Students with positive views of their ability to achieve will undergo the inevitable failures and frustrations of the learning process and still be confident of their capacity to persevere. The opposite is also true. Plagued by failure, and with no confidence in their ability, such students are almost assured of nonfulfillment.

Finally, Cronbach (1963, p. 128) concludes that there is no one list of needs, and the needs that he describes do not act in isolation from each other.

V. Gordon W. Allport

Allport states that a motive is any internal condition in the person that induces action or thought (Allport, 1961, p. 196). He employs this definition as a criterion with which to evaluate other theories of motivation and as a foundation upon which he builds his own theory. Additionally, he specifies several requirements for an adequate motivational theory (see Allport, 1961, pp. 220–226):

1. It will acknowledge the contemporaneity of motives. That is, motivational theory should concern itself with the present state of the organism.
2. It will be a pluralistic theory—allowing for motives of many types. Motives cannot be reduced to one type since the complexity of motivation involves, at some time, any or all of the motives that many authors insist are *the* explanation of motivation. Motivational theory must be sufficiently inclusive to incorporate all levels of motives.
3. It will ascribe dynamic force to cognitive processes—e.g., planning and intention. Theories of motivation are gradually veering from the blind, irrational drives toward an acceptance of man's conscious involvement in his actions.
4. The theory will allow for the concrete uniqueness of motives. Here, Allport shows his reluctance to commit his theory to any given number of instincts or drives because such lists fail to encompass all of the goals which men pursue for their highly personal reasons.

To meet these demands, Allport turns to a concept of motivation which he believes will help to interpret the changing, spontaneous nature of motives. This is his belief in the notion of functional autonomy.

Allport defines his terms as follows (1961, p. 229):

Functional autonomy, then, refers to any acquired system of motivation in which the tensions involved are not of the same kind as the antecedent tensions from which the acquired system developed.

There seem to be two levels of functional autonomy, the perseverative and the propriate. The perseverative refers to the tendency to repeat behavior which originally satisfied a need, even when the need no longer exists. Both man and animals exhibit this predilection. Thus, when the rat has been fed and the hunger drive appeased, it will still run the maze correctly.

The propriate level, however, evolves from earlier, more basic drives and eventually becomes a source of motivation in itself, now distinct from its beginning tensions. This is what Allport means by "functionally autonomous." He gives several examples of the propriate level of functional autonomy, among which is the following (1961, pp. 235–236):

... a student who first undertakes a field of study in college because it is required, because it pleases his parents, or because it comes at a convenient hour may end by finding himself absorbed in the topic, perhaps for life. The original motives may be entirely lost. What was a means to an end becomes an end in itself.

Allport appreciates the limitations of present motivational knowledge and states that all motives are not functionally autonomous. Those which are not include drives, reflex action, constitutional equipment, habits, primary reinforcements, infantilisms, and fixations, some neuroses, and sublimation. So, any motive may be a compound of all these forces, but if a present motive seeks new goals (that is, manifests a different kind of tension from the motives from which it developed) it is functionally autonomous (Allport, 1961, p. 244). And, functionally autonomous motives are almost always wholly related to the self.

Allport's theory of motivation should hold a fascination for educators because the transformation of motives from childlike to mature is the goal of any teacher. How can the school shift needs and direct energies to remote and often abstract goals? It is much more difficult in the public school classroom than at the college level which is shown in Allport's example; however, it is precisely this transfer that teachers must accomplish. There are no infallible rules that explain how this may be done but the sheer recognition of the existence of a need change is progress for all levels and aspects of education.

MOTIVATION IN THE CLASSROOM

The reader will note, in the above discussion, that there was no attempt to select any one theory over the others. All offer appealing possibilities, while, similarly, all reveal inherent flaws. But knowledge of such theories, and their trends, is decisive in learning. For the incentives that the teacher employs have their rationale in theory, and, if an instructor is uncertain of the effect of any one of these incentives upon a student's personality, learning may be defective.

The incentives ordinarily adopted by teachers include reward and punishment, success and failure, praise and reproof, knowledge of results, and classroom competition. We could extend the list almost indefinitely but the uselessness of such categories is quite apparent. What is significant is that the teacher understands the artificial nature of incentives and utilizes them only as they relate to the unique needs of the student.

Otherwise, they will frustrate rather than aid, because of the inner and outer nature of motives. Recall the sequence of motivation—the person feels a need; this felt need arouses energy, which is directed toward a specific goal in the environment that will remove the feeling of dissatisfaction. Thus, there is a drive state, and there is also direction toward a goal. So, the essence of an incentive is to link the pupil's drive toward an educational objective by making it meaningful to the person. But this necessarily implies an acquaintance with human motives.

As our information about motives accumulates, our use of incentives is accordingly changing. Punishment, for example, was long frowned upon because of its psychological stigma. Today, many psychologists reason that punishment, properly applied, may be a desirable means for directing drives. Thus, it should be coupled almost simultaneously with positive action and reinforcement.

Any effective, positive incentive, however, is to be preferred, but, even judiciously used, there are dangers which all teachers should circumvent. The incentive should never become an end in itself, for example, marks, pleasing a teacher, honor rolls, and the like. This occurs easily, and a teacher may not become aware of it until the incentive is the goal. Nonetheless, incentives do have a place in the classroom; without them, it would be difficult, indeed, to connect student needs to school goals. All educators should guide their use of incentives as follows:

1. Know as much as possible about the nature of motivation. This will entail a constant reading of the literature, which is fundamental to a teacher's duties.

2. Recognize the needs of students. This is not to say that teachers must act as parents, counselors, and nurses, but the teacher must involve himself sufficiently to comprehend the wants of pupils.

3. From knowledge of motivation and knowledge of students, utilize incentives as they will help to integrate personal needs with educational objectives.

4. Recognize the pros and cons of incentives, and realize that what might be most potent with one pupil may be a total failure with another. In the application of incentives the teacher must accept the individuality and uniqueness of motivation.

CONCLUSION

There was no attempt in this chapter to shun the striking and formidable obstacles in any deliberations about motivation. Motivational theory is in its infancy, and techniques of evaluation are far from sophisticated. Still, this does not mitigate the importance of motives in learning. If a teacher successfully identifies a student's needs and forms an explicit connection between them and educational ends, he is able to direct the energies, initiated by needs, to higher, and it is hoped, more profitable goals. In so doing, the teacher's chore is greatly eased, and learning is greatly abetted.

CHAPTER IV

Types of Learning I — Motor

INTRODUCTION

An individual's ability to meet the demands made upon him by his environment depends upon the acquisition of a great many motor skills—skills that involve bodily movement. To possess such skills means to be able to act with dexterity and proficiency. Every normal individual acquires a large number of motor skills, some quite incidentally as various acts are performed again and again, others by dint of much effort and time spent in practice to achieve high levels of expertness for their monetary or social values. Their possession is an asset in many ways. They mean greater efficiency in one's work; they enhance self-esteem; they bring social recognition, and are the source of rich satisfaction and pleasures (Kingsley and Garry, 1957, pp. 297–298).

PERHAPS THE MOST neglected and underrated type of learning is that of motor learning. Frequently classified in psychology texts as motor skills, psychomotor skills, skills, and skill performances, motor learning forms the basis of much of man's behavior. In this chapter these terms will be used interchangeably. Very often, the average person regards motor learning as a gross type of operation which comprises the mechanical manipulation of some object. Unfortunately, this is a widely accepted oversimplification of a vastly more complicated procedure.

If we reflect momentarily upon the divisions of man's life, we soon realize the extent to which motor activities predominate in the successful adjustment to each venture. Recreation, education, and work are spheres of endeavor in which we all engage. Most people enjoy some kind of recreational activity that demands bodily movement, such as swimming, golf, tennis, bowling, skiing, skating, and the like. Such activities are relaxing; they contribute to good health, and they furnish necessary diversion. Each sport or game, whether indoor or outdoor, is a sequence of movements directed toward a specific goal. The more skilled the movements, the more successful the participant.

Skilled performance results in satisfaction and pleasure because the human being likes to do what he can do well. Even with a recreational type of motor activity, however, more is involved than the performance of steps 1, 2, 3, and 4, which will then conclude in a polished, refined skill. Recall the example of the golf swing which was described in Chapter I. No person who learns to play golf will ever achieve a measure of success unless he integrates the various parts of the swing. And the individual attains integration of parts only as he understands. He must interpret *and* comprehend the nature of the skill he is learning and its relation to the goal he is seeking.

The Extent of Motor Learning

The same principles are true for man's occupations. Is there any business or profession in which some degree of motor activity is unnecessary? Law, medicine, dentistry, teaching, office management, and sales are examples of employment which require the utilization of motor skills. Some professions and some aspects of business require less motor skill than others; the lawyer obviously exerts less motor activity during his day's work than does the carpenter. But the lawyer must manipulate books, tape recorders, and projectors; he must drive to court; he must present his case, which undoubtedly demands demonstration of some kind. These are the more undisguised motor skills our professional man uses; are there more subtle kinds of motor performance his career requires?

These more subtle skills are often overlooked because they are the foundations upon which more manifest verbal learning rests. Thus, when the lawyer presents his case to a jury, he speaks as dramatically and effectively as possible. This oral communication relies upon motor skills: management of the tongue, the use of teeth and lips in sounding, and control of essential muscles and breath in word formation. These skills are such an integral part of the growth pattern that it is almost impossible to indicate distinct stages of development. They begin at birth, continue through growth, and are refined in school.

Other motor skills which are cultivated in school are those of reading and writing. It is probably most difficult for the reader to associate reading with motor skills. The act of reading, however, is not the purely verbal response that it so often appears. Unless the muscles that control eye movement are properly trained, a pupil will experience severe difficulty in learning to read.

The eye does not move in a smooth sweep across and down the page. Rather, it moves in a series of jerks across the page; it stops several times on each line. These stops are called fixation pauses, and it is here that reading occurs because the eye "sees" a group of words. When the eye comes to the end of a line it must return across the page and begin at the next line. This is called return sweep, and lack of skill in this movement plagues some youngsters throughout the elementary school.

All readers have a tendency toward another eye movement which interferes with rapid, comprehensive reading. This is known as regression and is the inclination of the eye to reverse itself, that is, to return to words which were previously read. This movement is characteristic of both poor and beginning readers.

The proficient reader has mastered the movements which are indispensable for smooth, swift reading. He has few fixation pauses, few regressions, and is capable of an accurate return sweep. So, according to the quotation from Kingsley and Garry at the beginning of the chapter, the reader has acted with dexterity and proficiency.

The final skill mentioned was that of writing. The art of legible, intelligible writing is one that appears in many of man's efforts. Instruction in writing begins immediately in school and continues for all of the elementary grades. In grades one and two, materials and exercises are provided which encourage the training of the larger muscles. As the youngster matures, he is expected to conform to stricter standards which require greater control and precision in the expression of the written word.

The Retention of Motor Skills

Any consideration of writing, as motor learning, introduces a problem which emphasizes the importance of skilled performances, not only in school or sport, but also throughout the individual's lifetime. A study by Fleishman and Parker (1962) investigated the retention of motor learning (tracking) over intervals of one to fourteen months. The results substantiated the conclusion from previous studies that continuous motor responses are retained for a significant period of time. In the Fleishman and Parker study, the correlation between final learning and retention performance varied from .80 to .98 for the groups in the experiment.

Why, then, does writing suffer so much when the individual is reaching a peak of maturation and should be capable of performing skilled tasks at high levels of dexterity and proficiency? Garrison, Kingston, and McDonald (1964, p. 244) stress the conditions of writing as the main cause:

Much of the current criticism of instruction in handwriting stems from the fact that, although the skill improves with practice during the elementary school years, it rapidly declines during the later school years. Reasons for this rapid decline may be ascribed to (1) absence of guided practice, (2) lack of social pressure, (3) less favorable conditions for writing, and (4) increased demand for writing in the upper grades resulting in an emphasis on speed.

So, writing, a motor skill which enters into all phases of man's life, declines in quality when the conditions of performance are altered.

Identity of Principles

If motor learning is so important, the teaching of skills should strive for rapid, drastic improvement, particularly in the school. Unquestionably, the school can be a very difficult training ground for motor learning unless motivation is aroused and sustained. Success in writing, speaking, and reading depends upon skill in some kind of bodily movement, that is, verbal learning seems to flow from motor learning. *And the principles and characteristics of both are identical.*

Too often, this fact of learning is disregarded. Recall the characteristics of learning: a motivated individual, an obstacle, environmental stimuli, the person's perception of the stimuli, the response pattern, and the goal. The learning of a skill reflects these characteristics. It would be well for teachers never to forget this truth. Motor learning is more than a mere accumulation of acts, steps, stages, and the like. It entails perception, *without which* the skill is soon lost. Once overlearning of the skill occurs, there is a remarkable stability of response *provided* that the conditions of performance remain basically the same. This is what Garrison *et al.* accentuate in their quotation: the conditions of performing the skill of writing are *not* duplicated outside of the classroom.

Nonobservable Behavior in Motor Learning

Consistency of excellence in skill performance, under all conditions, is the work of the expert. Although schools are not designed to produce experts in all skills, there is, nevertheless, a certain level of stability that can be expected. It will be the task of the remaining part of this chapter to suggest insights and methods that will contribute to individual stability of response in skill performance.

For example, a major element in the stability of response is the feeling that one has about the skill and about the product of the performance. There is a feeling of satisfaction about skillful performance, but there may also be a desire to express some personal feeling in motor activity. In his classification of motor activities, Ragsdale (1950) postulates three divisions: object-motor activities, language-motor activities, and feeling-motor activities.

These feeling-motor activities may encompass man's affective disposition at any particular time. The feelings associated with these activities may or may not be conscious, that is, the individual may deliberately select a certain activity to portray a mood. Thus, the host at a party may play a dance record whose music is fast and jumpy to mirror the feeling of excitement and joviality. Or, the golfer who has had an irritating day at work may lunge savagely at the ball and thus destroy the rhythm of his swing. He may be totally unaware of the reason for his poor game. However, in both examples a feeling has been expressed through motor activity.

As analysis of a person's feelings toward, or through, motor learning occurs, one quickly realizes that an individual's mastery of a skill rests mainly upon his perception of the task and its use. This is the reason that recent texts now refer to skill learning as psychomotor. It is not only mechanical; it must command man's consciousness. Otherwise, the sum of the parts will never equal the whole.

As an illustration, think about the way in which a boy learns to hit a baseball. He tries to gauge the speed of the ball; he concentrates upon the way that he grips the bat; he attempts to achieve as comfortable a stance as possible. If he fails to comprehend the nature of the baseball swing, however, he will meet with indifferent success. He must appreciate the consequences of swinging his bat "up" toward the ball; he will constantly hit the ball high into the air. If he swings "down" or chops with his bat, he will unfailingly hit the ball into the ground. Only as he understands the swing, will he strive for a level stroke, one which will culminate in the desired "line drive."

If we continue our examination of the boy learning to play baseball, we soon conclude that performance will also be aided if there is an understanding of the purpose of this particular form of motor activity. This is likewise true for all types of learning. In our example, the better the boy is able to relate the specifics of the game to the overall purpose of baseball, the better will be his performance.

There no longer can be any doubt that perception is vital in motor learning. Recent studies have attempted to solve the problem of the psychological refractory period. Why will a subject attend to only one stimulus and disregard, or delay reaction to, a second stimulus following closely? Davis (1959, 1962) and Harrison (1960) showed that the mere presentation of one stimulus, even when *no* response was required, delayed the response to a second stimulus. The subject perceives the initial stimulus and is so attentive to it that the response pattern to the second declines significantly in reaction time.

Because the more complex skills that man exhibits are dependent upon either the obvious or subtle motor learnings, teachers should know as much as possible about the nature of these skills and the most effective method of teaching them.

THE NATURE OF MOTOR LEARNING

Before an analysis of skill is undertaken, the reader should remember that any psychology of learning text describes *the* student, that is, all students. Furthermore, in any presentation of a particular skill, for example, writing, there is an accepted standard excellence of form which is recognized for each skill. But we all vary within accepted standards, that is, we bring our individual differences to the learning and performance of each task.

Thus, it is the student's interpretation of form which is the goal of skill instruction. As growth and development differ with the individual, so must individual adaptation differ within standards. When the batter swings at the ball, he usually moves his forward foot and strides toward it. Naturally, a tall boy will have a longer stride than a shorter boy.

In the golf swing, there is a limit which each golfer imposes upon his backswing. Control of the club is essential, and, if the club is taken back excessively, control is lost. In an attempt to attain distance, some golfers take their swing back much more than others, mainly because they possess stronger arms and hands and, accordingly, maintain greater club control than other, less strong, golfers. To expect all golfers to swing their club through an arc with an identical distance is obviously ridiculous. The same is true for motor learning under educational auspices.

The Skill Itself

A motor skill is a smoothly integrated series of movements undertaken for a specific purpose. As knowledge of man's behavior advances, there is a corresponding recognition of the complexity of certain behavioral aspects, such as motor skills. As Adams (1964, p. 181) says:

Historically, American research on skills has tended to deal with behaviorally large units like tracking performance, and has given less emphasis to the constituent mechanisms that enter skilled sequences. British research, on the other hand, has taken a more molecular view and the impact of their work has grown during the past few years in the United States. The British have gotten a lot of kilometers out of communications and computer models, but those who are disposed toward other interpretations can set aside these analogies from engineering and find plenty of good ideas and data behind the models. The gist of their formulation, which seems to find a goodly amount of agreement in the United Kingdom, is that S (subject) has a number of sensory input channels, short- and long-term memory for storing these incoming data before responding if necessary, a decision mechanism of limited capacity for processing the environmental stimuli as well as the internal stimuli fed back from responses, a number of effector mechanisms to which the decision mechanism issues orders, and mechanisms of temporal expectancy that govern the timing of responses. One way or another, research on these topics by the British, and lately the Americans, has been probing the stuff out of which skills are made. Until recently, learning has been conspicuously neglected in their work, as it has been by all whose penchant is engineering models.

This quotation clarifies recent thinking about skill learning and emphasizes the commitment of the total organism to the acquisition and perfection of the skill. Often, to demonstrate, or to aid understanding, the skill is divided into parts. Such instruction is questionable unless the totality of the act and its relationship to the goal is consistently reaffirmed. Otherwise, the unity of performance is lost, and may be extremely difficult to recapture.

Since a part, as a portion of the whole act, may be completely different when studied separately, it could well affect the final performance of the act. For example, if we recollect the boy learning to play baseball, he must swing his bat along a line to meet the oncoming ball squarely. But before he starts his bat toward the ball, he usually moves his bat backward in an abbreviated backswing.

If an instructor decides to break the swing into parts (backswing, forward motion, stride, follow-through), he may have pupils practice just the backswing. Such a procedure conceivably could destroy the rhythm of the swing because the abridged backswing differs wholly when removed from the entire swing. The timing, the power, and the "feel" of the backswing are incompatible with the entire performance.

Similarly, some penmanship exercises which forced students to draw endless straight lines or circles within a prescribed space had little value when applied to the actual writing of letters. When a pupil forms letters, there is a discipline demanded that is lacking in drawing lines and circles, regardless of the requirements of space and slant.

There is a psychological difference between a part analyzed separately, and a part analyzed as an integral element of a whole. Not only does it relate to the whole but it also relates to other parts. The manner and purpose of a part are determined solely and entirely by the whole. The identification of specific motor abilities to perform certain motor tasks is a seemingly insurmountable task. The more obvious abilities can be readily identified for each skill, but the perfection of skill execution exacts more hidden resources.

Fleishman (1953), who has conducted extensive research into motor learning, attempted to identify needed motor abilities for United States Air Force personnel. He detected the more conspicuous abilities, but he also established several more vague classes, such as avoidination, ambidexterity, and psychomotor precision. A complicated motor skill requires some aptitudes which are not readily discovered.

Perception and Motor Learning

If there is a nonobservable depth to motor learning, man himself must provide the answer. If the acquisition of a skill requires more than summing the parts, man's reaction to the problem must hold the answer. A major share of the explanation must be in the individual's perception of his task. Although individual variables such as maturation, motivation, and past experiences exercise a considerable influence upon perception, the very existence of perception in motor learning is persistently slighted in skill teaching.

To understand the presence of perception in skill attainment, it is necessary to comprehend its multiple function here, as in other types of learning. The individual must perceive the goal for which the skill is utilized and he must also perceive the parts of which the skill is composed. It is only as the individual relates the parts to each other, and the intact skill to the goal, that true precision and refinement of movement is achieved.

Once the task is mastered, the person's perceptual involvement will decrease; the response becomes more automatic. This does not imply a rote, thoughtless kind of activity because perception is operative *as it is needed*. A person who has learned to type can work rapidly, and carefully, with little intellectual commitment. But if an employer, or teacher, stresses the importance of a particular assignment, perception becomes keener to avoid the likelihood of error. As conditions vary, so does the attention which is necessary for an adept performance.

Recent studies have confirmed the belief that man is consciously engaged in the execution of a motor act. The design of the studies has been to present pairs of stimuli to subjects, one closely following the other. The stimuli require motor responses by the subjects. The response to the second stimulus continually requires more time than the reaction to the initial stimulus. The cause of this is the psychological refractory period. In Chapter II, the refractory phase of nerve stimulation was discussed. A psychological refractory period has much the same meaning.

As you recall, the nerve fiber is unable to transmit any additional impulses for a brief period following the passage of a previous impulse. Similarly, once there is a motor response to a stimulus, the subject is unable to respond to a second stimulus that also elicits a motor response. Harrison (1960) establishes the delayed reaction time to the second stimulus when it too closely follows the first. Particularly interesting is Welford's work (1959), which further elaborates on the psychological refractory period. He shows that studies which demanded successive responses by the same hand have a longer psychological refractory period than those which permitted responses by *both* hands. There are notable implications for teaching in the theory of the psychological refractory period and these will be discussed later in the chapter.

The evidence, therefore, is conclusive that perceptual involvement is necessary for skill, as opposed to mechanical learning, and should be of vital concern in the instruction of motor skills.

Individual Differences and Motor Learning

Although a motor task may consist of several parts or stages and there may be an approved way of enacting the skill, there are, and must be, individual innovations brought to both the learning and execution of the skill. Individual differences today is, unfortunately, a stale term which has become relatively meaningless to students of psychology in the study of the learning process.

Some differences, more than others, are particularly observable in motor learning. This is especially true of physical growth. Since many of the motor skills require attributes such as strength and skill, the union of motor learning with growth and development is almost indivisible. Guilford (1958) has attempted to differentiate psychomotor factors and abilities. Among the psychomotor factors are: strength, impulsion, speed, static precision, dynamic precision, coordination, and flexibility. These are then related to parts of the body such as the trunk, hands, and so forth.

Until a certain phase of growth and development has occurred, motor learning is restricted, if not impossible. The teaching of writing is a good illustration. During the first years of instruction, the youngsters are allowed to form enlarged letters and they also use materials designed to aid muscular development. In these early school years, the muscles employed in writing and drawing have not developed sufficiently to permit more intricate work. As the growth process continues, more complex motor tasks can be mastered. A study by Sloane (1955), in which he administered the Lincoln-Oseretsky Motor Development Scale, showed a steady improvement of motor learning with age.

Thus, there must be a definite stage of physical growth before particular skills are taught. This is true of the more basic qualities. If you recall Guilford's list of psychomotor factors, strength was included. Obviously, the average freshman in high school will lack the strength and weight of the average senior. But some high schools, because of disproportionate enrollment, or faulty athletic scheduling, must play their freshmen against another school's seniors, perhaps, in football. This is not only senseless, but it could also be dangerous. The physical growth and development of both teams is irreconcilable.

There is another difference between individuals which approximates growth and development and yet is distinct from it. This is maturation, a force which often controls the type of motor learning that can be taught and the extent to which the student can practice or apply it. Basically, maturation is a matter of readiness. Is a student physically ready, emotionally ready, and mentally ready to begin a special kind of learning?

Commins and Fagin (1954) speak of maturation as an interaction between developing physiological functions and experiences. Each phase of behavior flows from an earlier phase, and is not merely added to it. There is an inherent dependence of one upon the other. The concept of maturation as a link between physical growth and experience is pertinent because it implies a conscious effort by the individual to forge such a link.

Baller and Charles (1961, p. 22) discuss maturation as follows:

What is the meaning of maturation? To say that it is a process of attaining full development does not help much to signify the basic features of the process. A satisfactory definition of maturation puts emphasis upon the refinements in the structure of the various parts of an individual's body—refinements that occur as the individual progresses toward his goal of adulthood. Maturation is an unfolding or "ripening" of potentials that an individual possesses by virtue of his being a member of a given species and by virtue, more specifically, of his biological inheritance from a particular parentage.

There is more to the full meaning of maturation. It is that maturation denotes change in function as well as change in the organism's physical equipment. The close relation of function and structure cannot be overemphasized in any description of development and behavior. We can hardly discuss (or think about) the ripening of an organism's potentials without extending the meaning of "potentials" to what the creature does with its more fully matured parts as well as the changes that are occurring in the parts.

When children of normal intelligence, but of different age and size, are asked to perform a motor skill, the results are startling. A small six year old and a large four year old, approximately the same size, vary noticeably in the manner in which they perform a motor skill. The greater dexterity and sureness which the older child evidences cannot be attributed to muscle growth but must relate to experience, and this we designate as maturation.

Other variables which were listed at the conclusion of Chapter I affect motor learning, but in a more elusive way. Sex differences, for example, depend upon the nature of the skill and the individual's experience, which includes practice. In skills requiring strength, gradually boys surpass girls. Some more refined tasks, such as hopscotch and jumprope, favor girls. But variables such as sex, experience, and motivation are more difficult to appraise. We accept their existence, and recognize their influence, but we also admit the perplexities they afford for specific analysis.

THE CHARACTERISTICS OF MOTOR LEARNING

Among the more interesting characteristics of motor learning are the changes which occur during the learning period. Some parts of the task are eliminated; other, more sophisticated, portions are added. Kingsley and Garry (1957) state that the changes which ensue because of repetition of a task are as follows:

1. Changes in the task
2. Changes in perception
3. Changes in accessory responses
4. Changes in feeling tone
5. Integration of movements
6. Changes in speed and accuracy
7. Changes in fatigue effects

When a person first tries to learn a motor task, his movements usually are awkward, particularly if the skill is not closely related to his experience. Learning to type is a good example of a motor skill that normally is unrelated to any previous learning by the student. In the classic study by Book (1908) of learning to typewrite, the difficulties and differences which the subjects encountered are a striking illustration of initial crudeness.

Subjects differed in the manner in which they learned the keyboard; they experienced a major obstacle in moving the right finger to the right key, and the final movement which produced the desired letter. Similar hindrances were met when they had to transfer from letters to words.

Modification of the Task

Another frequently quoted study is that conducted by Longwell (1938). The subjects were expected to capture rolling balls, to duplicate "silhouette" figures, and to trace reflected patterns. Within the total skill three different kinds of distinct tasks were identified: general, specific, and secondary. The general task establishes a comprehensive overview of the task and what is needed to complete it.

The secondary tasks are those which contribute to the refinement of performance and which remain after attention to the general task is eliminated. Thus, in learning to swim, the neophyte is mainly conscious of staying afloat. After he becomes more familiar with the water and more confident of his own buoyancy, he concentrates on proper leg and arm movements. Slowly, these secondary tasks will likewise disappear.

Longwell (1938, pp. 265–266) describes the tasks as follows:

Problem I. Capturing rolling balls. The tasks are general, specific, and secondary.

(1) *General task*. The general task is an undetailed reference to a total and imminent problem. It may be definite or indefinite . . .

(2) *Specific task*. The specific task is a detailed reference to a phase of performance. It is set before resolution-by-movement occurs . . .

(3) *Secondary task*. The secondary task is a sub-task which occurs as a phase of the determination during the course of resolution . . .

It appears that definite and indefinite *general* tasks were set with about equal frequency (13, 12); that *specific* tasks were least frequently set (9), while secondary tasks occurred most often (98) . . .

Modifications of the task occurred because of practice. Longwell (1938, pp. 270–271) summarizes them:

Our most important phase of the comparison still remains. It concerns the modifications of the task under repetition from the first to the last member of the series of actional performances. This progressive change has now to be described.

In capturing rolling balls the trend in modification was as follows. Either a general or secondary task was set at first. After a few repetitions the general task dropped out and the secondary persisted. After many repetitions there is, as a rule, no task remaining. Rarely a general task may reappear or a secondary task persist.

Such task changes are often called "the dropping out" of movements, or tasks. Some authors (Commins and Fagin, 1954) object to this usage because a person frequently may add movements in his perfection of the skill. For example, most readers of this text possess a driver's license which was the objective of instruction that was given at home or at high school in a driver education class.

When you first sat behind the wheel your chief aim was to avoid hitting anybody or anything. Caution, almost paralyzing caution, characterized your actions. You thought—start the car, do not let it stall, watch for signs, lights, and people, and drive very slowly. You undoubtedly gripped the steering wheel so tightly that your hands became tired and moist with perspiration.

However, with repetition, your crude attempts at parking became more skillful, you applied the brake at the right time and with only the necessary amount of force, and you mastered the use of the gear selector and the directional signals; you became more expert. Finally, you were able to drive the car as well as your instructor and you were able to secure your driver's license.

In the transition from awkwardness to expertise, it is quite conceivable that you actually increased your movements. The good driver always adjusts his rearview mirror; if there is a sideview mirror, he will do likewise; often the driver will be dissatisfied with the temperature of the car and may pull switches or push buttons to turn the heater off or on; he may also regulate air intake by rolling up or down the car window; he may turn on or off the car radio.

He would never have tried to execute these tasks when he was learning to drive. Now he is expert, but the total number of movements has multiplied. Has he dropped or added tasks? Obviously, the learner has done both. He has abolished the unnecessary movements; he has added those which he thinks will improve his performance.

The key word in understanding the elimination and addition of tasks is "unnecessary." As the learner understands the relation of parts to whole, he combines his movements into a smooth and finished execution of the task, and it is here that the process of "dropping out" happens. As the learner understands the relation of the particular task to a particular goal, he concentrates the task upon the attainment of the goal, and it is here that the process of "addition" may occur. As Longwell (1938, p. 280) says:

Elaboration of task occurred in the setting of secondary tasks during resolution. The general initial task especially called for subdivision and recasting to attain a satisfactory resolution. Elaboration was also apparent in the intermediate stage, when determination was released. Here new and detailed directions for resolution were profitable, e.g., "go around to the right carefully and keep the pencil-point on the line." Here task lasts over into the determining phase.

When the individual achieves a degree of dexterity that allows him to focus upon secondary tasks, which will continually improve his performance, he is engaged in polishing his rendering of the act until it is as perfect as possible, given his individual limitations.

The same is true when attention is shifted from task execution to task usage, that is, goal achievement. Both these properties are the mark of the expert. In the typing class, for example, attention moves from the task itself to the speed with which the task may be executed. How many words per minute can the student type? Or, in the shop class, it is not how the tools are to be used but rather how finished will the object be?

If both elimination and addition of tasks occur, other changes manifest themselves. If the task can be done well, unquestionably the student will enjoy it; his facility of performance will leave him relatively untired, compared to his initial efforts. These were among the changes suggested by Kingsley and Garry, but they cannot develop until there are changes in the task.

The Learning Curve

Logically, then, as desirable changes materialize during the learning period, performance changes. These changes in performance may be diagrammed and are called learning curves. Psychologists have long studied learning curves and have shown inordinate fascination for them. Perhaps the safest statement we can make today is that there is no single learning curve. It is not possible for a single learning curve to exist because we fully accept the implications of individual differences. We can sketch a curve which is *representative* of the changes which occur in learning.

Such a curve will show fairly consistent traits. There will be a period of initial rapid rise after a slow start, continued improvements interspersed with a leveling tendency, and a final level of attainment. These leveling tendencies are called plateaus during which there is no visible improvement. These trends may be plotted in various ways. As Deese (1952, p. 148) says:

Learning curves can be classed roughly into three types, which depend upon what aspect of improvement in performance is measured. One type of learning curve is an error curve, a second type is a time curve, and a third type is an accuracy curve.

The accuracy or improvement curve is shown in Figure 4-1. The slow start is caused by the difficulties of initial learning, that is, lack of familiarity with the task and no established response pattern. The rapid rise occurs when there is some mastery of the grosser aspects of the task; in motor learning this would be the initial refinement of the task. Following the initial spurt, learning slows and improvement becomes more difficult because continued refinement entails mastery of detail as the person acquires greater perception of the process. Occasionally, a plateau will appear because of carelessness, decreasing motivation, or a shift to different units of the task (the transfer from typing letters to typing words). Finally, of course, there is a limit beyond which we are unable to achieve, so here the curve trails off into a straight line.

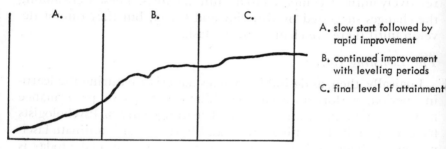

A. slow start followed by rapid improvement

B. continued improvement with leveling periods

C. final level of attainment

FIGURE 4-1. *A Learning Curve*

Feedback

Interesting and informative research has provided fresh insights into the cause of these changes. One of the most promising of these theories is that of "feedback." Any motor act consists of many integrated parts for which the individual acquires a "feel" when he begins to master the skill. He comprehends the sequence and correctness of each movement or part. When any part feels incorrect, the person realizes it immediately and instantly tries to remedy the faulty movement. Since we never repeat an act exactly in the same manner, this correction during the skill is a continual process.

It is as if knowledge of results were built into the performance. Feedback is an indication of sophisticated skill execution because it requires a thorough knowledge of the act and its movements before the person can respond to the change stimuli we have designated as feedback. As you read these pages, feedback is governing the rate of your reading. If you understand the material you have just read, you will be satisfied with your speed and will not seek to vary your rate. Here, feedback is acting as a reinforcer of your behavior.

If, however, as you scan these pages, you become aware that you are not grasping the material as you should, perhaps you sense that your eyes are traveling too rapidly for adequate comprehension, or perhaps you realize you were daydreaming, because of feedback, you slow your rate of reading and strive for greater comprehension. Here, feedback is acting as a regulator of your behavior.

Studies conducted by Chase and his associates (1961) verify the significance of feedback. They delayed feedback for repetitions of a speech sound and key tapping. Both types of responses had more errors because of the delay. Feedback was disrupted by such disturbances as tapping the subject on the arm because the person lost contact with the "feel" of his task. He could not judge if his performance was correct or not, and the entire response pattern suffered accordingly.

This concludes our analysis of the nature and characteristics of motor skills. From our discussion, how can we hope to improve the teaching of these skills?

TEACHING MOTOR SKILLS

Any teacher, entrusted with the instruction of motor skills, must be as expert in the performance of the skill as is possible. Although this may appear to be such an obvious statement as to be unnecessary, knowledge of a subject is not always a criterion for assignment to teach it. Very often, a prospective faculty member is hired to teach one subject, and, quite casually, another, perhaps unrelated, subject is included in the teaching load.

In the elementary school, this frequently happens with such subjects as music, sewing, shop, and the like. At the secondary level, a man may be asked to help with physical education; a woman may be asked to assist with home economics. The folly of such a procedure is apparent when we consider the complicated process of motor learning.

Before anyone attempts instruction in a motor skill, he should be thoroughly expert in its performance. He must understand all the details of the whole; he must understand the correct form for performing the task; he must also appreciate the individual differences which each person brings to the task. Such competence is the one norm which never can be excluded.

Without this proficiency, an instructor is unable to analyze the act into its parts and to present these parts, always in relation to the whole, as an intelligent sequence to a class. If an instructor does possess this adequacy, he is sufficiently familiar with the task to describe it to the class, to demonstrate it for the class, and to guide the class (as a class and as individuals) through its first crude efforts and to adjust the task to individual variations.

Guidance of Motor Learning

Assuming expertise, the usual procedure in beginning skill instruction is to explain the essence and purpose of the task. Verbal instruction is an essential part of motor learning, and, as such, it should achieve a definite purpose. The goal of verbal instruction is understanding so that, primarily, learners may comprehend why they are learning a particular task, and, secondarily, they may apprehend the parts and their relation to the whole.

Such verbal instruction will help to stimulate motivation because through verbal instruction the instructor enables the students to realize the value of the task. Motivation is usually not a problem in motor learning because knowledge of results is instantly obtained. The chief danger in the use of verbal instruction during the introduction of a motor skill is that the teacher may include excessive facts and thus confuse students.

When the instructor thinks that the learner understands the vital relationships of the task, he may *show* how it is to be done. Pictures, diagrams, movies, models, or whatever is deemed effective should be used. These tools should emphasize the *form* of the skill and should be presented with continued verbal instruction to reinforce understanding. Here, the learner actually sees what the correct form is, that is, how the expert performs his task. But demonstration can only be used to increase comprehension, to grasp the total act, or to enhance the learner's perception of the part-whole relationship.

Finally, the instructor must launch the beginner on his own way, and it is here that superfluous instruction may create a feeling of dependency. Frequently, instructors aid the student too quickly. Instructors should allow the learner to make mistakes; this is part of the learning process. But, he should be there to discourage frustration or permanent error.

How can this best be accomplished? Not by physically manipulating the learner through the act! The golf instructor who moves the beginner's arms through the swing or the teacher who guides the pupil's hand during penmanship class are not teaching properly because this kind of instruction creates an entirely different task. Perhaps the only time when such instruction is warranted is if the pupil has a physical handicap and needs aid in sensory adaptation.

After beginners initiate the task themselves, the best method of instruction is verbal *together* with the actual movements the learner is discharging.

Part versus Whole Instruction

There has been so much written about learning the whole task, here as well as elsewhere, that the reader may receive the impression that a teacher should never focus upon a part in instruction. This is obviously incorrect for a complex task. For abbreviated, simple tasks, the pure, whole method is desirable. A complex task, however, will require practice upon a part; otherwise the skill will not be perfected.

This kind of part instruction (often called the progressive part method) always relates the part to the whole, and, by so doing, forms a "psychological whole." These are then combined to form the true or pure whole. Momentarily, then, the learner considers these parts to be a total task, always remembering that they "belong" to a whole. If parts are learned as parts, with no effort to relate them to the whole, learning the total skill is hampered, and performance becomes mechanical.

The progressive part method is one reason why it is so difficult to predict final performance of a motor skill from initial trials. Parker and Fleishman (1960) discovered that initial performance correlated very poorly with final performance. Their study also verified an earlier study by Adams (1957) which indicated that unrelated measures of motor ability were a more accurate standard of prediction than initial performance on the task itself.

Practice

If one word could be found to summarize the conditions of practice, that word would be *meaningful*. The setting for practice must be as real as the limitation of the educational milieu allows, and the task practiced must be the task which requires the desired skill. Pushing a pen up and down, forming hundreds of straight lines, is a dubious way of practicing handwriting, to say nothing of the disastrous effect on motivation. Another example is the student in the physical education class who learns all the necessary rules and movements of a particular game but does not practice them under game conditions.

The student cannot be a spectator; he must participate. He must engage in purposeful activity because it is precisely here that he is applying the parts and the whole to the attainment of the goal. He understands the relations of the task to the goal, and, unless he has the opportunity to utilize his skill, there will be a loss of motivation and a corresponding disintegration of expertise.

The conditions of practice, although as real and meaningful as possible, must also encourage and not discourage. Fatigue and dismay at early errors must be avoided by brief, carefully spaced practice periods. As skill increases, the periods of practice may be longer and more frequent until the point where additional overlearning might lead to boredom and carelessness. Then, widely spaced practice periods to insure retention of a high degree of skill are all that will be needed.

CONCLUSION

Psychomotor skills are the foundation of much of man's behavior, both physical and verbal. Any difficulty with motor learning, either because of physical handicap or faulty learning will greatly hinder man's adjustment to his environment. The motor skills are learned in the identical way as other kinds of learning, but, because of the more obvious physical characteristics of skill acquisition, the notion of understanding is often omitted. Yet true motor learning occurs only when there is perception of the task and the purpose for which the skill is to be used. Finally, to a certain extent, all teachers are teachers of motor skills.

CHAPTER V

Types of Learning II — Cognitive

INTRODUCTION

But were we to utilize fully our capacity for registering the differences in things and to respond to each event encountered as unique, we would soon be overwhelmed by the complexity of our environment. Consider only the linguistic task of acquiring a vocabulary fully adequate to cope with the world of color differences! The resolution of this seeming paradox—the existence of discrimination capacities which, if fully used, would make us slaves to the particular—is achieved by man's capacity to categorize. To categorize is to render discriminably different things equivalent, to group the objects and events and people around us into classes, and to respond to them in terms of their class membership rather than their uniqueness (Bruner, Goodnow, and Austin, 1956, p. 1).

ALTHOUGH MAN'S ABILITY to categorize, form, and utilize concepts shapes his adjustment to reality and determines the limits of his achievements, the nature and function of concept formation and concept attainment are often misinterpreted. Any division of learning is artificial, whether it is by motor, cognitive, and problem solving, or by sensation, perception, comprehension, and creative thinking.

Cognitive learning is the basis of *all* learning. It controls the extent of motor learning, that is, a skill is mastered only as the relations of the part to the whole, and the task to the objective, are understood. Problems are solved only as concepts are formed and employed in the search for resolution. Finally, since creative thought is the ultimate aim of instruction and learning, concepts must acquire new dimensions to cope with the riddles of the future.

Therefore, the process of concept formation is common to all kinds of learning. Regardless of the form which learning may assume, the principles and characteristics remain identical. If the element of cognition is removed, the degree of learning, if any, is questionable. Consequently, investigators, in order to acquire as much knowledge as possible, have arbitrarily divided the cognitive process into parts. Because concept formation is of the utmost importance, the more that is known about the process, the more ably will man learn and adjust. For man to comprehend, to acquire solutions to problems, and to explore new frontiers of knowledge demands facility with the use of concepts.

However, many will argue cognition, concept formation, problem solving, and creative thinking all may be classified as "thinking." Again, this is true, and again, the division is arbitrary. Yet, to aid understanding, and because concept formation is such a complicated procedure, distinct analysis seems both logical and legitimate.

The reader is reminded of the analysis and synthesis described in motor learning. A task was separated into parts but instructors were counseled to remind students that the parts were related to each other, to the whole, and the task itself was related to a specific objective. As we study cognition or thinking, there are so many substantial portions of the whole process that we may profitably detach *parts* for more concentrated analysis. Once again the reader is cautioned against analyzing the part as a whole. The parts of the cognitive process are related to each other, to the whole, and to the purpose for which it is to be used: problem solving or creative thinking.

Because concept formation is fundamental to all forms of higher mental activity, the developments which lead to the concept will be the subject of this chapter. The reader should be aware that it is precisely here, in our analysis of learning, that we attempt the impossible. Man's mental life is not an open book which can be read. Our analysis is of nonobservable phenomena. *I* know that I can form a concept of a tree, a dog, or **an** abstraction of beauty and truthfulness, the fireness of fire, or the fourness of four. I also know that you, the reader, can similarly perform the same task.

How do I accomplish this; how do I conceptualize and abstract? Of course, we realize that everything originates in the environment. The countless stimuli that bombard our sense organs are the beginning of our knowledge. Exactly *how* does this unique, discrete experience ultimately become a concept that represents everything in its particular category? This is the unanswerable question. However, it is the one question to which we must return if there is to be a deeper and more appreciative understanding of man's potentialities and limitations.

Piaget

To extend our information in this critical subject, investigators have studied concept formation with great interest and diligence. Among the most productive, as well as provocative, of these has been Piaget. The studies of Piaget, working with Inhelder at Geneva, indicate that intellectual development occurs by stages.

Some of the major points which emerge from Inhelder's paper and the discussion of it are:

(a) In the Geneva theory, the growth of knowledge is not regarded as a simple stockpiling of information. It is based on the activity of the child. Piaget is quoted as saying: "I only know an object to the extent that I act upon it."

(b) While "somatic and perceptual development seem to be continuous, intellectual development seems to take place in stages." The order of the stages is constant, and periods of relative continuity alternate with phases of discontinuity. The progression through stages is not viewed as a result of maturation alone, nor of trial-and-error learning alone, nor of "social transmission" alone, but is said to be governed to some degree by its own internal laws of organization. The period of transition from one stage to another is marked by disorganization (disequilibrium), and the achievement of a new stage by a higher state of organization among intellectual processes (equilibrium). A state of disequilibrium implies forces within the person for the restoration of equilibrium.

(c) In the description of distinctions among the stages, the concept of reversibility plays a central role. Two forms of reversibility are distinguished: inversion (negation), and reciprocity.

The reorganizations that occur at the point of attaining equilibrium in a new stage involve the attainment of a basic set of operations (such as reversibility) which generalize widely (Maccoby, 1964, p. 218).

The interpretation of intellectual development by stages has resulted in much criticism of the theory. Piaget, however, by stages, refers to the probability that a certain percentage of children will function intellectually in a certain way (Stendler, 1964). Such stages are not inflexible boundaries which apply uniformly to all children.

The first stage which Piaget identifies is the sensorimotor stage, and, here, the major development is the realization that objects exist even when removed from the child's field of vision. This phase lasts from birth to about two years.

The second stage continues from two to about seven years, and, during this time, the child begins to use language. He can abstract and apply symbols to the results of his abstraction. He is beginning to categorize, but his ability is quite limited. Stendler (1964) gives the example of a youngster who can classify a rose as a flower. He also may be able to identify other flowers by name. However, if the child is asked if all the roses in the world died, would any flowers be left, the answer is likely to be negative.

Particularly important at this stage is the notion of "reversibility." The child at this stage lacks the facility for reversing his mental operations. If a youngster sees two identical clay balls, he will identify them as equal. If the shape of one is changed (flattened, extended), to him, they are *not* now equal. This second phase is often called the preoperational stage.

The third stage, that of concrete operations (seven to about eleven years), permits the child to manipulate, mentally, concrete data to solve problems. He is still unable to think abstractly about a problem, or to consider possible combinations.

The fourth and final stage (eleven plus) reveals a growing independence of concrete data. The youth thinks about possibilities and combinations. The capacity to reason, to judge, to solve problems, and to think creatively is what we ordinarily mean by "thinking."

The impact of Piaget upon American psychological thought is great, especially in the past few years. The reader may wish to examine some of the original work conducted by the Geneva school (Piaget, 1950, 1952; Inhelder and Piaget, 1958). These works are difficult, and, fortunately, some excellent American commentary has been published recently. Particulary recommended are Hunt (1961) and Flavell (1963).

Bruner

Bruner and his associates at Harvard have made another significant contribution to the literature on concept formation (Bruner, Goodnow, and Austin, 1956; Bruner, 1957; Bruner, 1960). Bruner's work has caused notable advances not only in research about concept formation, but also in the daily teaching-learning process in the classroom. This is especially true of curriculum construction.

His work on structure (grasping the structure of a subject is understanding it in a way that permits many other things to be related to it meaningfully) relies upon his interpretation of concept formation and concept attainment. He assigns the indispensable function in learning and education to cognition when he states that all cognitive activity depends upon a prior placing of events in their category membership (Bruner, Goodnow, and Austin, 1956, p. 231).

When Bruner alludes to "categorizing" activity, his use of the term has a dual meaning. First, there is concept formation, or the construction of categories. Second, there is concept attainment, which is the search and testing of attributes that can be used to distinguish exemplars from nonexemplars of various categories, the search for good and valid anticipatory cues (Bruner, Goodnow, and Austin, 1956, p. 233).

When we trace Bruner's theory of categorizing and inferring to the school, we note that materials, curriculum, and methods will demand activity by pupils, and not responses to stimuli which may, or may not, require any kind of higher mental activity. If the transfer of general ideas is at the heart of the educational process (Bruner, 1960, p. 17), the formation and attainment of concepts is the foundation upon which education rests. This, in turn, advances the mastery of structure. As Bruner says (1960, p. 18):

The continuity of learning that is produced by the second type of transfer, transfer of principles, is dependent upon mastery of structure of the subject matter, as structure was described in the preceding chapter. That is to say, in order for a person to be able to recognize the applicability or inapplicability of an idea to a new situation and to broaden his learning, thereby, he must have clearly in mind the general nature of the phenomenon with which he is dealing. The more fundamental or basic is the idea he has learned, almost by definition, the greater will be its breadth of applicability to new problems. Indeed, this is almost a tautology, for what is meant by "fundamental" in this sense is precisely that an idea has wide as well as powerful applicability. It is simple enough to proclaim, of course, that school curricula and methods of teaching should be geared to the teaching of fundamental ideas in whatever subject is being taught. But as soon as one makes such a statement a host of problems arise, many of which can be solved only with the aid of considerably more research. We turn to some of these now.

He then suggests methods by which the underlying principles of the various disciplines can be incorporated into the curriculum. Such curriculum construction demands complete and exhaustive apprehension of a subject. To achieve this goal requires the cooperation of scholars, scientists, teachers, and experts in child development.

The scholar, scientist, or teacher must rely upon the student's ability to form and attain concepts for learning to occur. The works of Piaget and Bruner are outstanding examples of the importance of the place and function of cognitive activity in today's psychological and educational thought.

ABSTRACTION AND MEANING

Once a person forms a concept, it belongs to a category of a definite title. A word, then, symbolizes a classification (tree) or a generalization (loyalty). Whether the word "cloaks" or "molds" the category (Bruner, Goodnow, Austin, 1956) is unimportant here. What is significant is that a word represents abstraction and a person's use of language is an excellent clue to the level of abstraction (Commins and Fagin, 1954, p. 62).

With an ascending level of abstraction, however, there is a constant danger that words will become meaningless symbols and the teachers will accept verbalism for knowledge. Since schools manipulate symbols so frequently in the presentation of information, the issue of meaning is particularly pertinent for the teaching-learning milieu. The school must ultimately transmit its knowledge by symbols, but every teacher has the responsibility to insure that a symbol possesses as much meaning for the students as is possible.

If a word symbolizes a concept, the substance of the concept will define the meaning of the word. Eventually, all meaning originates in the individual's experiences. Effective teaching attempts to fill any gap between a student's experiences and the symbols, representing concepts, which he encounters in the classroom. The way in which a person's experiences become concepts by the process of abstraction leads us to an examination of the most elementary act in concept formation: sensation.

SENSATION

The source of all our knowledge is in the sense organs. Unless physical stimuli act on sense organs and produce a nerve impulse which is interpreted by a central nervous system, there will be no higher mental activity. As Kingsley and Garry state (1957, p. 332):

These widely differing qualities of sensory experience depend upon the organs of sense and upon the nervous system. They are the basis of our knowledge of the world about us. Without them there would be no awareness of anything.

In this section, we are not concerned with the mechanics of nervous activity because a physiological analysis was presented in Chapter II. We are concerned about the function of the stimuli, how the individual reacts, and how the stimuli are used by the person. The person receives and apprehends certain simple stimuli by senses such as sight, sound, smell, taste, heat, cold, pressure, and the like. The sensations that stimuli cause have a basic and direct influence upon the accuracy and applicability of concepts. If there is any distortion of sensation, there is likely to be distortion of concept unless a sustained and concentrated effort is made to overcome such a handicap. Garrison, Kingston, and McDonald (1964, p. 56) say:

The sense organs have at times been referred to as "the gateways of the mind." Without the sense organs man would have no way to interpret his world. One has only to observe the deaf or blind person to realize the importance of a single sensory function in the life of an individual. People like Helen Keller, without vision or hearing, are able, under optimal conditions, to interpret their world through the other senses. Such individuals cannot visualize the colors and forms about them or hear the sounds coming from various sources.

Sensory Deprivation

Not only the distortion of sensation, but also the degree of sensation, affects the nature of the person's response to stimuli, and thus these factors also affect his behavorial pattern. Every human being needs a certain amount of stimulation to maintain a necessary level of intellectual and emotional competency. A study by Heron (1961) reported the results of an experiment which sharply diminished the amount of sensory input.

The subjects were placed in a cubicle, and sight, sound, and touch sensations were eliminated. As a result of confinement, the individuals showed a decreased capacity in intellectual abilities and twenty-five of the twenty-nine subjects stated that they experienced hallucinations.

This study supports the work of Hebb (1958) that was summarized in Chapter III. From their investigation of the studies of sensory deprivation, Kubzansky and Leiderman (1961) conclude that the cognitive, perceptual, and emotional changes accompanying deprivation leave the subject less able to adjust to the demands of the environment.

The above discussion of sensory distortion and deprivation suggests the obvious: teachers must be aware of the physical condition of students. This applies to both elementary and secondary schools. There is little difference between the elementary school child who refuses to take prescribed medicine during the school day and the secondary school boy or girl who declines to wear glasses in school because of an adolescent concern with appearance. Still, any examination of sensory functions in education seems to imply more than the obvious.

Recent studies, such as those mentioned, have significant inferences for curriculum, materials, and methods. *An unchanging environment approaches the boundaries of sensory deprivation.* Stimuli must be varied to produce maximum results. If a teacher uses the same techniques, day after day, the material he is presenting gradually becomes meaningless.

Instructors must continually alter their methods and appeal to as many senses as possible; the materials of instruction must allow for sensory differentiation. The teacher should vary the program with texts, films, field trips, guest speakers, projects, and the like. Similarly, the curriculum should suggest procedures that have the greatest possible attraction. Classes steadily taught in identical fashion become useless and boring to students, discouraging to teachers, and a fertile source of disciplinary problems.

Sensory Discrimination

Sensory distortion and deprivation suggest stimulation or the lack of it. If stimuli are to be effectively employed, the individual must be capable of sensing something. This is not the trite statement it may appear on first reading. If the school environment is sufficiently placid, or unchanging, stimuli from an instructor may simply be ignored. Or, if the environment is too distracting because of the simultaneous presentation of multiple stimuli, the student again may be unresponsive.

Psychologists call the ability to sense something the absolute threshold. When there is excessive stimulation the individual is unable to detect a stimulus of minor intensity. For example, there may be construction near the school. So, the teacher is forced to raise his voice to be heard. This, together with the construction noise, causes the student to concentrate upon the loudest stimulus. Any stimulus which fails to attain this intensity is ignored, which undoubtedly means that much of value is lost.

Conversely, as stimulation decreases, sensitivity increases, and the absolute threshold is lowered until a point of maximum sensitivity is reached. Recall the last time you went to the movies. When you first entered the theater, your vision was quite restricted. As you became accustomed to the dark (decreasing stimuli), you were able to see more and more objects (increasing sensitivity).

Such examples signify a remarkable degree of sensitivity for human sense organs. What does this denote for educators? For teachers the lesson is obvious, that is, they must search for the proper degree of stimulation which permits maximum sensitivity for all pupils. This is not easy. Individuals vary in their degree of sensitivity. What may be maximum sensitivity for one student may result in sensory deprivation for another. The teacher must ascertain and compromise this where necessary. The fundamental question remains: under what conditions can there be maximum sensitivity for a class?

There seems to be much more inherent in our knowledge of the absolute threshold than the above suggestion for teachers. Here, once more, we see the results of psychological experiments extending far beyond the laboratory and reaching into all aspects of the educational structure. Should not knowledge of the absolute threshold affect the planning of school buildings? Classrooms should be constructed to eliminate unnecessary noise and permit the introduction of only controlled stimuli. Perhaps this is impossible, but new building materials can aid in achieving this objective and should be considered in the planning stage of school construction. Similar forethought should be given to laboratory facilities, language labs, library space, the auditorium, and so forth.

Much the same is true of the ability to detect differences between stimuli. This is called the differential threshold. The differential threshold also depends upon the sensitivity of the sense organ as well as the intensity of the various stimuli from which the person must discriminate. Thus, the individual is responding to relative intensity.

No stimuli, some stimuli, and differences between stimuli are the variations that have resulted in the identification of the absolute and differential thresholds. They should engender better teaching and learning by the conscious manipulation of stimuli by teachers.

PERCEPTION

Although sensory experiences are an indispensable element for cognition, sensation is unable to unify and interpret reality as we know the average human being can do. We do not respond to our environment on a one-to-one basis. When you look at a person's face, for example, you do not respond to the left eye, the right eye, the left ear, the right ear, and so forth. You respond to the face. How? The answer rests upon the psychological fact called perception.

Present sensory experiences combine with past experiences of the individual and result in a more meaningful response to the environment. Bruner, Goodnow, and Austin refer to this as "going beyond the information given." They say:

> In the preceding chapter much was made of the anticipatory nature of cognitive activity. We constantly "go beyond the information given." We hear a familiar voice in the passage and call out "Hello, Bill" (Bruner, Goodnow, Austin, 1956, p. 25).

Bruner's statement is an excellent description of what occurs after sensation. The person begins to "work on" the sensation; he interprets it according to his own background and gives it meaning.

Two features of perception which are conspicuously relevant for educators are the manner in which a person chooses from the countless stimuli of the environment as well as the manner in which he organizes discrete stimuli into meaningful patterns.

Perception is an intermediate step in the transition from sensation to concept. It is neither pure sensation nor a product of abstraction. It is not pure sensation because we do not experience reality as a series, or accumulation, of separate stimuli. Rather, we respond to things, to objects, and eventually to symbols. It is not an abstract entity because perception always occurs in the presence of the object or thing.

So, perception is a process by which the individual transforms the separate stimuli of the environment into an *awareness* of objects. His personal, *past* experiences merge with *this* sensation and organize them into a pattern which produces awareness. If you meet for the first time a boy, or girl, with bright red hair, you do not react to hair, then eyes, nose, mouth, and so forth. But, because of your extensive experience with people, you respond to a *person* whose outstanding characteristic might be flaming hair.

Kingsley and Garry (1957, pp. 331–335) discuss what they believe are the essential features of perception.

1. *Sensory experience.* Unless sensory experiences occur, there can be no perceptual activity. There can be no awareness unless discrimination and differentiation of stimuli happen.

2. *Meaning.* The meaning which we attribute to an object, person, thing, or event is chiefly the result of learning. For example, something external is sensation; environmental stimuli have acted upon sense organs and caused a sensation. The chair out there is

perception. (It is extremely doubtful if the human, once he grows beyond infancy, ever experiences pure sensation. Even the most frightening and outlandish object would evoke the reaction, "It looks like..." He would combine this sensation with past experiences. This is exactly what is meant by perception.)

3. *Patterning of the sensory qualities.* The organization of the sensory field will affect the perceptual meaning derived from it. What we concentrate upon in our immediate environment and how we relate it to its surroundings determines organization, and thus meaning.

4. *Sensory discrimination.* Before a pattern in the person's field is ascertained, the person must possess the ability to distinguish among stimuli. Here, again, the richness of perceptual meaning will depend upon differences, at times minute, in sensory experiences. Smith and Smith (1961) report that in a study of surface convexity, subjects merely described a flat surface when there was an absence of depth cues.

Selection

Of the innumerable stimuli which strike the individual, we know that any person reacts to but a small fraction. Some stimuli may pass the absolute threshold but never reach the level of awareness. For the most part, however, man selects the stimuli he desires. This is often called perceptual readiness.

Readiness to perceive depends upon the type of stimuli present, the motivation of the person at a specific time, and the organism's background. Brown (1961) has concluded that a person's capability to respond to some stimuli rather than to others is affected by "emotionality." The threshold for recognizing certain stimuli is lowered by the feelings of the person. Kragh (1962) found that threat attributes of stimuli had a noticeable influence upon threshold.

Although experiments about the emotional aspect of perception are not as conclusive as one would like, there is every sign that motivation is a part of perception. What a person desires, or wishes to avoid, certainly affects his discrimination of stimuli. A study by Wiener (1955) disclosed that words with both sexual and nonsexual implication were more quickly recognized in unclear copy when they had recently been presented to the subjects in sexual rather than nonsexual content.

The remaining two items which aid in the selection of stimuli are the type of stimuli and a person's background. A stimulus which *demands* a person's attention is readily understandable. Our attention is drawn to a striking stimulus because of its intensity; this lowers the differential threshold. Also, a person who has previously experienced a certain stimulus is more apt to recognize it on future occasions.

Kingsley and Garry (1957) refer to this phenomenon as primary and acquired determiners of attention. Certain objects are so large, novel, or intense that they are potent attractions. Experience may have shown that certain other objects are more valuable to us than others; these gradually control our attention. Therefore, we can safely presume that a person selects those stimuli which are irresistibly thrust upon him, or those which he desires.

Organization

Throughout this section, we have emphasized the wholeness, or pattern, which the individual imposes upon the sensory field. Stimuli, selection, sensation, and next patterning, or organization, are the perceptual phases which we can note. How the individual structures a sensory field will undoubtedly control the range of both perceptual and conceptual meaning.

Once stimuli have aroused sensation, we become aware of more prominent properties of the object, person, or event which is the source of stimulation. These outstanding qualities are, nevertheless, part of the entire, immediate perceptual environment. They are *parts* of a *whole*. Psychologists today think of this relationship as figure to ground. The characteristic which holds our attention is the figure, while the more indistinct setting (background to figure) is the ground.

The figure-ground relationship may change, but, if it does, perceptual meaning also changes. For example, consider the following changes in meaning as the figure-ground relationship changes:

1a.	1	(Is this a straight line, the number one, or possibly the l in yell?)
1b.	1964	(The figure-ground relationship changes, and the meaning also changes.)
1c.	look	(Again, meaning has changed as organization of the sensory field changes.)

Kingsley and Garry (1957, pp. 106–107) summarize shifts in perceptual meaning as follows:

> It is to be noted that the change in figure-ground relations appears without a change in the designs themselves, but with this change comes a different meaning. Something different is seen. Thus, the figure-ground aspect of perception is an arrangement of the sensory field, or the way in which the individual organizes the situation for himself. It is a fundamental determiner of what one sees and of what one learns by way of observation.

Although each person structures his sensory field as *he* sees it, there are undeniable traits in the stimuli which, of themselves, further organization. We tend to group those things which are close together (proximity), those which resemble one another (similarity), and those which we know (familiarity). What do you see in the diagram shown below?

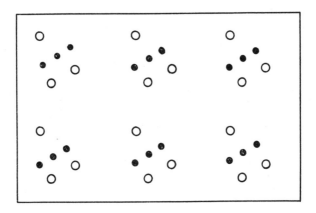

Is your initial reaction to three circles, and three dots? Or, did you instantaneously see eighteen circles and eighteen dots? This usually comes with further analysis when you would *deliberately* change the figure-ground relationship and search for a deeper insight into the diagram.

Another tendency which the individual possesses is that of closure. Now what do you see?

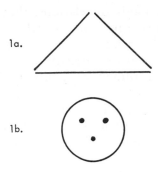

1a.

1b.

In Figure 1a, you certainly identified a triangle, and in 1b you probably saw a face. We all tend toward the completed picture, and parts which logically *could* be a whole *become* a whole in our perceptual field. There is a feeling of satisfaction and a sense of accomplishment when we complete something.

As we climb the conceptual ladder one important fact is beginning to emerge with clarity and urgency, that is, the human being is constantly responding to relationships. When accruing relationships are observed, perceptual meaning becomes more keen and richer for the person. Admittedly, there is much to learn about perception. As Berelson and Steiner (1964, p. 88) say:

Ultimately, the neurological locus of the activity that translates and integrates sensory data into intelligible pictures of the world may be established. At present the distinction is helpful but hazy: sensation shades into perception as experience goes from the isolated and simple (a pinprick, a flash of light) to the complex interpretations characteristic of normal, ongoing awareness of the world.

Despite the limitations, there is much for any instructor to contemplate in our present, limited knowledge of perception. Cognitive learning will grow and be more effective as perceptions are more penetrating and meaningful. Teachers must help pupils to organize their fields and to perceive relationships by skillful presentation of materials as well as a wide variety of methods. The sequence and technique of presentation will do much to aid pupils in the organization of their fields when we recall the principles of proximity, similarity, and familiarity. If teachers remember that the human being responds to relations, they will attempt to unravel a subject by teaching parts which will logically (and, of course, psychologically) relate to the next part of the discipline. The same is true of the entire curriculum. Subjects should relate to subjects. If high school students are studying the American Revolution in history, it would be well to study eighteenth-century literature in English. Here, an effort is made to relate subjects chronologically, which surely will lead to the discussion of many other relationships, for example, social and economic events of the time.

CONCEPT FORMATION

As man grapples with his environment, economy of movement becomes a pivotal issue for his adjustment and inventiveness. Thus, his talent for solving problems and responding creatively to the pressures of his surroundings depend mainly upon his mental aptitude. The physical presence of stimuli is often lacking when the individual must make some decision, commitment, or involvement. How successsful his decision will be is largely the result of his thought process, that is, concept formation. He cannot always go to a source for information, or advice, but, by forming concepts, reasoning, and reaching decisions, he avoids random trial and error endeavors. This is the meaning of economy of movement.

Desirable economy requires the capacity to categorize, or to conceptualize, when objects are no longer present to the senses. Because of this, you, the reader, can understand exactly what I mean if I ask you to think of the following concepts—a house, a tree, or the number five. You have responded, not to the distinct object itself, but to a symbol which represents a class of objects.

How, precisely, does the human being form his concepts? There is no positive answer. Description, based on careful observation, is the only method which investigators can use. From what man does, we can only infer *how* he does it. Man's nervous system reacts to stimuli and his sensations are then transformed into perceptions. It is also apparent, however, that he has additional abilities: he can express himself so that it is apparent that he is reacting to objects or events that are not in his immediate environment. His activities are thus subject to observation and description, but are not yet subject to explanation.

Scrupulous surveillance of man's behavior has yielded some definite clues as to the manner of concept formation. One of the most interesting conclusions is that a person may form a concept and be completely unaware that he has developed it, perhaps he has even retained and used it over a period of time. The individual has, however, consciously reacted to the objects in his environment to be able to form the concept, that is, sensation has led to perception. The person simply is unaware that he has classified several characteristics and fashioned a group (Leeper, 1951).

Discovery

Usually, concepts are organized in a more systematic, orderly, and conscious manner. The person actively pursues the properties which will allow him to classify. Many terms are employed to portray this procedure, for example, search, strategy selection, and discovery, among others. Smedslund (1964) comments that discovery in concept formation has acquired a significant position in the literature. Discovery is opposed to a more inactive role played by the learner, that is, he tends to be a searcher instead of a receiver of information.

The advantages claimed for discovery are that it is more intellectually stimulating; the person gains a sense of inner satisfaction and need not depend upon extrinsic rewards. It is a powerful stimulant to both memory and transfer.

An interesting study was conducted by Kersh (1962) in which he taught high school students new approaches to addition. The method was by programming. Of the subjects, one-third was encouraged to discover the principle involved; one-third learned the explanation by the programmed procedure; one-third was simply told, and given no additional instruction. He found that the subjects who learned by discovery were inclined to practice more and, consequently, remembered and transferred more effectively.

Bruner (1960 and 1961) has devoted much thought to discovery. He states:

Just as a physicist has certain attitudes about the ultimate orderliness of nature and a conviction that order can be discovered, so a young physics student needs some working version of these attitudes if he is to organize his learning in such a way as to make what he learns usable and meaningful in his thinking. To instill such attitudes by teaching requires something more than the mere presentation of fundamental ideas. Just what it takes to bring off such teaching is something on which a great deal of research is needed, but it would seem that an important ingredient is a sense of excitement about discovery—discovery of regularities of previously unrecognized relations and similarities between ideas, with a resulting sense of self-confidence in one's abilities (Bruner, 1960, p. 20).

Ausubel and Fitzgerald (1961), however, take issue with Bruner. They suggest that, in the vast majority of classroom situations, reception learning was more appropriate for the learning and retention of presented verbal material than was discovery learning.

It does appear, nevertheless, that activity, search, or discovery by the student would contribute to more meaningful concepts. Although all indications favor discovery as a more potent method of concept formation, Smedslund (1964, p. 273) wisely concludes that the belief in the superiority of discovery rests more on intuitive conviction than on well-established experimental generalizations.

In addition, the time element cannot be discounted. Even Bruner, who has done so much to advance the value of discovery, urges caution:

It is particularly the Committee on School Mathematics and the Arithmetic Project of the University of Illinois that have emphasized the importance of discovery as an aid to teaching. They have been active in devising methods that permit a student to discover for himself the generalization that lies behind a particular mathematical operation, and they contrast this approach with the "method of assertion and proof" in which the generalization is first stated by the teacher and the class asked to proceed through the proof. It has also been pointed out by the Illinois group that the method of discovery would be too time-consuming for presenting all of what a student must cover in mathematics. The proper balance between the two is anything but plain, and research is in progress to elucidate the matter, though more is needed. Is the inductive approach a better technique for teaching principles? Does it have a desirable effect on attitudes? (Bruner, 1960, p. 21).

Cognitive Style

A promising method of probing man's cognitive activities is that of cognitive style. Do individuals differ in their form of organization and solution of problems that compel human beings to engage in thought, reasoning, and judgment? Ausubel and Fitzgerald (1961, p. 507) define cognitive style as follows:

Research interest continued to be active in the area of "cognitive style," i.e., self-consistent and enduring individual differences in cognitive organization and functioning. Cognitive style refers both to individual differences in general principles of cognitive organization (e.g., simplification and consistency trends) and to self-consistent idiosyncratic tendencies that are not reflective of human cognitive functioning in general (e.g., intolerance for ambiguity; memory for particular kinds of experience). It reflects differences in personality organization as well as genetically and experientially determined differences in cognitive capacity and functioning.

Witkin and his associates (1962) published an important book about this subject, *Psychological Differentiation*, in which they studied ten year old boys and attempted to identify factors which are related to cognitive style. This study as well as others leave unsolved the reason *why* these relationships with cognitive style exist at all.

Does cognitive style depend upon the growth of differentiation as the Witkin study assumes? Or, are there several, independent cognitive styles? Zigler (1963) claims that the entire enigma of cognitive style is nothing more than the presence of one element: general intelligence.

Although disagreement is current, mainly because of the lack of experimental evidence, it is encouraging to note the continued seeking of more adequate explanations of man's cognitive life. As Maccoby (1964, p. 226) says:

In the search for dimensions which underlie intellectual performance, then, the devotees of the cognitive style point of view are dissatisfied with the previous factor-analytic approaches which have limited themselves to performance on intelligence-test items in their search for primary abilities. They argue that a different but meaningful set of genotypes will be uncovered by including a wider range of scores on perceptual functioning and on dimensions of individual differences which have previously been thought of as relevant only to personality. In this way they hope to produce a more satisfactory theory of the development of "intelligence" than has been produced so far through the study of intelligence test scores alone.

The Concept

Analysis of discovery and cognitive style, while promising tangible results with continued experimentation, nevertheless still confronts the basic question: how do unique sensory experiences develop into concepts? The first knowledge about a book that a youngster obtains is probably of something with a rectangular shape, hard cover, things that can be moved, and a particular color. These stimuli are experienced as sensations.

As the child's world expands, his experiences grow both in number and complexity. Slowly, he realizes that a book is something his mother and father look at; something his brothers and sister use in school, and for their homework. Now he begins to discover characteristics that are common to all books.

All books have covers; all have pages that move; all seem to be the same shape. Simultaneously, the child discards the elements that made the book a particular book, for example, the color, pictures on the jacket, title words, specific size, a unique cover design, and the like. Again, the processes of analysis and synthesis occur. The youngster carefully analyzes objects (books) for those qualities which are present in all books, and then he groups them to form classes.

The process continues as his contacts with books multiply. He discovers that the pages have marks on them; these marks tell something; they are words. A book tells something; people read it. Finally, the concept is well defined. A book is a bound set of printed pages enclosed between covers.

Next, he begins to refine his concept. He learns to distinguish among hardcover books, magazines, and paperbacks. He realizes that not all printed material between covers belongs in his classification of books.

Bruner, Goodnow, and Austin link concept formation and concept refinement when they discuss the psychological controversy about definition. They feel that the division between those who believe that a concept is defined by its common elements and those who believe it is defined by a relationship between part processes is unnecessary. They state:

The principal psychological controversy has been between two views: There are those who urge that a concept, psychologically, is defined by the common elements shared by an array of objects and that arriving at a concept inductively is much like "arriving at" a composite photograph by superimposing instances on a common photographic plate until all that is idiosyncratic is washed out and all that is common emerges. A second school of thought holds that a concept is not the common elements in an array, but rather is a relational thing, a relationship between constituent part processes.

We submit that such a controversy is relatively fruitless. We have found it more meaningful to regard a concept as a network of sign-significate inferences by which one goes beyond a set of *observed* criterial properties exhibited by an object or event to the class identity of the object or event in question, and thence to additional inferences about other unobserved properties of the object or event. We see an object that is red, shiny, and roundish and infer that it is an apple; we are then enabled to infer further that "if it is an apple, it is also edible, juicy, will rot if left unrefrigerated, etc." The working definition of a concept is the network of inferences that are or may be set into play by an act of categorization (Bruner, Goodnow, and Austin, 1956, p. 244).

Thus, both methods merge according to this statement, which seems to be a very logical conclusion.

A study by Shore and Sechrest (1961) investigated the facility of concept formation when a subject repeatedly examined a few instances of the concept, as compared to a single examination of many instances. They concluded that, if the characteristics of the concept are not obvious, repetition of instances is necessary. However, if the characteristics are obvious, less repetition is required.

The above study seems to stress the nature of the concept itself. That is, some concepts are, of themselves, easier to learn than others. Admittedly, the example of a youngster forming the concept of a book was a simple one. Concepts which are derived from common properties (as was the concept of book) are called conjunctive concepts. Other concepts are fashioned from relationships such as loyalty, references to size, degree, and the like where there is no tangible unifying element, but rather a state of mutuality. These are referred to as relational concepts. Concepts which possess characteristics so that any one characteristic may be used in classification are called disjunctive concepts. Bruner, Goodnow, and Austin (1956, p. 156) define disjunctive concepts as follows:

Members of a disjunctive class exhibit defining attributes such that one or another of these attributes can be used in identifying or categorizing them. Thus, the class of substances capable of producing an identical allergic reaction in an individual may include *either* cat hair or chalk dust *or* sepia ink. A substance containing *any one* or *any combination* of these defining attributes is necessary and sufficient for producing the class-defining effect.

There are several manifest facts about concept formation which teachers should note. Perhaps the most basic fact is that, the more concrete is the concept, the more easily does the student acquire it. The familiar study of Heidbreder, Bensley, and Ivy (1948) illustrates the increasing difficulty of concept attainment with decreasing concreteness. Nonsense syllables were given meanings, ranging from a more concrete concept such as shoe to a more abstract concept such as the number five. The more concrete concepts (such as shoe) were acquired with far less trials than the more abstract concepts (such as five).

Recall the work of Piaget, which was mentioned at the outset of the chapter. His theory of stages of intellectual development seems to agree with the conclusion that more concrete concepts are grasped more easily. Schools, then, bear the burden of analyzing a curriculum to assume that the type of concept demanded is within the capability of the age level of the students who are involved.

Granted that the curriculum must encompass all youth of a given age or grade, teachers must adapt the material to the ability of their students. Both curriculum planners and teachers, therefore, will benefit from knowledge about the way in which concepts are formed as well as the techniques of concept presentation which facilitate their acquisition by students.

CONCLUSION

Because cognitive activity is the very essence of learning, the more that teachers know about the manner in which the human being forms and uses concepts, the more effective will they be in the classroom. Mechanical responses and verbalisms are too often present in our schools because understanding is frequently disguised by "adequate" performance. Adequate here refers to the apparent attainment of an objective, that is, the learning product is judged to be satisfactory.

There are many legitimate reasons for such an assessment; often present methods of evaluation permit only superficial examination, or the nature of the task makes accurate appraisal exceedingly difficult. It is inexcusable, however, for any teacher to neglect comprehension in any kind of instruction. Teachers bear the responsibility for gaining as much information as they can about the way in which students understand, solve problems, and undertake novel exploits. Consequently, teachers also must encourage students to form new categories and to scrutinize those categories they already possess so that they may probe and explore the limits of knowledge as well as their abilities allow.

Exciting, stimulating methods of instruction should challenge students in carefully planned and constructed buildings. The materials of instruction should offer, together with methods, a range and variety of stimuli that will insure the proper stimuli being selected by students in such a way that a magnitude of relationships may be perceived by the learner. This will entail a number of original experiences to instill the concept an instructor may wish.

Finally, the student himself should be an active participant in the search for wisdom. Whether it is called search or discovery, the goal is the same. An alert, inquiring mind tends to retain, apply, and transfer concepts swiftly and competently to new, perhaps, unprecedented problems. And concept formation is the base from which such behavior must spring.

CHAPTER VI

Types of Learning III — Problem Solving

INTRODUCTION

A problem arises when a living creature has a goal but does not know how this goal is to be reached. Whenever one cannot go from the given situation to the desired situation simply by action, then there has to be a recourse to thinking. (By action we here understand the performance of obvious operations.) Such thinking has the task of devising some action which may mediate between the existing and the desired situations. Thus the "solution" of a practical problem must fulfill two demands: in the first place, its realization must bring about the goal situation, and in the second place one must be able to arrive at it from the given situation simply through action (Duncker, 1945, p. 1).

As THIS QUOTATION from one of the classical experiments on problem solving indicates, man must acquire the capability to grapple with the uncertainties and riddles of his environment. What does man do when he confronts an issue which is completely new to him? How does the student react when more than a repetition of facts is required to answer a question? The explanation is as obvious as it is involved: he himself must respond in a novel manner.

How does he respond in a novel way? And, *what* is meant by novel? Again, there is the obligation to go beyond the product of learning and examine the process which permits man to solve problems in a manner which is unique only to him. Undoubtedly, his response will be creative, if not for society, at least for himself. Although problem solving and creativity are closely related, they are still distinct processes and will be discussed separately in this chapter.

Both processes are the summit of man's intellectual activity; all that we have previously discussed has been a preparation for our analysis of this inventive expression of man. Sensation, perception, memory, and cognition all combine to enable man to solve the unknown.

Problem Solving as Learning

As you read the opening quotation, the intent of the author becomes clear. The author says that man wants something; his path to the desired object or thing is blocked; his customary behavior is inadequate to achieve the goal; and a reorganization is needed. He must devise ways to remove obstacles, and he must also devise ways to test his solutions before he actually attempts them.

These words should sound familiar. The first chapter of this text described the characteristics of learning, that is, a motivated individual, a goal, obstacles, environmental stimuli, and the like. The position that there is no learning without an obstacle that requires a modification of behavior was taken. Is all learning, then, problem solving? Many authors think so. Among them is Getzels (1964, p. 240) who raises several questions:

All learning involves problems. What then do we mean when we distinguish between problem-solving and other forms of learning? Are these terms mere redundancies? Or is there a difference between learning to remember a date and learning to understand the meaning of a negative number? Between learning to apply a given formula and to conceive of a new relationship? Between learning to know the correct answer to an old question and to raise a new question about an old answer? And if there are differences among these, are there complementary differences in appropriate instructional method?

Sawrey and Telford (1964, p. 164) introduce their discussion of problem solving as follows:

Practically all forms of learning can be conceived of as problem-solving processes. Conditioning, association, and trial-and-error learning are forms of problem-solving. They may be motor, ideational, or both. The development of insights involves the discovery and understanding of the principles necessary for problem solving. Cognitive learning, as we have described it, is likewise concerned with ideational forms of problem solving. The development of functional conceptual categories provides answers to such questions as, "What available object can be used as a hammer?" A description of the problem-solving process is essentially a restatement of the learning process.

Finally, Travers (1963, p. 316) says:

The term "problem solving" is a generic term which includes within its scope a great many different forms of complex behavior. Problem-solving behavior occurs in the presence of a task, a goal to be achieved in relation to the task, and a problem solver who is not equipped with the appropriate response required for solving the task. The solution to the problem is "learned" through the occurrence of a complex mediating process sometimes referred to as thinking.

There can be little argument with the above statements. If we designate the obstacle as the problem, learning is problem solving because modification of behavior has occurred to solve the problem, or to remove the obstacle. Learning the golf swing is certainly problem solving because customary behavioral patterns do not achieve the objective of a masterful golf game. Memorizing a poem is problem solving because the proper association of words is lacking, and the problem is to learn them.

The reader must be aware that each of these examples represents a different *level* of problem solving: motor learning and rote learning. The position taken here is that problem solving is the highest level of man's intellectual life. Thus, the term is reserved for a description of the *process* by which man mentally manipulates his environment, mentally tests his tentative solutions, and finally determines his course of action.

Again, we are dividing the whole into parts for the purpose of analysis, and we are assuming that, within the whole of the learning process, there is a hierarchy of stages, the highest of which is problem solving and creative thinking. Although there is a difference between the latter processes, both are distinctive of man at his intellectual heights.

At this pinnacle of mental life, man acquires his greatest economy of effort. The person who operates at a lower level, that is, does not mentally manipulate his environment, becomes enmeshed in the tangles of random movements. He must *do* everything; he must actually *try* each possible solution. Figure 6-1 depicts the contrast in the two types of response when a person's customary behavior does not achieve the goal.

Admittedly, the paradigm below is a simplification, but it does portray the discrepancies in behavior that function at a level lower

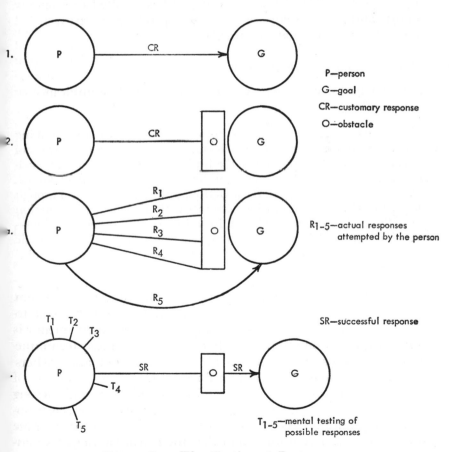

FIGURE 6-1. *The Testing of Responses*

than that of problem solving. The individual who engages in what Bruner, Goodnow, and Austin (1956) refer to as the "all and none response" attempts to reach his goal by the first response that seems appropriate. He does not reflect and consider the possibility of alternate, more suitable responses.

A person who functions at the problem-solving level ponders the consequences of several responses, and he *then* acts to test his response pattern. Unquestionably, he will discount certain responses, such as 1 to 5, as being impossible for goal attainment. Thus, his mental manipulation of the environment has resulted in economy of effort, and, as we shall see later, may produce the truly novel response that we designate as creative.

Problem Solving and the Schools

Kingsley and Garry (1957, p. 419) summarize the significance of problem solving:

The most exalted of all the psychological functions is the thinking out of the solutions of problems. Through it, under the directive and selective influence of the problem, the individual draws upon his knowledge and observations to produce for himself some new bit of knowledge, or to formulate some new conviction, opinion, or doubt. Through it he devises new ways of settling accounts with a problematic situation for which established methods are insufficient. The other functions—perception, memory, imagination, comprehension, and action—are basic to this activity, for the search for the solution of a problem may involve the use of any or all of them.

It is unlikely that anyone in the American educational system would disagree with this observation; yet the application of it to daily classroom procedures is very difficult. Assignment, memorization, and recitation are frequently an evident and easy technique that is used. This is not true in all classrooms, nor are teachers always at fault when this condition does exist.

Overcrowded classrooms and gruelling teaching schedules often restrict a teacher's freedom of action so that instruction becomes merely mechanical. Tasks are presented to a class, and habit indicates the answer. The information that the teacher anticipates may be different, but his manner of presenting it as well as the students' manner of acquiring the needed facts remain the same. Thus, habit dictates the type of response which will be accepted and the study skills which are necessary to secure it.

There is nothing stimulating here. Where is the variety of presentation that requires a variety of responses from the students? Where is the challenge that will motivate students to change their pattern of response and to recombine elements of experience in an endeavor to accept the dare proposed by the teacher? Teachers must strive to lift students from the ordinary, to widen their vision, and to encourage their probing of the unknown. This cannot be accomplished by the common task which tolerates the common response. As Berelson and Steiner (1964, p. 200) say:

This section deals with what happens when people are faced with problems as opposed to tasks—that is, with situations where standard approaches either do not work or do not work well, where new or creative approaches must be developed.

Once the concepts are formed and the facts mastered, teachers must insure that students use them. The mind is not simply a retrieval unit. It is alive and dynamic, but it must be inspired to remain alert and productive. It is the teacher's job to make sure that the students possess a spirit of inquiry which will remain with them for life.

In no sense does this denigrate the importance of factual knowledge. Unless a student possesses the ideas which are pertinent to a particular topic, he will be unable to apply and, perhaps, reorganize the concepts which are necessary for problem solving. Bloom *et al.* (1956) state that the justification for teaching knowledge is its breadth of application to all the objectives of education. Problem solving does not occur "by itself," but must depend upon facts, that is, knowledge is a prerequisite to man's highest intellectual activities.

They continue:

Although information or knowledge is recognized as an important outcome of education, very few teachers would be satisfied to regard this as the primary or the sole outcome of instruction. What is needed is some evidence that the students can do something with their knowledge, that is, that they can apply the information to new situations and problems. It is also expected that students will acquire generalized techniques for dealing with new problems and new materials. Thus, it is expected that when the student encounters a new problem or situation, he will select an appropriate technique for attacking it and will bring to bear the necessary information, both facts and principles. This has been labeled "critical thinking" by some, "reflective thinking" by Dewey and others, and "problem solving" by still others (Bloom *et al.*, 1956, p. 38).

Unless man can utilize his concepts and enhance his adjustment to his environment, the school will fail to achieve its objectives. Perhaps this is the ultimate rationale for a psychology of learning course and a learning text. The more knowledge teachers gain about the nature of learning, about the characteristics of the process, about the nature of motivation, and about the method by which students may transfer and use their knowledge, the more able they will be to aid students in the fulfillment of their intellectual capacities.

The Improvement of Performance

Such a fulfillment of intellectual capacities develops only if man succeeds in reducing his mistakes when he is confronted by a novel situation. A person who carefully reflects, rather than instantly responds (compare 3a and 3b of Figure 6-1), is concerned with eliminating incorrect responses.

The random response (the "all and none") is typical of the person who refuses to use all of his personal resources. In an effort to diminish mistakes, some authors have concentrated upon man's error factor in his attempts at problem solution.

Bruner, Goodnow, and Austin (1956) assert that concern about error is a requirement for problem-solving behavior. Only when a person has the opportunity to validate his decision will he become aware of the possibility of error. These authors further affirm that problem solving proceeds as one tests his tentative solutions and thus examines the success or failure of his behavioral pattern in pursuit of a particular goal. They declare that reduction of opportunity to validate decisions serves to diminish problem-solving activity (Bruner, Goodnow, and Austin, 1956, p. 210).

If a person remains unconcerned about error, he adopts the random response pattern which these authors call the all and none response. The individual plunges ahead and is either right or wrong on a *single response* only. The student may select just one cue in the examination question, for example, and respond to that single item, disregarding the possible alternatives. Such an individual disregards error and does not manifest problem-solving behavior.

In much the same manner, Duncker (1945) claims that learning from errors is essential for problem solving. He states that lack of problem solution, or even lack of progress, forces the person to consider other alternatives. Another tentative solution, as clearly defined as possible, is sought. The transition from one possible solution to another demands a variety of mental manipulations. Will it work; why not; did it previously? In answering these questions, Duncker says that the individual returns to earlier stages of the problem.

From this immediate mistake, an earlier hypothesis is seen differently; fresh perspective is brought to it. The earlier hypothesis may be one that occurred in the initial stages of seeking a solution, or it could be the hypothesis that just failed. However, such thinking is not *exactly* identical with its first appearance; one "tries in another way." The clue which proved unsatisfactory is now avoided.

Both of these examples illustrate several significant qualities of problem solving: the individual's perception of the problem, the problem itself, tentative solutions, and the testing of these solutions. All of these elements will be discussed throughout the chapter, but the problem itself is worthy of separate consideration.

The Problem

What is a problem? There is no easy answer to this question because, often, what one person considers a problem is not a problem to another. The individual perceives the problem, and for this reason problem solving was designated among the highest of man's mental activities. For, in problem solving we see the fruition of the stimuli which initiated the sensations that traveled the neural pathways to a definite section of the brain and then were organized into perception.

Man, through his power of abstraction, next formed concepts, which are the "stuff" he uses in his response to the challenges of the environment. And it must be recognized as a challenge or else the person will fail to realize that a problem exists. This is especially true of the educational environment, where the "problem" may be so divorced from a student's background that it is unreal to him, and hence not worthy of any effort.

The problem must motivate the person. This is true of all educational levels. There must be *something* in the situation presented to a student which is perplexing; something which makes him want to overcome it. It may be an elementary school youngster attempting to solve an arithmetic problem based on a descriptive presentation that is familiar to him. It may be a secondary school student attempting to relate some current event to a certain period in history. It may be a business man attempting to improve sales, or it may be a teacher attempting to devise situations which will be problems for his class.

There must be a sense of urgency about solving a problem that is characteristic of all learning because problem-solving behavior is goal-seeking behavior. The solution to the problem is the goal. Thus, youngsters are taught how to improve their performance, and the school, it is hoped, will encourage in them the tendency to appraise all situations in an inquisitive manner, always searching for better alternatives.

ANALYSIS OF PROBLEM-SOLVING BEHAVIOR

After an individual recognizes that a problem exists and begins his search for alternatives, what happens to him? The mere realization that a problem exists is insufficient in itself; the problem must possess the ingredients which drive the individual toward a solution. Then he will begin the "search." Initially, he must decide if there are several responses which could conceivably attain the goal. If so, which response appears to be the most appropriate?

What will be the consequences of a particular response? This is a crucial question in problem-solving behavior. The individual who is highly skilled in the techniques of problem analysis will not only attempt to select the most suitable response, but will also weigh the results of his decision. Here, his thought process probes the ramifications of his choice: this appears to be the best action, but are there other variables that should be considered; for example, will this get me directly to the goal, or will other steps be required; should I focus on a single clue, or should I endeavor to react to a combination of clues?

As the student decides, questions his decision, and contemplates other options, he is unquestionably reducing his percentage of error. To explain the process that the student is experiencing, investigators have followed two clearly defined methods: the descriptive and the experimental. In the descriptive technique, thinkers have focused upon their own thought processes and tried to relate what happened when they encountered a problem. Experimental studies have presented subjects with problems, and then they closely observed reactions, or they had subjects say aloud exactly what they were thinking as they searched for a solution. Both methods deserve careful inspection. They are offered here with Dewey's classic analysis of problem solving representing the descriptive method and studies by Duncker, and Bloom and Broder, representing the experimental methods.

Logical Analysis

Dewey's theory of problem solving (1910) has had an impact upon education and teaching methods that is as influential today as it was in 1910. Many educators would deny their adherence to his five stages to solution, but observation of their actions refutes their words.

Travers (1963) recounts a visit he made to the Air Force Academy, which is designed to educate the future leaders of this branch of the armed forces. On the walls of the classrooms which he visited were the five steps of Dewey's problem-solving process. Teachers followed his outline in the presentation of material, and students were expected to solve military problems by using the same procedure.

In a discussion of the scientific method, a noted authority in educational research states that a brief list of steps in research would be as follows:

1. Definition and development of the problem, including the survey of the related literature and formulation of the working hypotheses.
2. Selection, or creation, of appropriate data-gathering techniques and actual collection of data.
3. Classification and analysis of data.
4. Conclusions, generalizations, and applications (with due attention to reporting) (Good, 1959, p. 4).

Both of these examples reflect the continuing acceptance of Dewey's view and also show its remarkable consistency. None of the more modern scholars have departed radically from his five steps, which were:

1. Recognition that a problem exists
2. Identifying the nature of the problem
3. Searching for possible solutions
4. Analyzing the adequacy of the tentative solutions
5. Testing the most promising of the tentative solutions

Dewey's classification distinguishes the five separate stages through which problem-solving behavior passes. Failure to solve a problem suggests that one of the steps is either incomplete or incorrect. The fact that there has been little change in Dewey's sequence is shown by an examination of recent recommendations for the solution of problems.

Garrison, Kingston, and McDonald (1964, p. 285) state that the problem-solving process involves four essential functions:

1. an orientation function—understanding of the nature of the problem
2. an information gathering function
3. an hypothesis-formation function
4. an hypothesis-testing function

The authors declare that these steps are not necessarily sequential because a more difficult problem will require the formation and testing of more tentative solutions than a simple problem.

Kingsley and Garry (1957, pp. 421–422) observe that these stages are characteristic of the process:

1. a difficulty is felt
2. the problem is clarified and defined
3. a search for clues is made
4. various suggestions appear and are evaluated
5. a suggested solution is accepted or the thinker gives up in defeat
6. the solution is tested

These authors join problem solving and learning in a dual fashion: we learn by thinking and we improve our ability to think by means of learning.

Finally, Bigge and Hunt (1962, p. 308) list five series of steps:

1. Recognition and definition of a problem
2. Formulation of hypotheses
3. Elaboration of logical implications of hypotheses
4. Testing of hypotheses
5. Drawing conclusions

They also caution that no one actually moves through these steps in a consecutive and orderly manner; instead, the process is usually difficult and confusing. They summarize their attitude toward the use of logical analysis in a pointed statement:

There is a great deal more to understanding the reflective process than merely listing the steps. Experience of the past few centuries has led to certain conventions concerning how a reflective or scientific process is to be pursued. We use the term "conventions" because there is nothing absolutistic about the rules which govern testing of hypotheses. Pragmatically, the rules accepted at present have been shown to lead to more productive results than any alternative rules which have yet been devised. But there is no reason to suppose that the rules of reflection will not continue to evolve as mankind gains more experience (Bigge and Hunt, 1962, pp. 308–309).

If our understanding of the problem-solving process is to increase, will it be because of improvement of the "steps" in problem solution, as Bigge and Hunt suggest, or will it be because of entirely different methods of study? Criticism directed at the logical analysis technique reveals several inconsistencies, the chief inconsistency being that problem solving does not seem to occur in such an ordered fashion.

Testing of hypotheses is not an unfailing source of problem solution; often the answer appears where least expected, for example, away from the environment where the problem might be expected to be solved or while engaged in a radically dissimilar task. Ghiselin (1955) reports a series of interviews in which outstanding thinkers describe the origin of their ideas. Consistently, they mention the answer or solution that came in a flash. Solution, then, would appear to be by insight and not by logical analysis.

However, could the "flash" or insight be the result of information gathering or hypotheses testing? This is a distinct possibility; yet, it leaves unsolved the unconscious or subconscious nature of the manner of solution. Something is happening *within* the person which logical analysis is incapable of explaining.

Perhaps the chief obstacle to problem-solving steps is that the interpreter reviews his thought processes after the solution. It is easy to find explanations, which might originally have been lacking, when the answer is known. We "understand" that, when sufficient information was gathered, we then proceeded to formulate hypotheses, after which we assessed their consequences. This is too simple because it omits any psychological explanation of *how* the solution was derived.

Experimental Methods: A. Karl Duncker

In an attempt to discover more about the process itself, some authors have turned to experimentation. Such research with humans entails much the same procedure: the subjects are presented with a problem and asked to say aloud whatever enters their minds as they seek a solution. Duncker, particularly, emphasized this direction when he states that it is not identical with introspection because the subject remains in contact with the problem and does not remove himself and then "look back." Even incomplete, or apparently inconsequential, remarks are desired since they could signify a common trend, or step, toward the solution.

The most famous of his problems (1945) posed this question for students: if a human being has an inoperable stomach tumor, how can the tumor be removed by rays which destroy organic tissue at sufficient intensity without destroying the healthy tissue surrounding it? The range of replies showed a steady refinement of thought as the problem was reevaluated and tentative solutions became more pertinent. One subject first suggested sending rays through the esophagus, later wondered about changing the location of the tumor, and, finally, determined to send scattered rays through a lens and focus them at the point of the tumor.

The subject made several other recommendations in the sequence leading to solution, and, in his analysis, Duncker insists that they were not random, trial-and-error, responses. Each, although incorrect, was actually sensible, but not for the particular problem. The correct solution was attained only when its functional value became clear. The solution functions in removing the obstacle and achieving the goal.

The functional value of the solution does not occur immediately, but it is associated with a more penetrating insight into the problem itself. The problem is becoming more concrete and more specific to the subject. Tentative solutions which are unsuccessful serve to narrow the problem, to reformulate it. As the subject better comprehends the problems, his suggestions for solution become more relevant and accurate.

Duncker reaches the interesting conclusion that each stage, in retrospect, represents a solution, and, when proven incorrect, in prospect, represents a refinement of the problem. Here, again, error becomes a factor. It forces the subjects back to some preceding phase of the problem, but with added insights. As the subject questions the reasons for failure of a particular response he is reorganizing his process to correct his mistakes. Thus, the problem is reformulated until the functional value of a solution is clearly evident.

Experimental Methods: B. Bloom and Broder (1950)

During the spring of 1945 a study of the problem-solving process was conducted at the University of Chicago, which has earned a lasting place in the literature of this subject. Twelve students were presented with a series of problems selected from tests and examinations used at the University of Chicago. Six of the students were classified as academically nonsuccessful. Both groups were identified by aptitude test scores and achievement test grades.

The authors were concerned with obtaining evidence on both the processes and the product of thought through an analysis of problem-solving behavior. They regarded as a problem any task which the subject could understand but which he could not immediately solve. Test items which depended on memory were omitted because they furnished little information about the mental processes. Puzzles, which demanded trial-and-error responses, were eliminated because it was impossible to estimate the consequences of actions.

Problems that were included had definite goals to attain and required considerable thought to solve because several alternate routes to the goal could be utilized. Problems were selected which made unnecessary any value judgment by the student which could conceivably influence an answer. Problems were used which an expert in the particular subject would be able to judge as most acceptable.

Again, the subjects were urged to "think aloud" as they searched for a solution. They were given some sample questions to aid them in the method of thinking aloud. The authors report the interesting result that the best answers were mumbled. When a subject spoke distinctly and loudly he appeared to be repeating a process that had occurred previously, that is, he forgot to think aloud for the observer and then tried to go back and relate what had happened.

The account of the students' reactions was extremely revealing. For example, one girl professed total ignorance of a particular question and said that she would have to guess. Her attack, however, indicated something other than guesses was operating, although she was totally unaware of it. Another student had difficulty in solving problems because he relied on authority for his answers (texts, lectures) and exercised little freedom in his thought. One student consistently asked himself questions, and then answered them. This method seemed to reshape the problem and aid him in its solution.

From their analysis of the various methods of problem solving used by the students, the authors concluded that four major categories of behavior were evident:

1. Comprehension of the essence of the problem
2. The ideas that are inherent in the problem
3. The style of problem-solving behavior
4. Bias toward problem solving

1. Here, the students showed a wide difference in their grasp of the type of problem and this was reflected in their ability to begin a pattern of responses. Those who were successful problem-solvers seized upon some element in the problem (word or phrase) as a beginning, while the nonsuccessful students were confused; they were unable to initiate attack. For many students, the authors attribute the lack of initial attack to a failure to understand directions.

2. The subjects required a certain amount of knowledge to solve any problem, and, what is even more important, they had to be able to utilize their knowledge in the solution of problems. A notice-

able contrast was seen between the two classes of response. Frequently, the nonsuccessful subject possessed all the information needed to solve a problem, but was incapable of employing it. This, the authors say, was because the subject was unable to comprehend the ideas in the problem. For example, when students were questioned about "corporate enterprise in America," they were confused; when they were told that this meant a company similar to Ford, they were able to understand the question.

3. The students differed as follows in the manner in which they attacked problems:

a. Extent of thought about the problem—the authors state that this was active or passive. The successful students formed hypotheses and made assumptions where they lacked knowledge. The nonsuccessful students manifested very little search; they tended to guess the correct answer because of their own prejudice.

b. The strategy of thought—the successful subjects showed an orderliness in their manner of attack. They attempted to simplify the problem and, if necessary, would grapple with parts rather than a complicated whole. The nonsuccessful subjects, however, appeared to have no method of attack; they constantly retraced their steps, hoping for an insight. They were unable to sustain their thought process to reach a conclusion, and they "jumped" at an answer (similar to Bruner's "all-and-none" response).

4. A significant difference emerged between successful and nonsuccessful students in their attitude toward problem solving. The authors state that the nonsuccessful students decided that reason was no help in solution and they often "felt" they were powerless to gain a solution, when, in reality, they lacked assurance in their own capacity to master the problem. They did not trust the answers that they derived, and, accordingly, they often projected themselves into the problem. Thus, their own feelings repeatedly led them into error.

Both of these studies present detailed observations of the thought processes involved in problem solving, and it is interesting to note that neither contradicts the sequence proposed by Dewey. The sequence of importance apparent from our discussion is the reorganization of elements in a person's background, their combination with cues in the problem, and, finally, a novel response.

Unless the response is novel, it is doubtful if the experience can be designated as problem solving. The individual's reaction may be novel to him, but not to society, or it may be novel to both. Which response should be termed creative?

Problem Solving and Creativity

Creativity can apply only to those learning products which are unique to both the individual and society, and not merely to the individual. Creativity can also apply to any learning outcome that is original for the individual alone. Instead of restricting ourselves to this "either-or" classification, more freedom is offered by an acceptance of both categories as creative. If creativity is so defined, perhaps educators will be encouraged to exert greater effort to inspire creative work in their students.

If creativity is recognized in the personal work of students, both teachers and pupils can share a common objective of developing the creative student. Perhaps this is a fine distinction, but it is important. To judge a pupil's products for their social creativity is to restrict originality and inventiveness to a select few. What is urged here is the advancement of all pupils' creative talents so that *more* students will eventually fashion *more* socially usable, original products.

This will happen only if creativity is accepted on an individual basis. If it is, its close association with problem solving is conceded. To solve problems requires a response unparalleled in the person's experience. It is exactly this kind of behavior that teachers should encourage.

To do so, teachers should be familiar with current findings about the creative process. Such individuals as Guilford (1959), Torrance (1962), and Getzels and Jackson (1962) have contributed substantially to our present meager knowledge of methods of identifying the creative child, and of the creative process itself.

While it is difficult to assess creativity because of relatively recent studies using widely varying subjects, techniques, and different definitions of creativity, one fact emerges that is extremely significant for teachers. Creativity and intelligence are not identical. Almost every investigation has found highly intelligent individuals in a low creativity category. Therefore, creative and less creative individuals will achieve quite similar results on intelligence tests.

Research on the relationship between creativity and intelligence is far from definitive. Too often the subjects of such studies have been highly intelligent as a group. Thus, scientists, mathematicians, engineers, and the like are in a superior IQ range by professional requirements, that is, they would be incapable of acceptance and achievement in these occupations unless they were highly intelligent. Since superior intelligence is a requirement for this particular subject, there will be a questionable correlation between intelligence test scores and creativity; all of the group are intellectually superior.

If studies could show that the creative members of a group, which represented a range of low-high intelligence, were those members possessing superior intellectual abilities, there would be a definite relation between creativity and intelligence. There is a lack of results which encourages authors, cautiously, to state that such a relationship seems to be missing.

PROBLEM SOLVING AND TEACHING

The lack of experimental evidence about the most effective method of aiding the development of problem-solving behavior makes one hesitant about proffering advice. But, from our analysis of what is observed in problem-solving behavior, these conclusions seem both logical and, hopefully, productive for teachers:

1. A problem-solving attitude can be taught
2. There is a personal equation in problem solving
3. Students must have both knowledge and techniques
4. Students should use their mistakes to improve their style of attack on problems
5. Teachers should be aware of barriers to the development of problem-solving behavior

If we examine each of these statements, we see that they encompass all the principles of learning thus far discussed.

1. Memorization and recitation of facts are unequal to the task of completely describing man's mental activity. It is only when he uses his store of knowledge in modifying his reactions and conquering the unknown that he functions most efficiently. Students can be helped in the development of their problem-solving and creative behavior when schools insist that pupils master the fundamentals and when they also insist that teachers propose classroom exercises

that challenge, but do not frustrate, the students. Teachers must also instruct in the method of attacking obstacles and then present a wide variety of problems that will allow students to engage in this desired behavior.

2. For teachers to excite students and make them active participants in the search for solutions, pupils must first realize that a problem exists. The characteristics of a problem were discussed earlier in this chapter, and great emphasis was placed upon motivation. Unless students discover that a problem exists and that, somehow, it is meaningful to them, there will be little creative activity. A problem advanced by a teacher, or one that interests adults, of itself, may not provoke students to action. Teachers must be able to refer the problem to something in a student's experience which is real to him, and accordingly, makes the problem real. If one student evinces genuine interest and enthusiasm, it often spreads very quickly to others. As was mentioned in the chapter on motivation, however, teachers must appreciate the events, people, and things which are significant to youngsters and teenagers.

3. Earlier in this chapter, the dependence of problem-solving behavior upon facts was stressed. Individuals are successful with problems only to the extent that they possess ample information. Technique implies use of something: objects or ideas. There is a certain hard core of basic material which demands mastery before more complex manipulation is feasible. If such knowledge is lacking, problem-solving behavior must necessarily fail. Recall that, in both logical and experimental studies of problem solving, the search for information was accentuated. If students are permitted to engage in activity which is designed to encourage creativity, but given few tools with which to work, they will be helpless in any endeavor to transfer such behavior. There will be no problem-solving behavior. If sufficient knowledge is acquired, teachers can direct the student's attention to an analysis of the problem for clues, to the quest for pertinent information, to the formulation of tentative solutions, and to the testing of these solutions. Thus, technique will merge with knowledge.

4. Repeatedly, the error factor has appeared in cognitive activity. Here, as both Duncker and Bruner urge, mistakes should help in solutions. Teachers should not respond to students' mistakes by furnishing them with the correct answer or solution. Rather, mistakes

should be used to force students to reevaluate the problem, to check the accuracy of their information, and to judge the means of attack. Errors should make students determine if they understand the nature of the problem or if they possess material that is necessary for solution. If properly handled, exposure to error can aid students in improving their techniques if they are urged to discover why they made a particular mistake and how to avoid it in the future.

5. Garrison, Kingston, and McDonald (1964), in an excellent analysis of barriers to problem-solving ability, make several relevant comments. First, as we have also warned, they state that lack of motivation will restrain problem-solving behavior. Second, they state that students who feel the need of authority before they reach a conclusion are limited in their freedom of expression. These students must learn to evaluate a problem by utilizing their total resources, and not just one textbook or one teacher. Third, they feel that the lack of an organized technique of pursuing the solution to a problem will result in random, trial-and-error behavior. Fourth, they suggest that students must learn that a successful behavioral pattern in one problem may not be successful in another. Students must adopt a critical, flexible view of problem solving which enables them to adjust to the conditions imposed by the problem. Fifth, they realize that students must gain confidence in their ability to solve problems. If, for reasons we have mentioned, because of a lack of knowledge, technique, and the like, they consistently fail to achieve success, this becomes a major obstacle in future attempts at solution.

As the reader can discern, these barriers stand between a teacher's endeavors to aid students to acquire a critical and creative attitude and a student's successful response pattern to diversified problems.

CONCLUSION

Just at this time I left Caen, where I was then living, to go on a geologic excursion under the auspices of the school of mines. The change of travel made me forget my mathematical work. Having reached Coutances, we entered an omnibus to go some place or other. At the moment when I put my foot on the step the idea came to me, without anything in my former thoughts seeming to have paved the way for it, that the transformations I had used to define the Fuchsian functions were identical with those of non-Euclidean geometry. I did not verify the idea; I should not have had time, as upon taking my seat on the omnibus, I went on with a conversation already commenced, but I felt a perfect certainty. On my return to Caen, for conscience's sake I verified the result at my leisure (Poincaré, in Ghiselin, 1955, p. 37).

This famous passage, so frequently quoted in psychological literature, poses the problem which we have discussed in this chapter: man is capable of magnificent, creative effort, but how? Is it, as Poincaré suggests, by a sudden flash, or is it a more systematic process than we realize?

Examine the following quotation, and again see the analysis of inspiration:

So far as I can describe with any accuracy, the progress of that winter's work in England was not along the lines of planned design, but along this line that I have mentioned—writing some of the sections which I knew would have to be in the book. Meanwhile what was really going on in my whole creative consciousness, during all this time, although I did not realize it at the moment, was this: What I was really doing, what I had been doing all the time since my discovery of my America in Paris the summer before, was to explore day by day and month by month with a fanatical intensity, the whole material domain of my resources as a man and as a writer. This exploration went on for a period which I can estimate conservatively as two years and a half. It is still going on, although not with the same all-absorbing concentration, because the work it led to, the work that after infinite waste and labor it helped me wonderfully to define, that work has reached such a state of final definition that the immediate task of finishing it is the one that now occupies the energy and interest of my life (Wolfe, in Ghiselin, 1955, pp. 188–189).

Both of these examples agree, and yet disagree, with Dewey's explanation. They agree that there is recognition of a problem that requires search; they disagree in that systematic solutions were not apparent in all three descriptions. Undeniably, all three combine the essentials of problem solving and creativity, but, upon reflection, the philosopher, the mathematician, and the writer reach different interpretations. The experimental evidence quoted in this chapter would seem to support both conclusions. Such mental activity exists, and research will continue to scrutinize the problem-solving process and will continue to supply educators and psychologists with added insights. Meanwhile, teachers must gather as much knowledge as they can about the educational implications of such theoretical investigations and apply it to classroom instruction. Recognition and acceptance of the importance of contributing to the development of critical and creative behavior will assist teachers in seeking measures to improve their instructional methods for just such an objective.

CHAPTER VII

The Transfer of Learning

INTRODUCTION

There is no more important topic in the whole of the psychology of learning than that of transfer of training. Practically all educational and training programs are built upon the premise that human beings have the ability to transfer what they have learned in one situation to another. This assumption is evident in everything from the curriculum of the college of classical tradition to the adolescent who is persuaded by his mother to attend dancing school on the fond hope that training in the graces of ballroom dancing will permit him to navigate the length of the house without danger to the less sturdy furniture (Deese, 1952, p. 214).

WHEN PREVIOUS LEARNING influences subsequent learning or activity, the phenomenon of transfer occurs. There no longer is any doubt that transfer exists, but the extent, method, content, and conditions of transfer pose genuine and substantial problems.

For example, the extent of transfer depends upon such variables as the intelligence of the learner, his physical condition at the time of learning, his attitude toward the material to be learned, his emotional state at the time, and many other similar, personal variables.

The method of transfer suggests that the teacher deliberately strives for transfer by students, or relies on incidental transfer. If the method is deliberate, the teacher will insure that the student grasps principles and is afforded an opportunity to apply these principles in different circumstances. If the method is incidental, the teacher concentrates only on a particular task. Later, if the pupil encounters a similar problem, he will not have a systematic approach to the solution, but rather a chance application of isolated fragments of knowledge. What exactly is the most productive manner of teaching for transfer?

In addition, the content of the material learned will modify transfer. If the material is quite dissimilar, there will be little, if any, transfer other than that of technique or style. If the content to be learned is similar to that originally learned, and if the responses in both situations are similar, unquestionably there will be a significant amount of transfer. But, if the content in both learning situations is similar, and if the responses required are noticeably different, interference is likely to result, and, consequently, transfer will be negative and will definitely hinder learning. Therefore, teachers must carefully judge the learning material to determine if, and to what type of content, it can be transferred.

Finally, the conditions of transfer actually encompass all of the above variables. To what degree should learning occur? Should overlearning be the objective to assure transfer? How carefully should the teacher indicate the possibility of transfer? How much practice, and of what kind, should there be? If students realize that transfer does occur, and it is desirable, and it may be improved, motivation becomes an issue. Students, therefore, must acquire the need to transfer their learning to different problems. Again, teachers must utilize any such need as effectively as possible.

Is there a hierarchy which dictates a series of logical steps which should be followed to provide maximum transfer? Thus, should we present questions, problems, and the like which gradually become dissimilar until students must diligently search for any content or technique to transfer? Or should there be a repetition of relatively similar puzzles which will slowly reinforce the fundamental nature of transfer? Ultimately, schools and teachers must face the reality of transfer—it will vary as the individual varies, and the conditions of transfer must be adapted to individual differences.

Continued research will progressively answer these questions, but, meanwhile, teachers must consciously direct their instruction to accomplish transfer. It is not confined to educational subjects alone. What is learned in a specific instance spreads into many parts of a person's daily response pattern. For example, there is a laudable trend in American secondary education to introduce more geography at all levels. So students learn more about landforms, water bodies, weather, climate, and the like. After youngsters understand that temperature is an essential element in weather change, after they comprehend the concept of humidity, and after they grasp the thought that warm air holds more moisture than cold, they can then perceive the how and why of precipitation. They also can discern the cause of rain or snow in one city, and a lack of precipitation in another city only ten or fifteen miles away.

Transfer also results when the student is watching a news program on television and the meteorologist explains the reasons for the weather conditions and predicts what tomorrow's weather will be. Now the student perceives the reasons why an air mass changes its characteristics as it moves, for example, from south to north. Thus, tomorrow's forecast for Massachusetts is snow, although the air mass that will bring the snow is presently causing rain in the Carolinas.

The implication here is obvious. The student has understood the principles that govern the relationship among temperature, precipitation, and weather changes. Now, when a similar, but slightly different, situation appears, the student applies previous learning in an attempt to solve a new riddle, to understand more fully, or to perform more efficiently. Transfer is evident.

Or consider the youngster who is endeavoring to master the fundamentals of letter writing. In his class work, he has discovered that a sentence is a group of words expressing a complete thought; a paragraph is a group of sentences about one idea. He then analyzes the parts of a letter: heading, body, closing, and signature. Next, he applies what he has learned about sentences and paragraphs to the writing of letters. Under the guidance of his teacher, he writes sample letters in class, and then writes letters to classmates, parents, and relatives.

When Christmas comes the pupil's mother decides that he can write thank-you letters himself this year. So, the boy writes a sample letter which he can use for all circumstances, and, in so doing, he utilizes the principles which he previously learned in school. Again, transfer is evident. The situations are similar, but slightly different; he has previously mastered the required class material, and he now recognizes its relevancy for this new episode. The rapidity with which he transfers his former learning will likewise depend upon the range and scope of the teacher's efforts to prompt transfer.

Caution is required, however, in the attempt to stimulate transfer. Unless teachers appreciate the intricacies of transfer, they themselves are in danger of frustrating their own purpose. For transfer, like everything in the learning process, must be as precisely controlled as possible; otherwise there is the very real contingency that it will be detrimental to learning. What is carried from one situation to another may interfere with present learning.

As an illustration, recall the familiar post office work in which many college students engage during Christmas vacation. One particular chore is a striking instance of negative transfer. Those who receive positions sorting mail as it arrives at the post office must pass an examination on a "scheme." This is an elaborate listing of all the streets in a city or town, accompanied by a code number for each street. The person who takes this test must memorize the corresponding number for each street. As you can imagine, this is a long, tedious, and difficult task.

If successful, the combination of studying for the test and actually using the code for many weeks results in thorough mastery of the scheme material. All the indispensable components of transfer are present. The individual must be of sufficiently high intelligence to attempt such mastery. He will learn far beyond the point of mere competence—overlearning becomes an objective. There is a high degree of similarity in the study and test structure, yet there is enough difference to avert identity. Certainly the person is motivated because the money earned may defer expenses such as tuition, books, clothes, and so forth.

If these conditions are fulfilled, therefore, there is every reason to expect a high degree of transfer from study to test, and also to the next year if the qualifications remain the same. But, what will happen if the post office department decides to change the code, as it frequently does? Obviously, if a person memorizes to the stage of overlearning that Plymouth Street is 14 and Adams Street is 2, when he is required to respond that Plymouth Street is 26 and Adams Street is 6, he encounters a formidable obstacle. His previous learning interferes with his mastery of the immediate task because the two problems are so similar, but demand radically different responses. A major share of forgetting is caused by the phenomenon of negative transfer, which actually is a kind of inhibition. (A discussion of the distinctive classes of inhibition will be presented under Experimental Designs.)

There are several inescapable conclusions to be drawn from these cases. First, and by far the most important, transfer of learning does happen. Second, it is a very complex process about which we have much to learn. Third, the identification of variables which influence transfer has contributed steadily to refinements in advancing the theory of transfer. A growing body of literature has eliminated many historical and theoretical inconsistencies and has gradually evolved a theoretical structure which is generally accepted as the basis for transfer. More will be said about theoretical agreement when we trace the history of transfer theory. Fourth, teaching for transfer must be a conscious objective of the teacher if it is to be accomplished as proficiently as possible. If left to their own devices, students often fail to understand that application of former learning may aid in the solution of a seemingly novel problem. Yet, independence of intellectual endeavors is a major ambition of the school. Ultimately, the success or failure of education hinges upon the ability of students to employ the knowledge and techniques of formal education to problems that exist in unique circumstances far removed from the classroom.

Does the school have any other reason for its being? Should the mission of the school be to insist upon knowledge for its own sake, or to prepare students to exercise their talent and knowledge in practical application? Philosophers have pondered this question for centuries and today are no closer to providing an absolutely acceptable answer than in any past period of history.

Those who advocate the pursuit of knowledge for its own sake believe that a classical curriculum makes the whole man. Those who oppose this philosophy of education presume that, in the twentieth century, the schools have an obligation to prepare students for specific professions and occupations. Modern society is so fragmented and specialized that to refuse to equip the young for specialization is to render them a disservice.

Today, a compromise between those apparently conflicting positions seems to be evident. Even the most highly technical schools acknowledge the need for a liberal education. Man must do more than involve himself in the minutiae of employment; he must also communicate with his fellow man. If he is unable to establish rapport with colleagues and neighbors and if his intellectual horizons are limited by the restrictions of technical jargon, his capacity as a man is correspondingly confined.

Man inhabits two worlds, professional and personal, and he must be able to function productively in both if he is to experience satisfaction as a person. Therefore, the demands of society dictate that schools provide students with, at least, rudimentary tools to progress competently in both worlds.

If we accept the premise that schools must prepare students both personally and professionally, a dual role of transfer emerges. Students should be proficient in carrying knowledge from those subjects which are usually classified as liberal to the more professional studies; they also should be capable of conveying academic attainment from both professional and liberal studies to practical utilization.

Such a dualistic objective of transfer must be thoughtfully weighed by teachers when they determine goals of instruction. Admittedly, this is not a vital topic in the elementary school, where transfer is from theory to practice, that is, from learning numbers by rote, to using them in simple equations of addition and subtraction, to solving word problems, and so forth.

Schools must employ a dualistic exercise of transfer much more widely than before because the drop-out problem in American education becomes larger each year. Commitment to the fullest development of man's power, in addition to vocational training in the secondary schools, needs to receive more deliberative consideration than it has. Perhaps the development of the junior college in America reflects this need.

Regardless of the level of education, schools have no reason for existence other than the ability which they instill in pupils to transfer their knowledge to events outside of the school. Surely no one believes that schools survive merely because they afford youngsters a sheltered environment in which they may partake of abstract pursuits which are completely divorced from the world around them.

Instead, the members of all societies have concluded that there is an inherent and applicable value to education. Man's logic informs him that life is not an exact replica of the school; consequently, logically and historically, man has intended the school to ready youth for his contribution to society. Thus, he is expected to maintain himself and his family, and additionally, to promote the ventures of his society (familial, religious, national, and the like). If the school is to aid him in these endeavors, it can achieve such ends only as the student is able to transfer his newly acquired knowledge.

When transfer is viewed in this perspective, its importance to the student as a person, and as a worker, cannot be overemphasized. Certainly, such significance has attracted voluminous research and has aided considerably in a more scholarly investigation into its nature and function. Gradually, more admissible and scientific hypotheses have resulted, and, because teachers must be alert to all eventualities for transfer, they should be aware of the steady evaluation and discrimination in the speculations concerning transfer.

THEORIES OF TRANSFER

Formal Discipline

Since the theory of formal discipline seems to be the initial doctrine that can be distinguished as a definite attempt to explain transfer, most summaries of transfer history begin here. As Kolesnik (1963) convincingly argues, formal discipline has no specific time or origin, and yet we can deduce its vestiges from the Greeks. We can, nevertheless, argue that whenever man accepts the value of instruction, for whatever purpose, he acknowledges the existence and worth of transfer.

The theory of formal discipline urges that man's mind be exercised by the study of difficult subjects. The same principle applies to an athlete in training. Muscles should be vigorously exercised by subjecting them to periods of increasing strain and stress, and gradually they will become stronger and more efficient.

The formal discipline theory advocates much the same training for the mind. It, too, can be strengthened by exercise, and through stress and strain caused by studying formidable material. Thus, the faculties of which the mind was thought to be composed, such as memory, imagination, judgment, and reasoning, would be nourished by a curriculum containing such subjects as Latin, Greek, and geometry.

As Brubacher (1947, p. 140) says:

Improvement from the exercise of a faculty like memory was supposed to be generally available, not just in the specific area in which memorization took place. Increase in power from the exercise of a faculty in one field of endeavor was thought to "transfer" automatically or at will to endeavor in other fields. Indeed, certain subjects in the curriculum, notably Latin, Greek, and Mathematics, came to have the reputation of being peculiarly well suited to disciplining the mental faculties.

Consequently, certain subjects, especially Latin, were thought to be indispensable to any curriculum. The muscle, which is the mind, would be made keen and alert and would be able to function decisively under any conditions.

The more difficult the subject, the better. Those who believed in the formal discipline theory pointed with pride to their students. They were so much more astute; they were so much more able. Later, when more emphasis was placed on variables, educators appreciated that the students who qualified for a classical curriculum possessed more inherent intelligence.

Also, it is interesting to note that the intrinsic value of the subjects which best disciplined the mind was never a topic for discussion. Only their disciplinary worth, that is, their ability to exercise the mind, was thought to be significant. If certain subjects posed more severe obstacles, the faculties of memory, judgment, reasoning, and the like had to strive more strenuously for a solution. So these became the core of any "good" curriculum. As Kolesnik (1963, p. 271) says:

Mr. Dooley summed it up in his oft-quoted observation that it does not matter much what subject a student studies, so long as he doesn't like it.

The formal discipline theory carried within itself the elements for its own destruction. The starting date for the assault upon formal discipline is usually given as 1890. The battle was led by one of the towering figures in psychology—William James. Before we examine James' experiment, the reader should note the length of time during which the theory of formal discipline was unchallenged. We tentatively identified the beginnings of this theory with the Greeks, but also indicated that it could conceivably have been much earlier. And it is only in 1890 that we see the first questions being raised about the actual efficiency of the theory.

Returning to James, in his classic work, *The Principles of Psychology* (1890), he reports the results of an experiment he conducted to determine the accuracy of the claims of the adherents of the formal discipline school. He memorized 158 lines of poetry (Victor Hugo's *Satyr*) during a period of eight days. The time required was almost 132 minutes. According to the formal discipline theory, if he now exercised his memory by memorizing something else, he would then be able to memorize another 158 lines of the *Satyr* in less time than his original attempt.

He therefore practiced memorizing for twenty minutes a day for thirty-eight days by committing to memory Book I of Milton's *Paradise Lost*. If the formal discipline theory held true, future memorization of the *Satyr* should be easier and more rapid. He now memorized a second 158 lines, which took him 151½ minutes— several minutes longer than the initial trial!

How could this phenomenon be explained? There are many criticisms which we could make today, such as the lack of a control and no consideration of variables other than James' statement that fatigue must be a major element in any analysis of the results. Perhaps more significantly, James encouraged others to experiment with the formal discipline theory.

Identical Elements

When anyone investigates creative ideas and experiments in problems of education, he continually encounters the name of Edward Lee Thorndike. Studies of the transfer of learning are no exception. In 1901, Thorndike and Woodworth published the conclusions of a series of experiments which produced these remarkable outcomes.

1. They thoroughly refuted the apparent benefits of the formal discipline theory.
2. They provided the foundation upon which an entirely new theory of transfer could be formulated.
3. They penetrated into the materials and methods of instruction and established a pattern of teaching which is presently employed in many school systems.

The experiments which produced these drastic changes were relatively simple. Subjects were initially tested for their ability to perform certain tasks, for example, to calculate the size of various objects. They then received sufficient training to yield discernible improvement in a closely related chore. Finally, they were retested on the first task. Thus, training in estimating the size of one-half inch to one and one-half inch lines showed little, if any, transfer to estimating the size of lines from six to twelve inches in length.

The conclusions were inescapable. Training in the discernment of line lengths applied only to specifics and manifested no shift in ability to discriminate beyond the particular task in which training had occurred. So there are separate and distinct abilities associated with the calculation of length, each of which must be taught as separate and distinct lessons.

Consequently, what was true of these experiments must similarly be true of all learning. Training in one subject or task does not mechanically bring improvement to other subjects or tasks, regardless of what appears to be an exterior similarity between them. Thorndike, however, refused to dismiss transfer completely. There must be some explanation for the irrefutable evidence of transfer. Thorndike proposed his famous "Theory of Identical Elements" to account for any transfer that seemed to appear.

Training the mind requires the identification and mastery of thousands of precise capacities and habits, which will then improve some other task that has common elements. This belief, as we shall see, is compatible with his theory of learning, which construes learning as the formation of bonds between stimuli and response. Specific stimuli elicit specific responses, and similarly, transfer materializes when specific elements are present in two separate experiences. Travers (1963, p. 193) summarizes the connection between Thorndike's theory of learning and his theory of transfer as follows:

The reader will remember that learning, for Thorndike, involves the development of bonds between stimuli and responses. According to him, what is learned is a bond which may be considered a connection in the nervous system between an input on the stimulus end and an output on the response end. In Thorndike's version (1923) of his theory, transfer of training will occur from an activity involving certain bonds, say XYZ, to another activity, if that activity involves also the bonds XYZ. This is the famous theory of identical elements, but Thorndike is actually vague concerning what he means by identical elements. In one sentence he speaks of identical elements as "mental processes which have the same cell action in the brain as their physical correlates" (p. 359). However, he does add, "It is of course often not possible to tell just what features of two mental abilities are thus identical."

The physiological rationalization of identical elements was too vague for lasting acceptance, but its effects are evident today. The subjects that afforded a "general" training for the mind were discarded; if transfer *were* limited, each objective must be attained by unique and explicit instruction. Rapp (1945, p. 470) describes the changing techniques of instruction as follows:

This was only a beginning. The movement toward particularization quickly spread into the field of personality. The line of argument was as follows. If training the mind means the development of thousands of particular independent capacities, and there is no general spread of training beyond that which is actually being taught, then surely training for honesty, bravery, neatness, or courtesy is a thousand separate trainings. You have to inculcate honesty separately in each separate type of situation. There can be no general trait of honesty, or bravery or neatness or courtesy.

Courses in the curriculum multiplied, the entire concept of learning sustained theoretical and practical readjustment, and philosophies of education were obliged to examine anew their goals since man's traditional method of learning had ostensibly changed. Subjects were admissible only if their pertinence to goals was clearly defined. Thus, Latin was taught only if it aided the development of English vocabulary by a comparison of roots, and so forth. If an instructor taught reading, why use anything else but words; meaning, subtleties of phrasing, and exploitation of visual clues were unimportant. If the student knows that 8 multiplied by 7 equals 56, we cannot assume that he will transfer this knowledge to 7 multiplied by 8. Thorndike's book on arithmetic testifies to the specificity of his theory. Education was on a "one-to-one" basis; one item taught, only one item learned.

Transfer by Generalization

Although the identical elements concept achieved wide popularity and many teachers still resort, perhaps subconsciously, to this notion of transfer, another doctrine of transfer has become quite celebrated. This is the theory of generalization first advanced by Charles Judd (1908). In a renowned experiment, one group of boys received instruction in hitting a target under water. The principles of refraction were explained to these boys; they were not explained to a control group. Both groups of boys were about eleven years old.

The first trials were with the target submerged twelve inches. Initially, both groups did well with little difference between them. But, when the target was raised from twelve inches to four inches, a significant difference between the two groups was apparent. The boys who were not afforded the explanation of the theory of refraction were unable to respond effectively to what appeared to be a completely new problem. When the target was moved to eight inches, confusion was compounded.

The importance of this experiment is immediately evident. Although both groups performed adequately on the first trial, when the conditions were changed, the performance of both groups was considerably altered. The training that was provided by the first attempts to hit the target did not transfer to the second problem when the depth of the submerged object was changed. Therefore, even the identical elements did not transfer.

Recall the essentials in both tests: boys of approximately the same age and ability; use of the same instrument to hit the same target, a submerged object in both instances. The one variable was the instruction given to the first group, and, when the conditions in the test differed, even as little as four inches, the specific elements of the first trial did *not* aid in the second.

Consequently, training to hit a target twelve inches under water would transfer only to other targets twelve inches under water unless the theory, or the generalization, underlying the act is also learned. Then, and only then, could a successful adjustment be made by those taking the test. So, Thorndike's experiments were doomed from the beginning. Since no effort was made to inform the subjects in his experiments of any principles involved in the discrimination of size, they could transfer their original learning only to situations that were identical. If the slightest change occurred in the two tasks, no transfer was evident.

Thus, Judd refuted the formal discipline theory and the doctrine of identical elements. Transfer depends, instead, upon an individ ual's grasp of the principles or generalizations which are inherent in any learning task. Abstractions, generalizations, and application are vital to his theory. A student must comprehend the fundamental ideas of a subject; he must recognize the possibilities of applying these principles; he must have the opportunity to employ the generalizations of one problem, subject, or task to another which possesses various degrees of similarity to the original learning experience.

Although any discipline demands an exhaustive mastery of detail, it is the manner in which the resultant knowledge is treated that will determine the extent of transfer. For example, the student of geography must have certain essential information about a nation, such as location, population, resources, and economy, to analyze intelligently its power position in the twentieth century. Yet, mastery of this knowledge for the sake of mastery is insufficient. The instructor should guide his students to realize that economic diversity, for instance, in modern society is a necessity for any nation. Dependence upon one crop is disastrous if the world market should shift its need for this single item.

The teacher should also introduce a cautionary note and indicate that some economic diversity can result in segments of one nation competing among themselves. The American Civil War is a good illustration. Now, when students examine a country's economy, there will be repercussions from past learnings; principles of the subject will be operating and useless memorization of products will cease to be the only method of study, a technique which has caused more students to rebel against the remoteness of formal education than any other single reason.

The Unity of Transfer Theory

When our limited knowledge of concept formation and learning is admitted, the process of transfer becomes more intelligible and less subject to a rigid dichotomy. That is, solution is not purely identical elements, or strictly generalization, with acceptance of one theory completely discarding the other. Thus, theorists and practitioners today select the best of available speculations, while research into the nature of the entire question continues. But one conclusion is inescapable: knowledge of transfer will increase only as knowledge of the learning process itself grows.

Recall the identical elements and generalization theories. Each relied upon learning in its experimentation: Thorndike teaching his subjects to discern between differences in size, and Judd teaching boys how to hit a submerged object. In each theory, regardless of hypotheses, the results depended upon learning. Now, if our knowledge of learning is incomplete, our knowledge of the essence and operation of transfer must be limited.

Accepting the restrictions imposed by the inadequacy of current facts has caused educators and psychologists to study existing theories more intently than otherwise might have been done. And, the surprising result is that none of the present theories is actually incompatible. There must be something identical in Situation I for anything to transfer to Situation II, but more than specific items may transfer. It may be an entity as intangible as an attitude derived from a specific experience; it may be a technique, or a method of attacking any problem, such as the "what do I have, what do I need?" manner of seeking a solution in any endeavor.

Unless the individual forms a concept of the item to be transferred, be it fact, principle, attitude, or ideal, failure will be the product. Hence, ideal transfer demands a conscious realization by the student that he may apply a specific detail to other activities. It then becomes a principle or generalization which the individual may use in a variety of functions. There *must* be a conscious commitment to transfer, that is, somehow, the student must be aware that particular facts learned in classroom study are pertinent in other, seemingly diverse, cases.

Because consciousness is an indispensable ingredient in our transfer formula, the burden again falls on the school. Teachers must make a more resolute effort to teach for transfer; they must alert students to be constantly striving to envisage new opportunities to utilize hard-won knowledge. And teachers must force themselves to scan work and materials diligently for similarities and generalizations which they can hopefully transmit to students.

TRANSFER IN THE CLASSROOM

Once we acknowledge the reality of transfer and utilize the most appropriate findings of transfer theory, research can provide teachers with more acute insights into the actual workings of transfer.

The paradigms used in the analysis of transfer will help the reader to understand the design of recent research; they will also aid in teaching because the notions of interference with and facilitation of learning are more easily seen. The two basic designs are proactive and retroactive. Proaction refers to the influence that learning task A now will have on learning task B in the future. Retroaction refers to the effect that learning task Z now will have on previously learned task Y. In either example, it may be positive or negative. The designs are as follows.

I. Proaction

Experimental Group—Learn task 1   Learn task 2   Test task 2

Control Group—Rest (neutral activity)   Learn task 2   Test task 2

For these experiments to be valid, the experimental and control groups must be as closely matched as possible. Thus, any variation in the test results of task 2 can be attributed to the learning of task 1 by the experimental group. Perhaps, after examining the proactive design, the reader can better comprehend the possibility of transfer being either positive or negative. Learning task 1 may have assisted the experimental group to achieve superior results in mastering task 2. Or, there is the definite eventuality that it might have hindered the study of task 2. This is what is meant by interference.

II. Retroaction

Experimental Group—Learns task 1   Learns task 2   Test task 1

Control Group—Learns task 1   Rest (neutral activity)   Test task 1

In this design, the effects of task 2 on *previously* learned task 1 are measured. The effects of task 2 reach *back* on task 1 and may either aid or impede the recall of task 1. Again, the effects of the inter-polated task may either be positive or negative.

After examining both of these examples, the reader can comprehend the formidable obstacles facing those investigating transfer, and can appreciate the relative paucity of transfer research. It also helps to explain the reliance which is still placed upon the older experiments. Control of variables is presently an overwhelming barrier. Consider the individual variables involved: age, motivation, health, intelligence, emotional set, attitude at the time of study, and many others. Can we effectively control the nature of the tasks themselves: the equal impact of the selected tasks on the subjects, the effect of previous transfer upon present tasks, the influence of practice, and so forth? Again, as our techniques of research improve, knowledge about the process of transfer will improve accordingly.

This is steadily happening. Certain aspects of transfer are now deemed more important than others. For example, Deese (1952, pp. 216–217) says:

> In any situation in which transfer of training may occur, the major variable that determines whether positive or negative transfer will be achieved is the nature of the material being learned or practiced. The most important aspect of the material is its degree of similarity. Depending upon the similarity relationships between the two tasks involved in an experiment on transfer of training, negative or positive transfer will be the result.

So, the essence of the material which will occasion the transfer causes differences in the amount of transfer, not by chance, but because of the relationship of stimuli to responses in both cases. How similar are the stimuli in both instances; how similar are the responses?

Note the similarity of stimuli and difference in responses in the following illustration. Correct English usage requires the placement of subject, verb, and object in one, two, three order, for example, John caught the ball. Then the student begins his study of foreign languages and discovers that the principles of word order are not identical. Unquestionably, the modification of word location will interfere with the proper phrasing of sentences in the new language. The stimuli were similar: a sentence was to be written. But the responses differed.

Or, picture the first-grade child learning to read. One of the first requirements is that he masters a sight vocabulary of a limited number of words. The teacher may present word cards to the youngster and ask him to name the word on each card. If he is successful in this type of activity, he will probably begin to use some kind of preprimer where he will encounter the same words. There is a slight difference in both stimuli and responses for reading but the similarity far outweighs any differences.

Thus, similar stimuli associated with similar responses will produce significant transfer. But similarity of stimuli associated with difference of responses produces negative transfer. The neutral zone remains, that is, stimuli which are dissimilar associated with dissimilar responses will produce no transfer. Similarity of stimuli and similarity of responses prompt a continuum of transfer from positive to zero to negative transfer.

Transfer of abstract knowledge, nevertheless, appears to be more complex than mere similarity of stimuli and responses would indicate. Ausubel and Fitzgerald (1961, p. 501) are concerned with the surface ease of explanation by these terms only:

Much more saliently than in experimental laboratory types of learning situations, typical school learning requires the incorporation of new concepts and information into an established cognitive framework with particular organizational properties. The transfer paradigm still applies here, and transfer still refers to the impact of prior experience upon current learning. But prior experience in this case is conceptualized as a cumulatively acquired, hierarchically organized, and established body of knowledge which is organically relatable to the new learning task, rather than as a recently experienced constellation of stimulus-response connections influencing the learning of another discrete set of such connections. Furthermore, the relevant aspects of past experience in this type of transfer paradigm are such organizational properties of the learner's subject-matter knowledge as clarity, stability, generalizability, inclusiveness, cohesiveness, and discriminability (i.e., cognitive structure variables)—not the degree of similarity between stimuli and responses in the two learning tasks. Further, recent prior experience is not regarded as influencing current learning by interacting *directly* with the stimulus-response components of the new learning task, except insofar as it modifies significant relevant attributes of cognitive structure. In an empirical test of this theoretical orientation, Ausubel and Blake (1958), using a proactive inhibition research design, demonstrated that meaningful learning and retention of a passage on Buddhism was not adversely affected by recent prior learning to interfering materials, for example, on Christianity.

Here the authors urge the student of transfer to appraise the personal variables as well as the task because it is not only the student's immediate state that is important, but also the nature of the past learning that is transferring to the present topic. Can unknown past experience be controlled? Subjects may be matched as closely as possible and experimental circumstances may be rigidly regulated, and yet, ultimately, there is the entire classification of past experience which remains beyond the eventuality of control.

Recent experiments testify to the need for caution in assessing the amount of transfer which results from specific stimulus-response connections. De Rivera (1959) had his subjects learn letters as the responses to fingerprint patterns, and later he had them learn numbers as their responses to the same stimuli. One group learned one letter for each print; two other groups learned only two letters, one letter for each half of the prints. Of these latter two groups, one was told to look for common characteristics. Transfer to the numbers was significantly lower for this group, while the other two groups were equal. The outcome was inconclusive, and the subjects still had to discriminate among stimuli for clues.

Another experiment by Rasmussen and Archer (1961) was conducted on concept identification. The subjects learned relevant labels for nonsense shapes on the assumption that the use of labels would aid discrimination and assist concept identification. This did not occur, but another group which examined the shapes for aesthetic qualities later showed improvement on the assigned task, probably because they inspected all phases of the shapes. Therefore, the transfer value of the specific relationship between stimulus and response is debatable, but an interpolated task that permits discrimination of characteristics seems to help transfer.

Transfer, however small or uncertain, does appear with sufficient frequency to warrant continued research and continued effort by teachers to inspire it in the classroom. Transfer should not be taken for granted; it must be deliberately cultivated. Consequently, a student must master a subject and consciously strive for transfer to insure effective usage under different conditions. Memorization of facts confined to one particular lesson or subject remains restricted to that specific stimulus situation. Transfer exacts more from the student and teacher: concept formation, reasoning, judgment, application of principles, and the like.

After the teacher decides that there are definite transfer potentialities in a certain subject (which should always occur), he then settles upon how to attain maximum transfer for *each* student. Individual differences assume great importance because pupils with high intelligence will undoubtedly transfer more easily and proficiently than students of lower intellectual capacity. That this statement is true becomes clear when we reflect upon our analysis of transfer. The discernment of principles requires a necessary ease with abstract notions which denotes additional work by the teacher for slower youngsters to benefit as much as ability permits from this aspect of instruction.

CONCLUSION

Probably the most significant proposition which could be advanced in any discussion of transfer is this: the student must ceaselessly search for similarity. He must learn to estimate each new problem, each new task, or each new activity for *anything* that might be familiar and would enable him to seek a rational solution based upon previous experience. The familiar item may be content; it may be method of study or problem solving; it may be principles. Whatever it is, the student must be alert to the possibility of transfer. He must pursue new answers by *consciously* utilizing prior learning.

It is not exaggerating to state unequivocally that future success in a society which is becoming increasingly more complex socially and technologically will rest primarily upon how well a student transfers his learning. As more and more students graduate from high school and college, competition grows more intense, and it is the person who is able to apply his knowledge and skill competently in society who will achieve the most.

And it is certainly no exaggeration to state that, in a world of social and technological revolution, the nation which produces imaginative, creative citizens will also provide security and prosperity for its population. Still, this will occur only if the graduates of its school system transfer their knowledge to modern, changing, problems; it is necessary for them to take the rudiments of their education and recombine them to achieve the new, dynamic ideas which any vital nation needs for its nourishment.

Therefore, the conclusion that transfer is critical is inescapable; the conclusion that the entire question of transfer poses enormous problems is also inescapable; the conclusion that transfer demands effort from both student and teacher is again inescapable. So, to terminate this chapter, a summary statement by Bigge and Hunt (1962, p. 393) is indeed pertinent:

Transfer of learning may be summarized in six crucial points:

1. Opportunity for transfer may occur in many situations. It is not inherent in any subject but is possible from any field of knowledge.
2. Transfer is not dependent upon exercise with disciplinary subjects.
3. Transfer is dependent upon methods of teaching and learning which use lifelike situations. It is facilitated by teaching for large generalizations which have transfer value.
4. Transfer is not automatic; opportunities for transfer must be recognized, and the person concerned must want to use them.
5. Transfer varies according to difficulty of generalization of subject matter and intellectual ability of individuals.
6. Insights need not be put into words for their transfer to occur.

CHAPTER VIII

Learning Theory — I

INTRODUCTION

THE BOY SQUIRMED uneasily. Restlessly, he chewed the top of his pencil. Which formula should he use? How could he tell which would offer the correct solution? He had studied them. The teacher had discussed them. But, now he had to use them. Gradually, his movements assumed a pattern. He had made his decision. Right or wrong, he had committed himself. He was applying his knowledge.

How can this process be explained? Is it a type of reflex action? Is the student simply responding to a stimulus? Or is he manifesting a superior type of activity? Psychologists have offered many and varied answers to these questions. Educators have been equally concerned. Nowhere are the two disciplines of education and psychology so closely united as in the study of learning. Each has much to offer; each has much to gain.

The psychologist realizes that learning is one of the basic operations of the human being. New information about the learning process will aid him in his investigations of the complexities of human behavior. The educator realizes that additional insights into learning will better the quality of instruction. It will strengthen the curriculum, improve teaching methods, and certainly assist in an understanding of the motivational process.

The increasing sophistication of research tools and techniques has led both the psychologist and educator to a deeper understanding of learning. Unfortunately, most studies have been confined to the animal level. There has been a tendency to apply animal findings to the human. If the findings of animal studies are used as a basis for further human study, the results would be most acceptable. To apply the conclusions of subhuman research to human action, however, is a dangerous oversimplification.

Research of the learning process must continue, and the problem warrants study in its proper setting. It is time for research on the human level, in the situation supposedly most conducive to learning —the school. Many topics urgently need careful and controlled examination. Among these are personality, motivation, and thinking (Buswell, 1956).

Such persistent scrutiny of animal behavior has caused many educators to dismiss theories of learning as too speculative to influence classroom procedure. Nevertheless, someone in a school system, at some time, has accepted a particular psychology of learning as the foundation of curriculum and instruction. This acceptance will be reflected in the materials and methods that the teacher uses daily.

It will also be reflected in the school's attitude toward the pupil. If the accepted psychology of learning is founded upon animal studies, the assumption is made that a youngster learns in the same manner as an animal. Methods of instruction will mirror this assumption. Phenomena such as conditioning, reinforcement, and the like will become a central part of classroom procedure.

If the school views the pupil as an individual who manifests activities that are superior to those of the animal, its goals will be significantly different. Man's creative abilities will be encouraged; knowledge will be used in problem-solving situations. These objectives will dictate different methodological approaches.

Thus, the conclusions of learning theories cannot be dismissed lightly. They must be inspected carefully. If the findings of a particular theory offer promise of improvement for the learning process they should be utilized wherever feasible.

An example of the impact that learning theory can have on the daily life of the school is seen in the teaching machine. A direct outgrowth of stimulus-response learning theory, teaching machines today are widely accepted in many communities.

Conflicting learning theories exist—they do exert influence, in a most practical way, upon the school. Therefore, individuals in the field of education, or contemplating a teaching career, should be familiar with the major theories and their educational implications.

Still, certain problems must be faced. An explanation of learning, agreed upon by all, is an objective that psychology has not achieved (Blair, 1948). Of the many theories that attempt to solve the intricacies of learning, some have had a greater impact on education than others. Certain of these theories belong to the association schools of learning. With their emphasis upon stimulus, response, reward, and conditioning, these theories view man as a machine. Perhaps man may be slightly more complex than the machine we ordinarily visualize; nevertheless, these theories state he operates on the same principles. Man's cognitive nature, if it exists, is unimportant. He must respond to the pressures of the environment in a determined manner.

Other theories see man evidencing behavior that is obviously superior to and more complicated than either mechanistic or animal activity. These are known as field theories. They recognize that man can solve problems and is capable of creative expression. This he does by a form of insightful behavior. However, his insight into a problem is structured by his perception of the environment which surrounds him. Man is able to respond to the pressure of his environment in a creative fashion. The more he knows of the subtleties of his environment (or field), the more acute is his perception of the problems, and their solutions. Consequently, his insight is sharper; his learning is faster and more accurate.

Neither classification of learning theory tells us all we need to know about the learning process. Yet, both have made significant contributions to classroom procedures and both deserve comment. The associationists, who have been so prominent in American psychological thought, shall receive first notice, followed by representatives of field theory. A theorist who exerted considerable control for many years upon curriculum and instruction of the schools is Edward Thorndike.

CONNECTIONISM

The bond psychology, or Connectionism, is so closely associated with the name of Edward Lee Thorndike that one has come to mean the other. Thorndike *is* Connectionism (Sandiford, 1942).

Early in his academic life, Thorndike fell under the spell of William James. His interest in psychology originally was inspired by reading James' *Principles of Psychology* (1890). When he went to Harvard for graduate work, he studied under James and became interested in animal intelligence. Boring tells the interesting story of the difficulties Thorndike encountered with his animals. When he was unable to find an agreeable landlord who would permit both Thorndike and his chicks to share a room, Thorndike moved his equipment and chicks into the cellar of James' home—much to the delight of the James children (Boring, 1950).

He continued his work with the chicks, establishing a trial-and-error form of learning in them. He investigated the place and function of reward in learning. Gradually his findings were systemized, and a formal theory of learning evolved from his substantial research.

The Laws of Learning

In the course of his work with animals, Thorndike formulated three major laws of learning based on the assumption that learning is connecting. The connection is a bond between stimulus and response. These connections have their physical basis in the nervous system, and the connection between neuron and neuron (synapse) accounts for learning. The more bonds, or connections, that a person possesses, the more intelligent is he.

Between 1898 and 1930, there were relatively few changes in Thorndike's system. During this time he was concerned with the application of his theory (Hilgard, 1956). His consistent position was that all learning functions in accordance with his major laws of learning: readiness, exercise, and effect.

The Law of Readiness

The law of readiness is closely linked to the law of effect. In fact, Hilgard considers it to be the physical basis for the law of effect (Hilgard, 1956). If a bond (connection) is ready to act, to act causes pleasure, and not to act causes annoyance. When the neural pathway is ready, the completed act is successful. If it is not successful, or does not act, a feeling of dissatisfaction or annoyance is aroused. One receives the impression that Thorndike considered readiness as an "On your mark-get-set-go" type of phenomenon.

One sees the obstacle that this theory of readiness does not remove. Regardless of environmental pressures, man retains the ability to choose. Although every indication suggests action, and a person's nervous system is prepared to act, the individual may decide that it is in his best interest not to act. Thus, for some reason not explained neurologically, he has restrained his action and selected what, for him, was a greater good, that is, not to act.

Such a problem persists for any mechanistic school. Clearly, there are aspects of man's behavior that cannot be explained in animal terms. Thorndike himself seems to have sensed this. Readiness refers not so much to the actual neural pathways, as to the conditions of these pathways. So, he does not entirely remove the possibility of such behavior as choice. He does ignore the issue, and, therefore, presents the troublesome task of reading into his writings what may not be there.

The Law of Exercise

"Practice makes perfect" is a saying so familiar that it is almost painful to repeat. Before 1930, Thorndike felt that a connection is strengthened by its practice, and little else. If practice is discontinued, the connection will become weakened, if not lost entirely.

This law brought swift and devastating criticism. Mere repetition of an act does not insure its permanence as a successful S–R bond. This is easily shown by many and different examples. Draw a six-inch line on a blackboard with chalk. Ask individuals to go to the board and look at the line. Next, ask them to close their eyes and draw a similar line. What will happen is apparent. The lines will get progressively worse. Yet, the act is being repeated.

According to Thorndike's original law of exercise, the successful S–R should be stamped into the nervous system by repeated trials. It became evident that repetition of a situation was not, of itself, sufficient for a continued successful response. What is needed is repetition of the actual connection (S–R). If this is accompanied by a reward, the result of the connection is such that the organism is eager to duplicate it.

Thorndike recognized the limitations of the law as originally postulated, and, after 1930, he revised it to include the law of effect.

The Law of Effect

The law of effect was undoubtedly the most important of Thorndike's laws. A bond is strengthened or weakened in accordance with the pleasure or pain that is associated with it. Although this has been regarded as the foundation of Connectionism, it was attacked early and often by others of the mechanistic schools. Terms such as pleasure, satisfaction, and the like are much too subjective to please some critics. What is pleasure? Who determines it? How can it be measured?

In his initial statement of the law of effect, Thorndike considered reward and punishment to have an equal and opposite result. Reward would encourage repetition of the behavior (S–R bond) that had resulted in a pleasant experience. Also, punishment would inhibit, with the same strength, behavior that resulted in a painful experience.

Dissatisfaction with the law of effect led Thorndike to further experimentation, both with chicks and with humans. In his *Fundamentals of Learning* (Thorndike, 1932), he reported that reward was much more potent in the shaping of behavior than was punishment. Learning occurs because of positive aftereffects. Consequently, the first duty of the school is to insure that the student makes the proper connection with his first attempt, if possible. This enables the bond to be made and a reward to be given immediately.

Conclusion

These are Thorndike's major laws of learning. He also formulated several subordinate laws which were mainly designed to clarify and expand upon his three basic premises. It is the three main laws, however, that give dimension and scope to his learning theory.

The educational implications of Thorndike's work were disruptive and far reaching. From a philosophy of idealism, the schools turned to an education that reflected the assumptions of associationist methods of instruction. Understanding and problem solving were virtually ignored.

One may well ask how and why this admittedly more restricted form of learning achieved such popularity. The main reason was that Thorndike gave educators a more practical and measurable theory of learning. The products of his learning could be tested and measured more accurately. A scientific aura began to settle over education.

Very slowly the weaknesses inherent in Connectionism became apparent. Today, they are recognized and admitted. This is in no way belittling Thorndike's contribution to learning theory and to the daily life of the classroom. In any classroom the impact of Thorndike can be seen.

BEHAVIORISM

Dissatisfaction with Thorndike's concept of pleasure caused many American psychologists to turn to the theory of conditioning. The impetus given to classical conditioning is due, primarily, to the work of Pavlov. His physiological study of the digestive glands of animals reported the occurrence that seemed to answer so many psychological questions—the conditioned reflex. He discovered that the mere anticipation of food caused the flow of saliva in dogs.

Saliva flowed at the sight of the attendant who was bringing the food. It even flowed at a sound the attendant might make. As Pavlov emphasized, these are not natural stimuli. A natural stimulus would be food placed in the mouth. When saliva flowed because of an unnatural stimulus, it must be a type of learned response. Pavlov designated this response as the conditioned reflex. He called any unnatural stimulus (sight of the dish, or of the attendant) the conditioned stimulus. The search for a substitute for consciousness seemed at an end. Introspection was unnecessary to explain this superior type of nervous activity.

A stimulus causes a response. Some neutral stimulus, associated with the original, unconditioned stimulus at the time of response, gradually acquires the power of eliciting the response by its own appearance. Thus:

1. S–R   (unconditioned stimulus causes response)
2. $\begin{array}{c} S \\ | \\ S_1 \end{array}$ –R   (unconditioned stimulus causes response in presence of neutral stimulus)
3. S_1–R   (after several repetitions, the conditioned stimulus, S_1, elicits the original response)

For John B. Watson, Pavlov's work solved many problems. Psychology as the study of behavior was replacing psychology as the study of consciousness. In America, the time was ripe for simpler explanations of behavior. Anything of a practical nature was quick to appeal. Anything of a philosophical nature was viewed with suspicion. Why waste time with exercises of futility? Pragmatic America was ready for Watson.

Although a reactionary, negative attitude prevailed at the turn of the century, Behaviorism did make a positive appeal. Watson felt that the study of behavior itself was significant and too often had been overlooked because of an obsession with man's mind. He never denied the existence of consciousness but simply ignored it. He refused to investigate the unobservable. To Watson, physiology was the study that most closely resembled psychology (Watson, 1930).

If psychology is to be limited to the observable, the stimulus and response are rudimentary concepts. The organism is bombarded by stimuli from its environment. From the many thousands of unlearned possible responses, our organized learned responses are formed by conditioning. By carefully selected stimuli, simple unconditioned responses can be linked together to form more complicated conditioned responses.

Conditioning is paramount in Watson's system. It not only is a method of investigating the intricacies of human behavior, but also is an explanation of the character of human behavior. Learning is synonymous with conditioning. For Watson, there were three kinds of learning: emotional, manual, and laryngeal.

Emotions

Fear, rage, and love are the basis for emotional learning. Watson hastens to assure his readers that he means nothing mentalistic by these terms (fear, rage, love). They are bodily responses of a visceral nature. From these few, unlearned responses, the human organism builds complicated emotional patterns. This is accomplished by conditioning. In all emotional reactions, visceral and glandular features are the most prominent.

Watson emphasizes that unconditioned stimuli with unconditioned responses are the means of acquiring the complex patterns of behavior that are designated emotions. These emotional reactions are identical to other bodily reactions, both by nature and development. That is, there is a conditioning of stimulus and response. The number of stimuli eliciting the response is increased, and the responses to any stimulus also multiply. The range of both stimulus and response is widened.

Manual Habits

By manual habits, Watson refers to the organization in the trunk, legs, arms, and feet. When the human body is stimulated, it moves. The body reacts to inner as well as outer stimuli, and it never responds to just one, or only to the other. If the body undergoes ceaseless stimulation, it responds with ceaseless movements. There is never a period of complete adjustment [Watson claimed that the only adjusted person is a dead person (Watson, 1930, p. 161)].

In his discussion of motor learning, the terms "frequency" and "recency" appear. The more a response is made to a certain stimulus, the more apt we are to repeat it.

Watson felt that the recency principle refuted Thorndike's law of effect. There is no need of a "feeling of satisfaction." Common sense tells us that the last response will appear more quickly in the next trial until, finally, it is elicited immediately.

He similarly analyzes the more integrated manual responses. There is a relationship between these and the simple conditioned response. It is a relationship of part to whole. The more involved response is merely a series of conditioned reflexes. The initial muscular response to an external stimulus serves as an inner stimulus to arouse the next motor response in the correct sequence. Watson called this second-order conditioning.

Laryngeal Habits

This is Watson's phrase for thinking, which reduces language to a manipulative habit. The larynx is manipulated by its attached muscles as we expel air. The human's laryngeal habits are developed as are the manual habits. The result is a conditioned vocal response that is acquired by learning (conditioning) from original unlearned responses.

The original unlearned stimulus is change in muscular or glandular tissue in the throat region. The unlearned response is an overt, vocal reply (ma ma). Watson claims that word conditioning is built upon this process. Conditioned word responses are established for all objects in the external environment. This is not true for the internal environment. Society has no terms for these inner objects or changes. As in manual activities, the unlearned response is the foundation for laryngeal habits.

Laryngeal habits enable man to move through his world with great economy. He no longer has to manipulate physically the things in his environment. He is able to do this by verbal substitution. For example, if I am in bed at night and am concerned because a pupil misbehaved in school, I am not forced to recreate in fact the same situation to ascertain what happened. I can use words to formulate once again the same troublesome situation.

Watson insists that laryngeal habits are only one phase of thought. Muscular habits learned in overt speech are the basis for internal speech. Thought, then, is not restricted to the larynx. Many more muscular responses occur in both the throat and chest. Removal of the larynx obviously does not inhibit a person's thought. Overt speech has resulted in a formidable complex of muscular organization. Slowly, they are internalized and new combinations arise. This is caused mainly by the pressures of society.

Eventually, any bodily response may become a word substitute. Shake your head for yes or no. Shrug your shoulders because you do not understand. Thought is not restricted to the larynx.

A person thinks when he wishes to escape a maladjustment. Often, manual activities will not aid a person in the solution of his problems. He is thrown upon his own resources. Are there any alternatives to action? He must think through the problem and determine a course for action. Thought, again, is used in the behavioral sense.

Conclusion

Although emotional, manual, and laryngeal habits were discussed as distinct entities, this was done for purposes of analysis. Watson repeatedly claimed that, when an individual reacts, his whole body reacts. All habit systems function together. Since man's life is so filled with thought reactions (subvocal speech), verbal organization rapidly predominates.

Integration of the three habit systems determines an individual's personality. To many people, personality means what makes this person a distinct individual. According to Watson, it is a composite of the parts we have mentioned—emotional, manual, and laryngeal.

Personality becomes the end product of our habit system. It is reduced to observable habits witnessed over a lengthy period of time. Some systems within the personality will become more dominant than others. Athletic ability may be superior in the manual domain; facility with the spoken word in the laryngeal; finally, withdrawal may be the most obvious reaction in the visceral domain. Stimuli determine the person's reaction pattern, but it (reaction pattern) is also influenced by the dominant factors in our habit systems.

Personality as the summation of our habit systems becomes all of the learned and unlearned responses of which the individual is capable. It is the duty of society, particularly the school, to determine the stimuli for each individual. Thus, society will direct the individual to goals that have been predetermined by the institutions in society. This was the ultimate objective of Behaviorism. The prediction and control of behavior must become a reality if society is to progress in an orderly fashion. The school should be instrumental in the process.

CONTIGUOUS CONDITIONING

One of the most intriguing and deceptively simple of the mechanistic theories is Guthrie's interpretation of conditioning. Similar to Pavlov's classical concept, but sufficiently different to warrant separate classification, Guthrie has created a lasting place for himself in American psychological thought.

Guthrie was for many years a professor at the University of Washington. His background and approach to psychology were remarkably similar to Watson's. Part of Guthrie's undisputed appeal has been his ability to phrase difficult notions in a manner that the reader can easily understand. He also possessed the capacity to write simply and clearly in a discipline known for its jargon and obscurity.

The most important premise of Guthrie's theory is that a response is conditioned to a stimulus pattern. Conditioning is between stimulus and responses, not between stimulus and stimulus. When the necessary stimulus and response occur together, learning or adaptation results.

Observable Behavior

Throughout his career, Guthrie was obsessed with the observable, understandable, and verifiable. The persuasiveness of Watson is clearly evident. A psychology of learning is unworthy of the name unless its rules are observable and subject to verification. Explanations of learning must concentrate on things—never on concepts, ideas, or judgments. Any interpretation that relies on synapses, differences in electrical potential, and the like is rejected. There is no way in which these theories may be tested.

Insight because of perception of the total situation is also rejected. Insight may be another way of expressing the association between stimulus and response. It is not observable; therefore, it must be excluded.

Inner Stimuli

We observe behavior rather than inner manifestations, which may or may not exist. When we observe behavior, we witness the occasion of the response (stimulus) and part of the response. Here is one example of the deceptive simplicity of Guthrie. A person reacts to more stimuli than those we see pressing on him from the environment. Clearly, he is also reacting to himself.

Guthrie states that a combination of stimuli which has accompanied a movement will on its recurrence tend to be followed by that movement (Guthrie, 1952, p. 23). Inner stimuli are a part of the combination. Undoubtedly, there are inner responses that are hidden: the reaction to a teacher's question may include a rapid heartbeat and a rise in blood pressure.

Inner stimuli are important to Guthrie. He claims that they can be observed but not shared. When we see the various postures of the person, we see the movements that stimulate the inner sense organs. These give rise to the inner stimuli. By postulating such stimuli, Guthrie offers a solution for different behavior in the same situation. Although the environment presented similar pressures to those which caused the original response, now the inner stimuli of the individual differ from those of the previous occasion.

One-Trial Association

Guthrie believed that a stimulus pattern gained its full associative strength on the occasion of its first pairing with a response (Guthrie, 1942). Since careful practice causes gradual improvement, this statement appears contradictory. The first attempt, in any field of endeavor, rarely results in instant perfection. Guthrie states that the movement is confused with the act. Practice does cause improvement. The improvement we see refers to an act and not to the movements that led to the act. One-trial association is our observation of a particular act. But there were many separate movements that led to the successful completion of the act. Many and diversified components of the reaction pattern were included in a successful response that was observed.

Learning—Doing

Guthrie insists that we learn only what we do, which is not the same as learning by doing. Here he refers to new situations calling out previously learned responses. How? The nonvital stimuli which were present at the first occurrence of the response, under new circumstances, have the capability of eliciting the original response. This is important for education. If S–R contiguity is the accepted theory of learning, the curriculum, methods, and materials must be specific to insure that their roles as stimuli cause the correct learning responses. The implication is that the classroom must be rigidly structured. There would be slight opportunity for the development of man's creative ability.

The specificity of Guthrie's theory demands that the objectives of education should be similar to those of society. Otherwise, the stimulus provided by the school will not, in a future and different circumstance, elicit the desired response. What is learned in school will not necessarily appear in the playground. The events are too dissimilar.

Associative Inhibition

Behavior is changed under the direction of the school. Such behavior is necessarily associated with the stimuli. Under this pressure certain elements of behavior seen in past responses may have vanished. The stimuli have lost their capacity to cause the original responses.

Guthrie asserts that this is a corollary of the principle of association. A stimulus becomes associated with a response that suppresses the former response. Eventually, it ceases to evoke the original response. This is associative inhibition.

The educational implications are obvious. The school must make provision not only for the positive association of the proper stimulus for the predetermined response, but it must also provide for the detachment of unwarranted responses. For Guthrie, associative inhibition is synonymous with forgetting. The positive and negative possibilities of associative inhibition must be considered in the teaching-learning environment.

Conclusion

Guthrie's theory of contiguous conditioning may be summarized as follows:

1. The study of behavior is confined to observable and nameable events. Most important for learning are the activation of sense organs (stimuli) and the contraction of muscles and the secretions of glands (responses). The internal sense organs that are sensitive to movement are also essential to Guthrie's theory. These movements become stimuli to action (movement-produced stimuli).

2. Guthrie adds another class of stimuli to his theory. These are "excitement-produced" stimuli. The excitement-produced stimuli are caused by the varying physiological conditions of the individual. This is Guthrie's term for emotions.

3. Movement and emotional response are subject to associative learning.

4. We learn what we do. We are unable to learn what we accomplish, but we are able to learn the definite movements and emotions in the circumstances which originally accompanied the response.

5. In associative learning, as Guthrie interprets it, the single most important fact is that a response is always associated with a stimulus, or a new combination of stimuli. Changes in behavior are the result of new response combinations becoming attached to new signals.

6. Associative inhibition is significant in the learning process. Forgetting and associative inhibition are identical.

7. Learning occurs by one-trial association. The seeming difficulty in grasping this concept is caused by man's concentration upon acts instead of movement.

8. Motives are stimuli. Guthrie calls them maintaining stimuli because they sustain activity until the goal has been reached. Goal-attainment removes the maintaining stimuli and thus preserves the successful movements from extinction. That is, these movements will not be associated with different stimuli that would cause new behavior.

Guthrie's lesson for education is simple and direct. Unless a response occurs, it cannot be attached to any situation as its cue. The school must elicit the desired movements and acts by presenting students with appropriate stimuli. Teachers and administrators must be aware of this general objective in their selection of curriculum, materials, and methods of instruction.

SKINNER'S BEHAVIORISM

The inner operations of the human are hidden from the observer. Thus, the only knowledge that can be obtained about learning is that which can be noticed in the person's behavioral pattern. B. F. Skinner, in his major works, *The Behavior of Organisms* (Skinner, 1938), and *Science and Human Behavior* (Skinner, 1953), has developed a stimulus-response psychology without hypothesizing intervening variables.

Skinner's work with rats, pigeons, and machines has made him one of the most well-known and controversial of the behaviorists. The "Skinner box" has become famous. The box contains a rat, a lever, and a device for producing a food pellet. When the rat pushes the lever, food appears, and hunger is appeased. The rat is being conditioned to push the lever when he is hungry. The animal learns rapidly in the box because there is so little else to do (Boring, 1950, p. 651). If the conditions of the experiment are changed, a wide variety of conditioned responses can be elicited.

The nature of Skinner's experiments sharply limits the interpretation and application of their results. Emphasis is placed upon stimulus-response psychology, and his work has been primarily with animals. That he recognizes his self-imposed restrictions is clear from a quote by Martin Mayer (1961, p. 82):

Skinner likes to cite a cartoon that appeared twenty years ago in the Columbia Jester showing a rat leaning against the puzzle-lever in his cage and telling another rat, "Boy, do we have that guy conditioned. Every time I press the bar down, he drops a pellet in."

Skinner's rat is well controlled in his unique box. If man's behavior can be controlled equally as well, man will progress in a smooth and orderly fashion. Manipulation of behavior is essential to Skinner's theory. The consequences could be startling. *Walden Two* (Skinner, 1948) illustrates Skinner's theory in action.

Respondent and Operant Behavior

Skinner departed from typical stimulus-response psychology by recognizing that man responds to stimuli not identifiable to the observer. The orthodox stimulus-response psychology assumed that environmental stimuli were acting but that man simply lacked the refined techniques to perceive them. Such a naive approach to science disturbed Skinner. If man responds to an unknown class of stimuli, such stimuli must be explained as they exist—not as observers imagine them to be.

Consequently, he advances two kinds of responses: elicited and emitted. When a response is elicited by known stimuli, it is called respondent behavior. A youngster giving an answer to a teacher's question is an example of respondent behavior.

Some responses, however, are apparently unrelated to any discernible stimuli. These responses are emitted by the organism and Skinner specifies them as operant behavior. This is the meaning of Skinner's classification of behavior as respondent or operant (Skinner, 1953, pp. 59–90).

Although operant behavior appears unrelated to a particular stimulus, it must have been associated with a stimulus, or stimuli pattern, on some prior occasion. Skinner then accepts associative shifting of stimuli. This is in the tradition of classical conditioning as accepted by Pavlov and Watson. In Skinner's theory, if the operant behavior becomes identified with the needed stimulus, it is called a discriminated operant.

Most human behavior is operant in character. The behavior of eating a meal, driving a car, or writing a letter shows little respondent behavior (Hilgard, 1956, p. 83). Skinner's belief in operant and respondent behavior raises many questions. Because the human reacts mostly to unknown stimuli on the majority of occasions, but part of the behavioral pattern is respondent behavior, the analysis of behavior into respondent and operant behavior segments is, and must be, artificial.

Driving an automobile, for example, reveals some illustrations of respondent behavior—the turning of the ignition key to start the car or the shifting of gears to move the car. But how can the decision to pass on a hill be explained? There is no identifiable stimulus to cause this reaction.

The internal and external states of the organism both contribute to goal drive. They are different parts of the same whole. They can be analyzed into parts only for purposes of description. Skinner realizes, as the early behaviorists did not, that a behavioristic psychology must attempt to explain certain parts of man's behavior that do not conform to traditional S–R theory. Operant behavior is an attempt to fill this void in mechanistic thought.

Conditioning

Two entirely different classes of responses must be conditioned in different ways (Skinner, 1953, pp. 62–68). Skinner proposes two forms of conditioning: Type S and Type R (Skinner, 1938).

Type S conditioning is related to respondent behavior. Pavlov's experiments were of Type S conditioning. The conditioned stimulus is paired with the unconditioned stimulus and eventually elicits the same response. Type S conditioning is the associative shifting of stimuli. Something is done to the organism to cause a reaction. Type S concentrates upon the something—the stimulus or stimuli patterns that will determine the direction of behavior to attain a goal.

Type S conditioning assumes a great deal. Is the environment manipulated so passively? Can it be so easily determined that this stimulus will always cause this response? Type S also ignores the character of the response. Will it always be of the same quality? Are there any intervening variables (internal factors) which will alter the response in varying circumstances?

The value of Type S conditioning is limited, if it exists at all, for the neo-behaviorist. It places too much emphasis upon stimuli and neglects the inner conditions of the organism which affect learning (Thorpe and Schmuller, 1954, p. 178).

Type R conditioning stresses the response and pertains to operant behavior. The response is combined with the reinforcement. It is important to understand the distinction between Type S and Type R conditioning.

1. In Type S, the stimulus relationship (S and S_1) is indispensable. Think of Pavlov's experiments. Food caused saliva to flow. Next, something linked with the original stimulus acquires the capability of eliciting the response. Finally, the sight of the attendant, or his voice, caused the response. The acquired stimulus will lose its ability to produce the response unless the unconditioned stimulus (food) continues to be presented with the conditioned stimulus. *The neutral stimulus is reinforced.* This is classical conditioning.

2. In Type R conditioning, Skinner attempts to interpret the appearance of operant behavior. A response appears. How? Why? There are no visible stimuli which account for operant behavior. The only tangible evidence which the psychologist has is the response. To suppose that there are environmental stimuli operating, but merely unnoticed, would be unscientific. The scientist must work with what he has.

Skinner maintains that the stimulus conditions, if any, are irrelevant to the understanding of operant behavior (Hilgard, 1956, p. 83). It is the *response* that is reinforced. The organism does something and is rewarded. Note that the organism acts on the environment. *If the response is correct, it is reinforced.* This is the psychological basis of programmed instruction.

When the organism acts on the environment and evokes a response, it is rewarded (if the response is correct). Such a pattern of action differs from the work of Pavlov's classical conditioning. This new sort of behavior is called instrumental conditioning. The organism does not respond passively to stimuli, or stimuli patterns. It acts on the environment to produce the response. If reinforcement is lacking the response gradually will be eliminated.

Conclusion

Although Skinner has formulated a detailed system to resolve the riddle of human behavior, his operant and respondent behavior, plus the manner of their conditioning, is the core of his theory.

Operant behavior and Type R conditioning are the more significant.

Most of man's responses cannot be attributed to identifiable stimuli. There is no one-for-one relation between stimulus and response. To insist that there must be a perceptible S–R connection is unnecessary and, in fact, misleading. Operant behavior, at some prior time, must have had the S–R link. But it is useless to appropriate stimuli that might or might not be responsible for the appearance of a particular response.

If we admit that man does evidence such a behavioral pattern and we observe and describe this behavior until sufficient knowledge is acquired so that human behavior can be predicted and controlled, education then becomes a process of control whereby the variables that affect an individual's behavior are regulated in accordance with the wishes of the school and society. Classroom materials must be selected accordingly. They must permit the student to respond correctly so that reinforcement occurs immediately. Because teachers frequently disregard the conditioning of pupil behavior, Skinner urges the adoption of programmed instruction. These "teaching machines" have reinforcement built into them, and they allow the pupil to proceed at his own pace.

PROGRAMMED INSTRUCTION

The psychological foundation of education is nowhere so clearly evidenced as in the current popularity of programmed learning. Impetus was given to the use of teaching machines by Skinner (1954), although their origin may be traced to the work of Pressey (1926).

The term "teaching machine" is deceptive. There is a wide range of programmed material available. These include machines that cost thousands of dollars, and printed matter that may be obtained for a few cents a copy. Any material that serves as a self-instruction device requiring an actual response by a student and in which the response is immediately scored may be termed a teaching machine.

The choice of instruments is of minor importance compared to the program that is fed into them. The program determines the quality of the automated method of instruction. The subject matter to be programmed must be prepared by specialists thoroughly conversant with their field. It is not enough to know only the material which will be taught in a given year. The person, or persons, responsible for programming must also know the outer regions of the subject. They must know its inner structure—its logic. Otherwise, pupils will flounder in a disorderly progression of stages. Unfortunately, in the initial enthusiasm, those responsible for the selection of the machine and material occasionally dismissed material to a secondary place. A machine, of whatever type, is only as good as its material.

Carefully programmed material breaks the subject into small, sequential steps that can be shown one by one in a machine or on the page of a book. Not only must the author of programmed material be a master of his subject, he must also write with precision and clarity. The student is questioned at each stage, and he is rewarded immediately with the pleasure of being correct. Such immediate reinforcement aids in the retention of knowledge.

It is clear that the student is not supposed to make many mistakes. If the rate of error is high, the purpose of programmed learning is defeated. This also places a burden on the program writer. How advanced can each step be? If the challenge is not sufficient, boredom will result. If the material is too difficult, the pupil will become discouraged and motivation will be lost.

Pressey and Skinner

The approach of Pressey and Skinner to automated instruction was quite different. Pressey's original objective was to score multiple-choice items as soon as they were answered. The student could teach himself drill material and so free the teacher from the more mechanical tasks that are required in every classroom.

This is a very inflexible and narrow concept of learning. It is S–R, trial-and-error learning, and little else. As a testing device (which Pressey originally constructed) it would be excellent. It saves time for the teacher and, by immediate correction, it does teach, to a limited extent. Today's Pressey-type machine presents multiple-choice or true-false questions which are to be answered by pressing a button or key. If the student's answer is correct, the machine presents the next question. If the answer is incorrect, the same question remains and the student must again select an answer. The next question in the sequence will not be presented until the right answer has been chosen.

These machines are faithful to Pressey's original objective. Since students who use test-scoring machines to grade their own papers learn more about the subject, mechanical devices must facilitate learning. If so, why? Pressey reasoned that the immediate feedback of results was the main cause of increased efficiency of learning (Pepinsky and Borow, 1961, p. 272). Note that the Pressey machine permits error.

It is the error factor that distinguishes the Skinner program from the Pressey program. Skinner's theory of learning emphasizes that a person retains the responses that are confirmed (Cronbach, 1963, p. 441). He must receive positive information consistently. So the Skinner-type program has the student construct his own response to questions that are arranged to avoid error. The Pressey multiple-choice form permits the student to err, and, even if the student corrects it, as he must, he still might remember the false answer. This is especially true if the alternate false answers appear credible.

A typical Skinner machine has the student pull a lever to have a frame appear in a window. The student must answer a question or fill in a missing word. He writes his answer, pulls a lever, and the answer slides under glass. Reinforcement occurs at once, when the student realizes his answer is correct (*Time,* March 24, 1961, p. 36).

Boehm (1960, p. 179) describes an English grammar text which consists of 2600 frames, each consisting of a statement with a blank to be filled with one or two words:

The student reads a frame. He fills in the blank. He turns the page, and there is the correct answer, together with the next frame. He can scarcely avoid a delightfully steady flicker of self-satisfaction as he plods through the program filling in a succession of blanks with obvious words.

The student presents his own response—he is not confronted with one, two, or three possible false answers that might lead him into possible future error. It is clear that the Skinner program must proceed in small steps. A large amount of content cannot be presented in one step since this would increase the possibility of error.

Branching

A third innovation has been advocated by Norman Crowder (1959). His programs follow the more conventional teaching method since they serve as a tutor. This is not a mechanical device. It is a "scrambled" book that utilizes the concept of "branching." The pages of such a book are numbered consecutively, as in any book, but they are not read in the normal sequential fashion. His progress depends upon his answers to multiple-choice questions.

If the student has selected a correct answer, he is directed to a page where more advanced material is found. If his answer is incorrect, he is sent to a "branch" which will review the material that he has not mastered.

Crowder schedules much larger amounts of material in each frame than does Skinner. He permits mistakes and plans for their correction as a vital part of learning. If a student makes a mistake, remedial work is built into the program. An interesting part of Crowder's programs are the comments which are inserted. The student is made to feel that the tutor is with him in his work. An incorrect answer may draw the remark, "Come now, you can do better than that." Or a correct answer merits encouragement—"That's the spirit." Boehm (1960, pp. 259–260) states:

Throughout the program Crowder carries his concept of the private tutor to extremes. He jollies his readers with a banter that some may find cloying, if not downright insulting.

The differences between Skinner and Crowder are apparent and reflect a wide variance of psychological theory. Conditioning is essential to Skinner's theory, but not to Crowder. The small, measured advances of the Skinner program are contrasted with the substantial presentations of Crowder; Crowder discounts mistakes, in fact he foresees them; a good Skinner-type program all but removes the possibility of error.

Pressey, Skinner, and Crowder offer three similar, but singularly distinctive, programs. The relative value of each is determined by the theory of learning held by those whose duty it is to select a form of programmed instruction.

Conclusion

It is much too early to assess the merits of programmed instruction. Verification of results seems to indicate that factual material can be effectively learned by some type of automated instruction. As a teaching aid, programming has earned a lasting place in the classroom. The question yet to be answered is to what extent should this device be employed?

The advantages of programming are clear.

1. The goal that the learner is to achieve as well as the steps he must take to reach this goal are evident. There is no vagueness about the amount of material to be learned to achieve the predetermined objectives.

2. Undoubtedly, the novel way of learning will appeal to students. How long this appeal will last and how successfully it cloaks the effects of conditioning are still unknown.

3. The student is required to participate actively in a learning milieu. Too often, in the typical classroom, a student can sit passively and be entirely unaware of the stimulation of teacher and materials.

4. The careful presentation of a limited amount of material insures successful responses. The rate of error varies according to the kind of program—Crowder or Skinner.

5. Reinforcement is prompt, which encourages the student in his learning. The emphasis placed upon reward again changes because of the nature of the program. The student, however, learns instantly if his response is correct or not, and thus he does not have an incorrect response entrenched in his mind for a day, or week, until the teacher returns the corrected paper.

6. The student proceeds at his own rate. Since most subjects require much factual knowledge as a basis for advanced work, programming is an ideal method of permitting students to master the fundamentals at their own rate, and then continue to the more difficult problems of the subject. This is as it should be. But here is an area that lacks experimental evidence.

In addition, there are negative aspects that must be considered.

1. Not all youngsters respond to this kind of academic reinforcement. Other means of motivation must be found for such youngsters.

2. What is the limit of the depth of material that can be programmed? When the conceptual stage of learning is reached, is the machine effective? Every indication thus far stresses the role of the teacher when the stage of creative thought is reached.

3. How will students function in problem-solving situations after they have been accustomed to programmed instruction? This is an

interesting question because the circumstances are quite different. The ability of students to make the transition will eventually decide the future of programming. If students can make the transition easily, the popularity of automated teaching will increase.

The goal of education is the comprehension of knowledge and its application in a creative manner. Can programming operate productively in securing these objectives? Certainly, it can. As an aid to the teacher, its possibilities are unlimited. As a replacement for the teacher, its possibilities are limited indeed. The opposite may well be true. When they are freed from routine tasks, teachers have the opportunity to widen the scope of knowledge in their classrooms. The demand will then be for more creative teachers. As one psychologist says: "Any teacher who can be replaced by a machine deserves to be replaced" (*Time,* March 24, 1961, p. 38).

CHAPTER IX

Learning Theory — II

As WE CONTINUE our analysis of the major learning theories which have contributed to a better teaching-learning environment in America, we shall conclude our brief survey of the associationist school with the work of Clark Hull. Next, we shall examine the writings of the Gestalt psychologists, and Lewin in an effort to understand learning as a process of organization and as the perception of relationships in the field.

HULL'S BEHAVIORAL SYSTEM

Hull received his doctorate at the University of Wisconsin in 1918 and remained there until 1929. He then moved to Yale where he undertook painstaking endeavors to explain the learning process in quantitative terms. The development of the theory was difficult. As Koch says:

From 1929 until his death in 1952, Hull was ceaselessly dedicated to the construction of his theory of behavior. The theory was developed in a tortuous, piecemeal way. General hypotheses advanced in the early phase of the program were under continuous revision and extension, and, from time to time, major modifications or realignments of the emerging theoretical structure were put forward (Koch, in Estes, 1954, p. 1).

In his theory, Hull has made a systematic, and often, mathematical attempt to explain learning. We know the stimulus—we can observe the response—but what happens within the individual that affects the response? Hull devised a set of postulates and corollaries by means of which he hoped to define and measure these intervening variables.

Postulates and Corollaries

The stimulus causes the response, but the process varies with each organism. Accurate measurement of response, in relation to stimulus, is impossible, unless the variables that influence the organism are taken into consideration. Inferences concerning the effect of these variables in the person are crucial. To incorporate these variables, Hull offers an elaborate series of postulates and corollaries. If the stimulus is measured, the response is measured, and the inferences concerning variables are related, much more depth is added to the resultant quantification.

A prolific writer, Hull's most influential works were *Principles of Behavior* (1943), *Essentials of Behavior* (1951), and *A Behavior System* (1952). The 1943 book is the most detailed presentation of a complex, quantified explanation of behavior and may have the greatest impact for theory construction. However, as Hull was constantly refining his theory, the 1951 and 1952 works represented the final exposition of his system.

As an example of his vigorous attempts to express man's behavior in mathematical fashion, consider the following postulate taken from his 1951 book.

Postulate IV.

Habit strength increases as a positive growth function of the number of trials, if reinforcements follow each other at evenly distributed intervals and everything else is constant.

The laws of reinforcement state the conditions under which habits are formed, but consideration must also be given to the number of reinforcements. Will one reinforcement bring about the maximum result, or will habit strength increase as the number of reinforcements increase? Hull chose the latter. Habit strength (SHR) varies from zero to 1.00 as a function of the number of trials:

$$
\begin{aligned}
\text{if } N &= 0, & SHR &= .0000 \\
\text{if } N &= 4, & SHR &= .2453 \\
\text{if } N &= 20, & SHR &= .7546 \\
\text{if } N &= \infty & SHR &= 1.0000
\end{aligned}
$$

In the 1951 book, there are eighteen postulates and twelve corollaries, yet Hull himself realized that his system was incomplete. He frankly admits that the constants in his equations are not necessarily constant. Individual differences and species differences appear in natural molar behavior laws as variable values of the constants involved.

Is it possible to interpret such a complicated system so that it may have practical educational value? Hull thought so, and, in the Forty-First Yearbook of the National Society for the Study of Education, he attempted to summarize his impressions of the learning process.

Learning

Throughout the lifetime of any individual there is a constant interaction between the organism and its environment. If we divide the organism's environment into internal and external segments, the external may be further subdivided into inanimate (physical sciences) and organismic (social sciences).

Frequently, in the life span of any individual organism, needs arise. Often, these needs can be satisfied only through an adjustment of the relationship between the organism and its external environment. Thus, the behavior of the organism has resulted in satisfaction. This changed relationship between organism and environment depends to a great extent upon the activity of the organism. To effect a satisfactory condition between organisms and environment, the individual's nervous, muscular, and glandular systems must be in accord. With this as a basis of Hull's learning theory, some of the major topics he discusses in the Forty-First NSSE Yearbook are summarized below.

Random Activity

Many of our needs are met by simple reflex action. If, however, the reflex does not still the disquieting stimuli, other bodily activity goes into action. It is as if the body were seeking the correct answer to a question by presenting many possible solutions. And, indeed, the impression of random activity is frequently given. But these activities are hardly random because they are goal-oriented. The apparent unlearned actions are usually pertinent enough for one of them, or a combination of them, to achieve the goal.

Stimulus Compounds

Any stimulus situation is exceedingly complex and frequently represents many different elements. A particular element within this stimulus compound may become dominant, but this is uncertain because of our present paucity of knowledge. What is important is that the *joint* action of stimulus compounds is much less effective than the sum of individual stimulus compounds taken separately. Thus, the cumulative effect is greater than the immediate joint effect. From the negative viewpoint the withdrawal of any element from the stimulus compound may drop the excitatory potential below the reaction threshold.

The educational implications of this aspect of Hull's theory are important because, in the teaching of any new portion of a subject, the teacher is constantly deluged with advice to use a multidimensional approach. Too often, teachers think this means simultaneously, and the result is apt to be confusion. The unidimensional approach, plus other, separate approaches, each presented in the unidimensional manner, provides a much more desirable learning product. In the final analysis, this is multidimensional, but by unidimensional stages.

External Inhibition

From the classroom, or practical point of view, Hull's treatment of external inhibition is significant. If a disturbing element is introduced into the stimulus compound, the excitatory potential is reduced and may be unable to surpass the reaction threshold. For example, if the teacher is introducing long division to a class and a discipline problem arises, the teacher acts swiftly and decisively. As a result, a new element has been introduced into the stimulus compound—tension. The attention of the students wanders, interest is lost, and the lesson bogs down. Why? Because a foreign element was introduced. This is the factor of external inhibition.

Behavior Variability

What of the irrelevant stimuli that constantly bombard the organism? There can be no question that distortion results from the impact of such stimuli. The lesson is taught, the habit is strengthened, and the conditions are kept as constant as possible ... but the reactions of the organism vary in a frequently unpredictable fashion. Hull designates this as behavior variability or oscillation. It explains the necessity for securing an extensive sample of a student's behavior before a teacher can determine that true learning has been achieved.

Trial-and-Error Learning

If man survives by his adjustment to a hostile environment, it appears that the manner of his adjustment is crucial. The primary importance of learning lies in its ability to aid the individual to survive because the individual often encounters novel situations. Therefore, a form of trial-and-error activity is indicated—not the trial and error of infancy but actually a form of randomness based upon prior learning. To circumvent the obvious difficulties involved in such an explanation, Hull refers to random as meaning "variable." Now, if variable behavior occurs (which must be the case), this often leads to maladaptation. How can this be overcome? Hull states that this results from certain elements in the stimulus compound dominating other elements which could lead to adaptation. Therefore, the maladaptive response occurs, but it is not reinforced. Gradually, the excitatory potential of this act declines until the former weaker reaction achieves ascendancy. This slow shift in favor of the adaptive reaction finally is strong enough to overwhelm the maladaptive act.

Behavioral Short Circuiting

For an organism to adjust to the environment, there should be an abbreviation of the involved series of steps necessary to secure an acceptable reaction. An example of the manner in which this occurs is that of the drive stimulus. Many reactions occur by chance, and it is the last step in the sequence that results in need reduction. By the gradient of reinforcement, this last act is most strongly reinforced, and the others less so. As a result, reinforcement will attach the last act very securely to the drive stimulus. At a later occurrence of the stimulus situation, the act that brought reinforcement will dominate the sequence and behavioral short circuiting has occurred.

The existence of this principle also poses a problem. Short circuiting can result in maladaptation. A given reaction may be called into existence only by an exceedingly complicated series of acts. Therefore, if reinforcement has previously been associated with the first act of the sequence, behavioral short circuiting may cause an abrupt reaction where it is undesirable. Thus, the gradient of reinforcement must be suppressed in some fashion. This is accomplished by the perseverative stimulus trace, that is, the continued action of the stimulus in the brain tissue, although the direct action of the stimulus upon the receptor organ has ceased. The activity of the trace in the brain tissue acts as a stabilizing element (resulting from a former successful response) in the stimulus situation, and, consequently, differentiated reinforcement occurs, terminating in the desired stimulus-response pattern. The goal reaction avoids separate, unrelated responses.

If, however, the goal reaction is easily divided into sections, any single, relatively unimportant component may initiate the behavioral sequence leading to reinforcement. Hull terms this "fractional anticipatory goal reaction," which actually is a dynamic element of the future goal. Accordingly, the fractional goal reaction is a pure stimulus act whose function is to produce a stimulus for control of other action. It is the "stuff" of the idea and the dynamic physical mechanism of intent.

The Habit-Family Hierarchy

Because the environment is immensely complicated, the behavior sequence which is actually reinforced will vary to a considerable degree. Therefore, a number of behavior sequences will be capable of achieving the suitable response, and in this sense they constitute a family. To determine which sequence is effective in a given situation, Hull turns to the principle of gradient of reinforcement. A behavior sequence that is more remote from the point of reinforcement than the others possesses a weaker excitatory potential than the others, and in this fashion the behavior sequences establish a dynamic hierarchy.

The Social Environment

Thus far, major consideration has been given to the relationship of the organism to its inanimate environment. One important point must be remembered in any discussion of the organism's social environment—the primary principles of behavior in social situations are identical with those of the inanimate environment. The chief difference lies in the conditions in which the principles operate, that is, the behavior of the organism must conform to the same laws as those according to which its own behavior occurs. Also, any form of social relationship involves reciprocal reinforcement. Something in the relationship must reinforce the activity; otherwise, the relationship will gradually perish.

Conclusion

The contribution of Hull to psychological theory has been great. It has been a dual contribution: theory construction and a theory of behavior. Perhaps his work has its greatest significance in its emphasis upon quantification. Not that he succeeded; no one has. However, he has forced psychologists to offer more than verbal explanation for proof of the development and expression of various kinds of behavior.

His reliance upon animal experimentation for his results caused much criticism of his theory. Also, inadequacy of definition and a neglect of individual differences raised many doubts. For example, Hull assigns numerical values to such items as stimulus intensity, but does this apply equally to pigeons, rats, and man?

Yet, when Hilgard (1956) says that it is easy to criticize Hull because his theory is so explicit and mathematical, we must agree because, in this kind of theory, omissions or weaknesses are readily apparent. Psychology, however, owes much to Hull for his leadership in attempting to construct a systematic and scientific theory.

CLASSICAL GESTALT THEORY

Not all psychologists were reconciled to theories, no matter how systematic, that reduced behavior to stimulus and response. Although Behaviorism was the predominant American psychology for the first quarter of this century, there were many psychologists and educators who were searching for another explanation of behavior and learning. Some psychologists were unhappy because the prevalent psychology overlooked man's cognitive processes; the educators were dissatisfied because man's capacity to solve problems and to engage in creative activity was neglected by theories dependent upon connections between stimuli and responses.

The work of the German psychologists, Max Wertheimer, Kurt Koffka, and Wolfgang Köhler, received a warm welcome in many parts of the American psychological scene. With their insistence upon perception, organization, and insight, they were a relief from mechanistic thought.

Gestalt

The Gestaltists claimed that actual experience was not a sum of the parts since it showed a wholeness, or "form," that any attempt at analysis would destroy. It is the totality of experience that sets the problem for psychology. This gives the facts that psychology must explain. Gestalt psychology insists that perception is not a summation of elements, but unified wholes.

The exact translation of the word Gestalt is difficult. "Configuration," "shape," and "form" have been used, but these do not seem to convey the true meaning of the term. According to Köhler, Gestalt has two meanings in German. At times it may be used to designate a shape or form as a property of something; at other times, it may denote something existing that has a shape or form as one of its properties. As a property of something, Gestalt is used to designate squareness or triangularity in figures, whereas, when applied to a being that has form, Gestalt refers to the square that possesses the quality of squareness, or the triangle that possesses the quality of triangularity. In the latter sense, it applies to the whole that possesses the property. This is the more appropriate meaning because the process that explains the construction of these wholes must also explain the properties of the whole.

Analysis

All events in nature occur within some field, and it is the totality of the field, its properties and structure, that explain all events transpiring within the field. Thus, there is no understanding of the individual until the individual's background is thoroughly comprehended.

Hartmann (1942, pp. 166–170) gives several examples to illustrate what a field is and how it operates.

A. The solar system is an outstanding example of the control of vast heavenly bodies and their movements by the organization to which they belong. It is impossible to understand one planet apart from its relationship to the entire system.

B. The living organism represents integration and regulation of part-reactions by the total structure. The unified nature of the body compels our lips, fingers, and shoulder blades to occupy approximately the same region of space as the rest of the frame—they are forced to go along with it and to be wherever it is, because, in a restricted but definite sense, they are it.

C. In the realm of the psychological, the presence of field forces is felt on every hand as soon as one has become sensitized to their reality. The characteristic intellectual activities of man reveal these whole-part dynamics to perfection. The character 1 on the typewriter has the same appearance in 11 as it does in love. But, the meaning differs because of the rest of the perceptual structure, that is, the totality of the field has attributed different functions to the same visual stimulus.

D. The classroom is a special kind of social field since the relationships involved in group dynamics, attention, discipline, and the like, permeate the atmosphere of the entire class and affect the learning process. The teacher's reaction to the discipline problem of one student is reflected in the "feeling" of the class. It is impossible to deal with just one youngster—the influence of the total classroom atmosphere is brought to bear on all students.

In the search for the unit of behavior, psychologists have analyzed to the point of destruction. Thus, the sensation, the bond, the reflex, and so forth, have been proposed as the basic explanatory unit. Yet these explanations describe a minute fraction of the complex of behavior. The quest for the simple has blocked the solution of the complex.

Gestaltists do not oppose analysis. To do so would be ridiculous. It is the nature of the analysis that is significant. To take a word from its context and attempt to comprehend the nuances of its meaning is as fruitless as ignoring a child's home environment in predicting behavior. Analysis is justified in relation to environment and background, that is, the field.

Within each field, the figure-ground relationship is of paramount importance. The process of attention enables the individual to be consciously aware of the thing, or person, as distinct from the background.

This is one of the basic, but most casually treated, factors in Gestalt thinking. The human being experiences wholes, or fields—the sum total of these fields we designate as nature. Because of the limited ability of man, independent, though related, fields are recognized. To understand an entire field is difficult, if not impossible. Therefore, analysis enables us to focus upon the figure in relation to the ground. Concentration is upon the figure, but *never* as an isolated entity. (It would be helpful here for the reader to return to Chapter V and review the principles of perceptual organization.)

Learning Theory

The acquisition of motor skills is a logical starting point for applying Gestalt thought to learning. The expression of such learning in writing, typing, sports, and the like, may be very misleading when analysis of the process occurs. Attention is focused on the motor aspect of the learning situation, and often the action of the total organism is neglected. Mastery of the skill does not depend solely upon the motor aspect; rather it results from the inner coordinating elements. The example is given of the person who normally writes with his right hand. If he writes his name with his left hand, although it may not be a thing of beauty, nevertheless, it is legible. Therefore, learning to write was not confined to the right hand, but was "spread over" to the left. In other words, the total organism was engaged in learning.

Although muscular coordination may be the objective, the function of the complete organism should be recognized and utilized if real learning is to take place. All of the disjointed parts of the skill must be "pulled togther" before unified action results. There must be some inner coordinating force which coordinates and directs. This is the insight phenomenon which is essential to all learning, but which is often overlooked in motor learning, because of the assemblylike arrangement of parts. The acquisition of each part is actually the acquisition of a whole at that particular stage of development. As each part is acquired, a new whole results.

Each motor skill has a characteristic structure, and it is only when insight operates that we see the composition of the structure differently because of the uniqueness of the human being. These differences in the operation of the skill are known as style.

Rote Learning

Gestaltists emphasize the concept of field and meaning in their interpretation of the manner in which rote memory operates. Although "brute" memory appears to be a purely mechanical operation, there are aspects involved that indicate functioning of a higher order. The type of material presented is extremely important for several reasons. If the student overlooks the unity of the material, or fails to comprehend the necessity of learning the task, mastery will be impossible. Unquestionably, the student will derive some meaning from the problem. But, what is the nature of the meaning? Undoubtedly, it will be negative, resulting in a distaste for all kinds of memorization. Again, there is a reaction, and there is a meaning. If meaning is considered a field property of any experience to which the organism responds and the response is one of dislike (negative), this feeling will characterize all future reactions to similar fields. In other words, purpose (system and order of the field) has not been perceived (Hartmann, 1942, p. 190).

Problem Solving

The learning that most educators and psychologists consider significant is that of problem solving. The solution of a problem depends upon the structure of a field. This is an important concept for teachers to understand because the fields of students and teachers, although similar, frequently are not identical. Since the structure of the two fields is different, the teacher doubts that the student has solved the problem.

The configurationist holds that fundamentally all problems are solved as soon as the learner has achieved insight into their essential relationships. The prominence of insight in Gestalt thought cannot be overemphasized. Insight is not restricted to any particular level of conduct, but cuts across all levels. Thus, insight is manifested when an algebraic problem is solved, and also when a knob is turned to open a door. Gestaltists insist that *insight is a form of perception*. It is a kind of neural organization that occurs when a goal is achieved. Closure has resulted from the organism being in a state of tension due to the incompleteness of the configuration (total situation). Once outer experimentation is coupled with inner maturation, the problem is solved, that is, insight has taken place (Hartmann, 1942, pp. 192–193).

Trial and error have occurred during the learning process, but they are not the explanation of the final learning. They are only the outer manifestation of the inner attempts at organization. Gestaltists state that such searching (trial and error) is not random, blind behavior, but is activity directed toward the hypothesized field that is structured as the individual sees it. Thinking is a process that goes beyond mere sense perception, but, nevertheless, as a mental process it is a perception of the organization of field forces.

Conclusion

That the Gestalt psychologists aided in the refinement of psychological thought concerning organization, meaning, and structure is undeniable. The recent emphasis upon problem solving, creative thinking, and structure owes much to Gestalt insistence upon insight as the explanation of learning. However, there would be little general agreement that all learning is so neatly explained. The Gestalt neglect of sensation, while understandable because of their attack on associationism, nevertheless is questionable in the development of a logical system.

Other criticisms were directed at specific parts of the theory, but Hilgard (1964) raises the fundamental question: is there a need for students to be taught about Gestalt psychology? Has the success of the theory eliminated its necessity to be offered as a separate unit of study? That is, are its ideas so much a part of Psychology (general) that there no longer remains a need for teaching "Gestalt Psychology"?

Hilgard poses a question that is difficult to answer. The solution probably is to be found in the objectives of the instructor. If the psychology course is basic, perhaps more recent developments should be presented. If time is not a problem, and students need to follow the historical changes in cognitive thought for a specific purpose, there is a sound argument for its study. Hilgard himself admits that, with the renewed interest in thinking, problem solving, and creativity, there is an aspect of Gestalt thought that remains very much alive (Hilgard, 1964, p. 63). It would be well worth the reader's time and effort to read Hilgard's provocative chapter (1964, pp. 54–77) about the future prospects of *a* Gestalt psychology.

KURT LEWIN AND FIELD THEORY

Kurt Lewin, so often associated with field theory, or topological psychology, was studying in Berlin when the original Gestalt group was developing an alternative to stimulus-response psychology. But Lewin's interests centered more on motivation, and it was here, with his emphasis on motivation, that Lewin differed from the others. His early publications were about motivation, and they were responsible for his already being known in America when he arrived in 1932.

He taught at Stanford, Cornell, and Iowa before moving to the Massachusetts Institute of Technology in 1945 for research in group dynamics. Unfortunately, the plan to utilize Lewin's great talents for the elaboration of social psychology abruptly ceased with his untimely death in 1947 at the age of fifty-seven (Boring, 1950, pp. 723–724).

Although Lewin's theory is a psychology of motivation, rather than learning, there is much in his theory that is pertinent for learning, and Lewin himself devoted a chapter to learning in the Forty-First Yearbook of the National Society for the Study of Education.

The main body of his work appeared in *A Dynamic Theory of Personality* (1935), which was a collection of his articles and papers, and *Principles of Topological Psychology,* which was published in 1936. One of the most important topics in his general theory was that of life space. This is the individual's immediate, personal environment, both physical and psychological. It is the person's relationship to everything in his environment, *but as he sees it.*

Another significant concept is that of valence. When an object exerts a force upon the person, it is termed a valence. Those objects which the individual desires have a positive valence. An object which repels has a negative valence. In Lewin's illustrations, the force to or from the object is represented by an arrow called a vector. When all of the positive and negative forces acting on a person, his needs, and goals are considered, there is a wide range of choices which the individual may make. This is the topology of his life space; it represents his options for action. Thus, knowledge of a person's field not only describes his actions, but it also explains them. Lewin was only slightly concerned with the individual's background. When the here and now are known and comprehended, a cause-effect relationship automatically is explained.

These are but a few of the highlights of a complicated system. Whatever its faults, it inspired continuing and productive research. The impact of the theory is admitted by most and challenged by a few. How much of its success was, and is, due to the warmth and charm of Lewin himself is difficult to estimate. Nevertheless, his influence still extends into varied disciplines, one of which is learning, and Lewin has commented upon the application of field theory to the learning process.

Field Theory and Learning

Writing in the Forty-First NSSE Yearbook, Lewin notes that there are several central aspects to his system:

1. It utilizes a constructive rather than a classificatory method.
2. It is concerned with dynamic factors.
3. It is interested in the psychological rather than the physical as the explanation of behavior.
4. It uses analysis but only after the whole has been surveyed.
5. It focuses upon the present, rather than the past.
6. It uses mathematical language to describe the activities of the field.

Lewin employs these basic ideas of field theory to formulate his impression of the learning process. For example, when he discusses the constructive method as opposed to the classificatory, he is challenging the entire order of concept formation. The classificatory system was presented in Chapter V: the concept is the nature of the thing, or the common characteristics of all objects of a particular class. Thus, we "fit" individual objects into classes by our experiences with them.

Lewin questions this method. He feels that, whatever makes the thing, object, or person, *this* individual thing is lost. Instead, he advocates better understanding of the individual by "elements" of construction, that is, psychological position, or forces. The relationships between the constructions, at any time, describe *and* explain the individual at that time.

These constructions are the dynamics of behavior. By this Lewin means the psychological forces that cause change. These are active within the individual's field. Thus, teachers are powerless to help the child unless they understand the psychological world of the child. There is a constant temptation to substitute the world of the teacher for the world of the child. But there are properties of the teacher's field which influence the tensions within the student's life space. A friendly classroom creates an atmosphere which encourages learning. So properties of one field influence another field when and where they meet.

Learning in General

The use of the term learning disturbs Lewin. Since learning refers to many varied processes and products, the universal acceptance of learning poses many problems. Is learning to high jump the same as learning to do without alcohol; are both of these identical with learning to be friendly with other people (Lewin, 1942, p. 220)?

There are at least four types of learning:

1. Learning as a change in cognitive structure
2. Learning as a change in motivation
3. Learning as a change in group belongingness
4. Learning as control of body muscles

Learning as Change in Knowledge

Here Lewin is referring to the differentiation of unstructured fields. He gives the example of a stranger learning his way around an unfamiliar city. Initially, the city is an unstructured area. Gradually, differentiation occurs and he learns how to get to work and other needed places.

There are ways other than differentiation by which cognitive structure is changed. Insight may alter the cognitive structure and so shape the psychological direction of the person. Behavior results from forces which have direction (Lewin, 1942, p. 228). When the field is unstructured, the individual has a precarious feeling; he is not certain of what to do because he has no knowledge of the results of his action.

Cognitive structure is also changed by the person's needs; he wants something (this refers to the concept of valence mentioned earlier). Thus, the goal exerts its influence upon cognitive structure.

Although Lewin's work encouraged much research, it does so

outside of the boundaries of the psychology of learning and, consequently, is not represented in current learning literature. He likewise has been severely criticized for his lack of precision with
language and the doubtful character of his mathematical terms.
Yet, of his influence there can be little doubt. Social psychology,
motivation, and group dynamics owe much to him. And, finally,
no analysis of learning theories is complete without some consideration of field theory.

CONCLUSION

Several learning theories were presented in these two chapters.
No attempt was made to analyze the entire field since that would
be impossible because of the proliferating interpretations and deri-
vations. The representatives of the major schools, both associationist
and field, were discussed so that the reader may grasp the basic differences between the two. Today, there are many and sophisticated
constructions of the classical schools; however, there is no understanding of the more modern views unless their origins are also
comprehended.

The significance of these differing theories for education was
mentioned in Chapter VIII. A theory of learning is predicated upon
the nature of man, and, as the theorist sees man, so will his learning
theory reflect the manner by which man should be instructed. If
the theorist firmly believes that there is no understanding of what
occurs within man, he will attend, most carefully, to what is observable in man's behavior. We can see the stimulus; we can see
the response; consequently, manipulation of the forces which cause
behavioral responses should, ultimately, result in the control of
behavior.

Conversely, the field theorist sees man acting upon his environment and constantly striving to structure it, that is, to better his
perception. What happens within man becomes vital. It is only as
man discerns his environment and changes the elements within his
field that he achieves insight and reaches his goal. But, man is
acting, not merely reacting.

There is more of a reconciliation between the two beliefs than
is usually realized. The associationists accept cognitive and purpos-
ive behavior; the field theorists have a deeper sense of the impor-

tance of stimuli than before. Yet, the fundamental cleavage remains, and each theory has its adherents who advocate educational methods in accordance with their theoretical beliefs. So the controversy rages about the merits of programmed instruction, or the encouragement of student search and discovery, or the components of a person's field, and many others.

The basic issues remain unresolved. How does man learn; how does he transfer his learning; what drives him toward a goal; can one explanation of learning explain all kinds of learning? These are the questions which have plagued the theorists, and will continue to do so. And the lack of resolution of issues should not cause the reader to disparage the efforts of the learning theorists. Without them, society would be far more primitive than it is today.

CHAPTER X

Learning and the Affective Domain

INTRODUCTION

The affective domain is, in retrospect, a virtual "Pandora's Box." One finds in it the objectives which were stated confidently at one time and then allowed to disappear from view. One finds in it the objectives on which disagreement is most likely within a school. One finds in it the vital points on which the society itself may be in disagreement. Much of the affective domain has been repressed, denied, and obscured. It is as though we have come upon the unconscious and begun to examine its contents. We are not entirely sure that opening our "box" is necessarily a good thing; we are certain that it is not likely to be a source of peace and harmony among the members of a school staff.

Some would question the desirability of a school's considering affective objectives. Some would wonder about the wisdom of making these objectives explicit rather than implicit, and more would doubt the possibility of the school's doing anything significant to develop affective objectives. If we obscure the objectives in the affective domain and bury them in platitudes, how can we examine them, determine their meaning, or do anything constructive about them? Our "box" must be opened if we are to face reality and take action.

It is in this "box" that the most influential controls are to be found. The affective domain contains the forces that determine the nature of an individual's life and ultimately the life of an entire people. To keep the "box" closed is to deny the existence of the powerful motivational forces that shape the life of each of us. To look the other way is to avoid coming to terms with the real. Education is not the rote memorization of meaningless material to be regurgitated on an examination paper. Perhaps the two *Taxonomy* structures may help us to see the awesome possibilities of the relations between students-ideas-teachers (Krathwohl *et al.,* 1964, p. 91).

IN 1956, a highly influential little book was published which concerned itself with clarity of goals, means, and techniques of assessment in the cognitive domain. This was the *Taxonomy* by Bloom *et al.,* which is referred to throughout this book. The second handbook, which investigates the affective domain, follows the same general procedures and, undoubtedly, is one of the most objective attempts to analyze these highly personal expressions of man.

The authors state that objectives in this domain have a feeling tone which varies considerably in range and intensity (Krathwohl *et al.,* 1964, p. 7). These are the objectives that are commonly classified as interests, attitudes, appreciations, values, opinions, prejudices, and the like. For our purposes, discussion will focus upon interests, attitudes, appreciations, and values. Admittedly, this is an arbitrary restriction, but it is necessary because of the amount of material which is available, because of the degree of repetition from one category to another, and, finally, because of the highly subjective nature of the writing in these categories.

Some Unresolved Problems

These reasons also help to explain the necessity for as unprejudiced an analysis of the affective domain as possible. The authors of the *Affective Domain Taxonomy* have attempted to do this. Any inquiry into interests, attitudes, and the like is faced with formidable obstacles. The very essence of behavioral characteristics such as values, attitudes, and so forth, makes accurate expression and actual attainment of desirable objectives extremely questionable. How far should the school go in changing the attitudes of students when such a change brings a student into conflict with his parents?

Should the school be active in the statement and attainment of affective objectives, or is this an infringement upon the home? Conversely, does the school have an obligation to foster learning of desirable affective objectives? These are not simple questions to answer since they cut to the heart of the entire educational process.

Yet, to deny the school's responsibility in the formulation and achievement of affective objectives is to disregard them as educational objectives, and, likewise, to put them beyond the learning process. But, as we shall see, behavioral manifestations such as interests and attitudes are learned just as cognitive objectives such as knowledge and comprehension are acquired. Unfortunately, most educators fail to see the advantages in time and effort spent in composing, teaching for, and measuring the attainment of affective objectives. How will it benefit the subjects which must be "covered"? The best answer to this question lies in reflection about the possibility of transfer, positive and negative.

This text urges that, not only is there a place for affective objectives in the school, but also they must be specifically stated and consciously strived for in classroom instruction. The difficulty is obvious. If time is given to aid students in the achievement of these objectives, where is the evidence that shows success or failure of such instruction? How do you grade interests or appreciations?

What measures are available that will precisely indicate whether or not a student appreciates good literature or the theatre? Almost without exception, we are reduced to asking or observing. In both instances, true interests, values, attitudes, and appreciations may easily be camouflaged. Students are well aware that an interest in school activities, or a desire for things that the school deems worthy, usually receives a tangible reward.

Does the lack of instruments that are not influenced by such surface properties dictate a policy of omitting any admission of affective goals in our schools? There seems to be a two-part answer to this question. First, youngsters have, and continue to acquire, interests, attitudes, values, and appreciations. Consequently, the school must determine in clear and definite objectives what it wishes to accomplish, and then it must seek the means to help students to attain such goals.

Second, educators and psychologists must continue to construct more adequate instruments which will reveal the actual affective characteristics possessed by students. As knowledge of human behavior accumulates, and as knowledge of more exact methods of measurement increases, educators and psychologists can better determine how, and if, adequate affective objectives can be realistically established and achieved.

Another serious issue is the personal nature of affective characteristics. Does anyone like to be told that his attitudes or values are incorrect, inconsistent, or, even worse, dangerous? As we shall see, these affective characteristics are learned early in life, and they manifest a remarkable degree of stability and persistency. Unless the school views the affective domain as a legitimate segment of the total learning process, any deliberate change toward more acceptable affective characteristics is only a remote possibility.

The internal quality of these affective behavioral expressions makes it exceedingly difficult to determine reliably what they are and how to change, eliminate, or substitute others. Krathwohl *et al.*, (1964, p. 18) state:

In contrast, one's beliefs, attitudes, values, and personality characteristics are more likely to be regarded as private matters, except in the most extreme instances already noted. My attitudes toward God, home, and family are private concerns, and this privacy is generally respected. My political attitudes are private; I may reveal them if I wish, but no one can force me to do so. In fact, my voting behavior is usually protected from public view. Each man's home is his castle, and his interests, values, beliefs, and personality may not be scrutinized unless he voluntarily gives permission to have them revealed. This public-private status of cognitive vs. affective behaviors is deeply rooted in the Judeo-Christian religion and is a value highly cherished in the democratic traditions of the Western world.

Affective versus Cognitive

Special emphasis should be placed upon the relationship between affective and cognitive objectives. Again, there are dual aspects to the existing association betwen the two categories. First, the reader is reminded that there is a very vital cognitive component to interests, attitudes, appreciations, and values. Such behavioral reactions, although mainly of a feeling or emotional character, nevertheless, do encompass some intellectual commitment. More will be said about this in our analysis of the individual categories of the affective domain.

Second, the attainment of desirable cognitive objectives (knowledge, comprehension, and so forth) does not, of itself, imply that desirable affective objectives are simultaneously and incidentally attained. If there is one fact about the properties of the affective upon which all writers agree, it is this. Such an assumption is one of the most prevalent, and false, conceptions held by teachers at all levels of education, elementary school through graduate school.

We have assumed that students can achieve knowledge and understanding of history or literature, for example, and can apply these objectives in test situations. We then assume that they likewise have acquired desirable interests in good reading and the drama, or proper attitudes toward a democracy and participation in elections. Yet, studies are showing that this is one of the most ill-founded assumptions about the learning process.

Admittedly, there are many variables that demand consideration in any discussion of cognitive and affective objectives. One of the most important, and widely recognized, influences is the social status of teachers. The public school systems of most nations are staffed primarily by individuals who represent a middle-class value system. (The reader's attention is once more drawn to the interdisciplinary quality of learning. We have previously seen the contributions of physiology, chemistry, and philosophy, among others, and here we see the benefits of sociology. This is true of each topic discussed in this text.)

Although faculties at all levels of education are predominantly middle-class persons, the school's population draws from all strata of society. Lower-class and upper-class children are exposed to the affective objectives of teachers which differ considerably from their own attitudes, values, and the like. If attainment of cognitive objectives automatically includes worthy affective objectives, the affective goals of the youngsters at the extremes of the social strata should be radically altered. This is not true.

Perhaps, in many instances, this represents the prejudices of teachers. In a study conducted in Great Britain (Himmelweit, 1954), British teachers consistently assigned a higher rating to middle-class students than to working-class students on such characteristics as industriousness, responsibility, and interest in school affairs. Was this because the affective characteristics of the lower-class children did not change and coincide with those of the teachers? The particular problem we are studying knows no national boundaries.

Another relevant study was that by Jacob (1957). In an extensive investigation of changes in the affective characteristics of college students after four years of college, he found little evidence that college learning experiences changed student values in any way. Prevailing college opinion seemed to be more effective in changing affective toning than did actual course work.

Krathwohl *et al.* (1964) go so far as to suggest that cognitive achievement may cause negative affective behavior. They believe that it is quite possible to achieve mastery of a subject and also develop a decided distaste for the same subject. Thus, cognitive learning experiences do not mechanically induce desirable affective characteristics in pupils.

The significance of such studies lies in their ability to jar the complacency of educators as well as to open doors for needed research in a most promising field of study. If intellectual attainment results from carefully selected and graded cognitive learning experience, it should now be quite apparent that worthy affective objectives will be achieved only by the direct teaching of appropriate affective learning experiences.

Intensity of Expression

Another major problem in studying man's affective behavior is raised by the intensity of each of the categories. For example, there is a wide range of interest in a student who manifests the minimum of interest in one subject, but eagerly seeks out a different discipline. Krathwohl *et al.* (1964) are unique in their endeavors to classify this spread of intensity. As a result of their studies, they have eliminated the more traditional titles (interests, attitudes, and so forth) to illustrate that what is termed interest, may, if sufficiently intense, reach into the category that is customarily designated as values.

They give the example of interest covering a range of behavior that extends from a student's awareness of something to his determinedly searching for it. Or, a student may admit that he has some feeling about a person, object, and the like, while at the other extreme he volunteers to express his feelings to others. Appreciation may stretch from mere permissiveness about something in the environment to pleasant feelings experienced when the object is perceived (Krathwohl *et al.*, 1964, p. 25).

If this range of intensity in each category does indeed exist, it would seem to dictate the need for some ordering element, or continuum. The search for such a guiding principle is similar to the attempt to locate the thread of continuity that helps to explain the development of emotional behavior. As we shall see, for the emotions, excitement seems to be the unifying element.

The authors of the *Affective Taxonomy*, after detailed search, decided upon the process known as internalization. Affective components extend from mere awareness of some phenomenon to an individual's use of an affective component as a basis for action. The authors (1964, pp. 27–28) state that, if it passes through all of these stages, it is absorbed into the person's internal controlling structure.

While this inclusion within one's behavioral structure is the fundamental meaning of internalization, it is a process of degree. External control by the environment gradually yields to inner control by the individual. Sheer awareness passes to active response even if external control is lacking. Internalization, then, refers not only to inclusion, but also to the *degree* of inclusion.

For example, a teacher of a particular subject may demand a student's interest. The student realizes that he must give a minimum of attention if he is to pass the course. He is aware at a low level, and he has incorporated within himself this demand of society. At a higher level, however, he is visiting the library for additional knowledge in the subject; there is no external control in this example but the student is actively responding. There is a wide difference in the degree of inclusion in these illustrations.

An excellent description of the manner in which internalization functions is offered by the authors of the *Affective Taxonomy*. They state (1964, p. 33) that the process of internalization commences when the student's attention is attracted by some phenomenon, characteristic, or value. As he attends to the stimulus, he differentiates it from any others that might be present in his perceptual field. Following this, he attaches emotional significance to the phenomenon and places a value upon it. He now relates this phenomenon to other similar phenomena that he values. Finally, he reacts automatically to it, and relates it to his other values. Thus, he formulates certain orientations to the changing pattern of his environmental stimuli.

The continuum was divided into the following stages (Krathwohl *et al.*, 1964, p. 35):

1.0   Receiving (attending)
    1.1   Awareness
    1.2   Willingness to receive
    1.3   Controlled or selected attention

2.0   Responding
    2.1   Acquiescence in responding
    2.2   Willingness to respond
    2.3   Satisfaction in response

3.0   Valuing
    3.1   Acceptance of a value
    3.2   Preference for a value
    3.3   Commitment (conviction)

4.0   Organization
    4.1   Conceptualization of a value
    4.2   Organization of a value system

5.0   Characterization by a value or value complex
    5.1   Generalized set
    5.2   Characterization

Because the *Affective Taxonomy,* from its date of publication, undoubtedly will be a potent factor in any consideration of these characteristics, ample space was taken in this introductory section to acquaint the reader with its goals as well as its problems. Throughout the remainder of the chapter, the affective categories will be presented under their traditional terminology, that is, interests, attitudes, appreciations, and values. But the conclusion of each section, where possible, will relate these more familiar interpretations to the relatively unfamiliar presentation that is found in the *Affective Taxonomy.*

One of the most different methods in the *Affective Taxonomy* of which the reader should be aware is the embodiment of the traditional categories of interest, attitudes, appreciations, and values in *more than one* category of the taxonomy. For example, interest extends from a student's consciousness that some phenomenon exists to the category which implies preference for a value. Attitudes and values proceed from a willingness to respond to circumstances in which the individual understands how the attitude or value relates to him. With these differences in mind, the first of the affective categories to be examined is that of interest.

INTERESTS

Interests have long occupied a special place in education. Very few textbooks on methods fail to urge that teachers capitalize upon the interests of their students. As we have seen, such utilization of student interests is of considerable value in motivating the individual members of a class. Unfortunately, there is an uncertainty about both the definition of the term and its application that has contributed to its neglect in educational planning.

Some authors recognize this failing and attempt to specify exactly what they mean by interests before they discuss the nature and application of them. For example, Commins and Fagin (1954) state that an interest is an emotional involvement of like-dislike which is associated with attention to some object.

Strong (1958) has stated that interests are directed toward activities, while attitudes focus upon concepts. However, Travers (1963) feels that definitions, although manifesting improvement, are still vague. In activities in which there are interests, the interest may be either shown by an expressed liking by the person, or it may be shown by the specific activity actually engaged in by the individual. Travers criticizes both means of defining interests because expressed interests are not always true interests, and a person's freedom of activity is restricted to a certain extent.

Another attempt to define interest is by means of a measuring instrument such as the Kuder Preference Record, or the Strong Vocational Interest Inventory. The Kuder forces a person to select among various kinds of activities; it then provides a total score which is indicative of a person's interests. The Strong differs from the Kuder in that it obtains a person's interests in certain activities and then endeavors to match his interests with those in certain occupations. For example, a person's interests expressed by his responses on the Strong may show that his interests resemble those of educators and social workers more than any other classification.

Whichever path we take in our search for a definition of interest, our limited knowledge causes a feeling of dissatisfaction. Persons have obvious preferences for one activity over another, and it is possible to secure accurate observations of such preferences. Beyond this, one hesitates to state that "interest means this, or that," or "this is a true interest." Perhaps the safest statement is that, when a person attends to a particular activity, rather than another, this is an interest.

The Nature of Interest

Our definition suggests that whatever activity an individual prefers is an interest. The implication is that true interest is voluntary. Yet the *Affective Taxonomy* places interest in a category as neutral as simple awareness. This kind of forced attention is an interest, but one can only question how lasting this interest will be.

If we view interest as an educational objective with several subdivisions, the possibility of conflict between cognitive and affective achievement may be lessened. The assumption that intellectual mastery, plus compelled interest, will result in worthwhile cognitive and affective attainment will not so easily be made. If teachers are aware that student interest varies from that demanded by a teacher to that gladly given by the student, this realization will make them more alert to the place of interest in motivation and learning.

Naturally, a voluntary commitment should be the goal of the instructor, and, the more that teachers know about the qualities of interests, the more able they will be to achieve this objective. The first characteristic to be noted is that interests are stable. If this seems surprising, it is because the development of an interest is usually overlooked.

For some reason, something in the environment attracts the attention of the person, and he slowly learns to distinguish it. Note that this capacity may be forced or voluntary. Then he acquires a like-dislike feeling that is associated with the object or activity. This is a process that occurs over a fairly long period of time; it is not the fleeting interest that youngsters pay to something in their environment that momentarily catches their attention. Rather, an interest pattern, or interest structure, grows that is not easily subject to quick change.

Throughout our discussion another significant concept has run—intensity. The range of feeling associated with an interest was mentioned earlier in the introductory section of this chapter. Strong

(1958) states that an individual not only evidences his like or dislike of an activity, but he can also indicate his relative preferences for different activities.

Strong also cites other characteristics of interest, among which are acceptance-rejection and readiness to act. The feeling that is associated with the activity ultimately decides whether it will be accepted or rejected, and, actually, whether the person will continue to respond to the original stimulus.

A further provocative comment on the nature of interests is seen in a statement by Smedslund (1964). He summarizes the recent work of experimental psychologists such as Berlyne (1960) and Fiske and Maddi (1961) who propose that interest results from the organism's inclination toward information processing. A person manifests interest, or not, in a subject according to the structure of the material presented, that is, whether or not it appears complete, consistent, and the like. As Smedslund concludes, the possibilities for education are tremendous.

The Affective Taxonomy

Thus far we have presented the analysis of interests in the customary manner. Here, a summary of the treatment afforded interests in the *Affective Taxonomy* by Krathwohl *et al.* (1964) would be valuable.

For these authors, interest is a phenomenon that begins at the low psychological level of awareness, proceeds to a willingness to receive, then differentiates the stimulus from others, next responds rather mechanically, then responds voluntarily, experiences a feeling of satisfaction, begins to respond consistently to the object, or activity, and, finally, the individual actively pursues the stimulus. In the language of the *Taxonomy*, interest extends from an awareness to a preference for a value.

What is particularly interesting is the authors' attempt to specify what other investigators have termed "range" or "intensity" of interest. What are the depths and heights of this range? If interests vary in intensity, does this mean that they assume some of the characteristics of other affective categories, such as attitudes, appreciations, and values? If there are multiple characteristics of the affective categories, is it logically and psychologically sound to categorize them as rigidly as we have done in the past?

The *Taxonomy* raises these questions; it does not answer them. This can only come with empirical studies that will attempt to verify the authors' conclusion. They themselves have tried to compare their classifications with recent studies such as that by Peck and Havighurst (1960). This study reported five stages of character development (amoral, expedient, conforming, irrational-conscientious, and rational-altruistic), the pertinent parts of which appear to correspond with the taxonomy.

There seems to be no contradiction between taxonomy and traditional methods of classification. All authors have recognized a wide range and intensity of interests. The *Affective Taxonomy* aims at exactness in formulating the limits of this particular category, and, to the extent that it is proven accurate, educators will have a more useful tool in formulating objectives.

Learning and Interests

From what has been said of interests, it is evident that, once a person attends to some object or activity in his environment, the persistence of this interest depends largely upon the satisfaction derived. Much was made, in Chapter III, of the need to link a student's goals with those of the school. Obviously, one method of doing this is to capitalize upon pupil interest. Note that the word used was "capitalize," not "guided by." Pupils often see nothing interesting in educational objectives; teachers frequently are dismayed by pupil interests. The school's task is to use student interest as a prod toward a worthy although more distant goal.

If this can be accomplished, interest is a definite stimulus to motivation. One hesitates to equate the two, particularly because of the need factor in motivation, and also because there is insufficient evidence to offer as proof. Perhaps the best way to summarize is to say that a school must channel a student's drives, and try to direct them to preferable goals, and that utilizing a pupil's interests is of great benefit to this process.

May we conclude, then, that high interest in a subject will insure rapid and lasting learning in the particular subject? Unfortunately, no. There is no substantial documentation to state that interest correlates with measured achievement in any discipline. There are far too many students who enjoy good literature, but are unable to write a decent composition. How many boys are fascinated by tales of outer space, but are unable to cope with the demands of mathematics and science? Interest in no way is a test of ability.

Is it ever fair to say that high ability shows a significant correlation with high interest? Probably not. A student may actually dislike a subject, but, if a teacher requires factual knowledge, and little else, and if the student possesses a retentive memory, he may obtain high grades in this course, in spite of his low interest.

Travers (1963, p. 179) gives the example of an investigator discovering a relationship between a student's increase in interest in a mathematics course, and a corresponding increase in mathematical achievement. Did interest in mathematics serve as a motivating force? Possibly, but this interest could have derived from *past* satisfactions in mathematics, and now success is producing interest.

Explanations for our present lack of evidence may lie in our inadequate knowledge of interest and thus our inability to measure its influence. Regardless, teachers should be aware of the uses to which a student's interests can be put, the complexity of interest, and the danger of assuming too much about pupil interest from any superficial investigation.

ATTITUDES

As we continue our analysis of man's affective qualities we can only wonder if there is any more important, lasting, and influential part of a student's personality than his attitudes. Pupils' attitudes may act as a stimulant to, or make a mockery of, the learning process. The attitudes they bring to school may well govern their reactions to their classmates, and even to the faculty. The attitudes they take from school may govern, or at least, influence decisions which they will make throughout their adult life.

Since attitudes assume such a vital function in our lives, the more knowledge that teachers possess about them, the more able are they to encourage the development of those attitudes that are in accord with moral and social acceptability. This is not to say that conformity is the goal of education. It is to say that there must be some standards toward which all members of society share a common attitude but which also permit the expression of dissenting attitudes.

The average student will often find himself caught between powerful and conflicting attitudes held by individuals who exercise an influence upon him. Parents, teachers, or friends all may pull in different directions. What action will a student take; whose attitudes will he adopt? His attitudes will probably be quite unstable. When he is with friends, he will likely accept their attitudes toward objects, or persons, but usually not sufficiently so as to bring him into conflict with parents and teachers. The same holds true when he is under the more direct influence of adults. Ultimately, he will adopt those attitudes which become most valuable to him.

These examples attest to the more discernible properties of attitudes. Perhaps this is why most authorities agree upon the meaning of the term "attitudes." McDonald (1959, p. 214) states that an attitude is a predisposition to action, a state of readiness to act in a particular way. Mouly (1960, p. 343) views attitudes as learned patterns of behavior which predispose the individual to act in a specific way when confronted with a given situation. Klausmeier (1961, p. 254) submits that an attitude is a learned, emotionally toned predisposition to react in a consistent way, favorable or unfavorable, toward a person, object, or idea.

Berelson and Steiner (1964, p. 557), however, refrain from such an exact definition. They maintain that opinions, attitudes, and beliefs do not have fixed meanings in the literature, but in general they refer to a person's preference for one or another side of a controversial matter in the public domain—a political issue, a religious idea, a moral position, an aesthetic taste, a certain practice.

Commins and Fagin (1954, p. 388) reflect the range of attitudes when they state:

If we define "attitude" as a set or tendency or predisposition to feel and act in a certain way, all personality traits, interests, and emotional reactions may be regarded as attitudes. "Inferiority" and "extroversion" are attitudes toward the self, and toward things, persons, and events in relation to one's self; interest in baseball is an attitude, and so is fear of the dark.

Attitudinal Elements

As we have seen, attitudes are concerned more with concepts and things, as opposed to the direction of interests toward activities. But recent studies and writings are inclined to move beyond such positive-negative tendencies. Travers (1963, pp. 372–373) summarizes the tentative conclusions thus far reached. Using Katz and Stotland (1959) as a guide, he asserts that attitudes possess an affective component which reveals the positive-negative feelings associated with the attitude, a cognitive component which reflects the degree of knowledge that a person has about an idea or object, and, finally, an action component that may or may not be consistent with the expressed attitude.

It is interesting to speculate upon an individual's attitude system which heavily favors one component at the expense of the other two. A person may have a very strong attitude toward Catholics, Protestants, Jews, or any other faith, but have relatively little information about the particular religion or experience with its members. The affective component is dominating the attitude system.

Another person may have carefully evaluated the differences between two political parties. He may have read the platforms of both, and attended rallies of each. After weighing the evidence presented by both parties, he has formed an attitude about them. This may, or may not, be linked with strong feelings about both parties. If not, the cognitive element is predominant.

Or, a person may say that he vigorously favors mass education and college for all who can qualify. He may be a college graduate himself. Despite this, he may be one of a disturbing number of college graduates who do not read one book a year.

The affective and cognitive components of attitude are undergoing continued study (Rhine, 1958). Westie and DeFleur (1959) speculate about the reaction of the autonomic nervous system in attitude expression. Sherif and Hovland (1961) question the nature of the stimulus that causes an attitudinal reaction. If the stimulus is definite, attitudinal reaction is limited; if the stimulus is vague, the attitude becomes intense because there are no standards and attitudinal reaction is less restricted.

Because the complexity of attitudes is more fully realized now, the question may well be asked: how does a person acquire attitudes?

The Development of Attitudes

If attitudes have the elements that were discussed in the preceding section, it is apparent that knowledge is not an essential requirement for attitude formation. Accordingly, we expect to discover that attitudes are derived from many and varied sources, within and without the school. Such ready accessibility of attitudinal sources helps to explain the conflicts in attitudes which many youngsters experience.

The most important point for the reader to appreciate is that attitudes are learned. None of us is born with positive or negative feelings toward religions, races, or politics, for example. These are acquired in the same manner as are facts and understandings. As such, they proceed through the same steps, meet the same obstacles, and encounter the same variables as do concepts, problems, and so forth. The content may be different; the process is the same.

For example, a person receives derogatory information about a politician he has long respected. His attitude toward this individual has been favorable. But now reliable reports reach him that this admired politician has acted contrary to the public good. He is motivated to investigate the charges. An obstacle is present: how can this story be checked for absolute verification?

He searches the environment for clues, and he establishes his response pattern according to his interpretation of the stimuli. This may be by seeking confirmation by other sources, reviewing newspaper articles, or discussing the problem with the politician. His goal has now been attained; he has adequate information upon which to make a judgment. If the information he initially received was correct, his attitude toward the politician probably will be very unfavorable. If he discovers that the information was false, his favorable attitude no doubt will be reinforced.

Here we see an attitude formed by a search for accurate information. Unfortunately, this is usually an exception. Attitudes are normally formed, retained, and strengthened on the basis of a minimum of information. Such formation often occurs in the home, where the attitudes of parents may be adopted at an early age, and quite unconsciously by the child. Or, most individuals tend to assume the attitudes of persons whom they admire. Again, attitude formation may happen without the awareness of the person involved. It is hoped that the attitudes of teachers would be adopted in this manner. Or, prevailing group attitudes may be acquired, especially if one is an active participant of the group.

Attitudes learned in this manner result from the process of conditioning. A student may like and admire his teacher and develop a positive attitude toward him. Since the school is the neutral stimulus with whom the teacher is associated, positive attitudes tend to develop about education in general. Or, this teacher may casually have remarked that he thought a certain political party had accomplished much for the country. A student, often politically naive, or maybe even negative toward politics, now finds himself with a favorable attitude toward the political party the teacher mentioned.

It is interesting to note the responsibility of the teacher in attitude formation. He himself should be a figure of sufficient stature to deserve admiration by the student. Not that he should engage in popularity contests, or heroics. Students are sharp and shrewd observers of human nature. They appreciate genuineness when they see it. A teacher's knowledge, teaching skill, and personality should command the respect and, hopefully, the admiration of students.

He also has a unique opportunity in his teaching to encourage the attainment of desirable attitudes. He can use the content of the course, outstanding figures in his discipline, and his own skill to foster this. He must also be conscious of the conflict he could cause in students. He should try to avoid it if possible, but, if impossible, he should make the desired attitudes so valuable that a student is forced to accept the validity of his presentation. From this brief description, one can see that teacher selection requires more than passing grades in college.

Berelson and Steiner (1964) trace the development of attitudes, among other affective characteristics, through several stages. The first is the historical setting where the impact of the type of society into which he is born is experienced by the individual. Next is the influence of the family where the influence of the parents is felt. This is followed by the pressure of the attitudes of his friends, that is, the group now makes itself felt. The final agent they see as decisive in attitude formation is that of the individual's social strata.

To conclude this section on attitude development, some suggestions by Klausmeier (1961) for the shaping of attitudes are offered:

1. Exactly what attitudes do you wish students to acquire?
2. Do students understand what the attitude means?
3. Do students have adequate information about the attitude?
4. Do students have desirable models to imitate?
5. Do students associate pleasant feelings with this attitude?
6. Does the attitude have real, practical significance to students?

7. Is the group being used to form desirable attitudes?
8. Are students encouraged to seek and cultivate desirable attitudes?

Attitude Change

The attitudes that a student develops are brought into the classroom and may permeate many of his activities within the school. Some of these may be deemed undesirable by the teacher. How can such attitudes be modified by the school, and particularly, by the teacher?

Initially, it is well to remember that attitudes are comparatively stable. They have developed over a period of several years and they are not easily dislodged. The more interested a person is, and the more emotionally involved, the more difficult will it be to accomplish attitude modification (Lane, 1959). To state the obvious, if a person is emotionally committed to an issue, and if the commitment is reinforced by his home, peers, and so forth, any attitude change is unlikely.

The first step in attempting to modify an attitude is to supply correct information. A previous section of this chapter remarked upon the relationship between affective and cognitive objectives. One does not insure the other, as the study by Jacob (1957) indicated. Supplying accurate information is merely furnishing a basis on which other work can be built.

A famous and frequently quoted study by Lewin (1943) is an excellent example of the limited effect of information upon attitudes. He wished to have a group of women change their food habits. Lecturing to them and giving them positive information about the new foods resulted in little change. When group discussion was initiated, with the women participating actively, considerable positive change was produced. Their opinions, attitudes, and beliefs were frankly analyzed; they moved from a within to a without consideration of the possibilities. Passive, intellectual acceptance changed to desirable practice. This study also illustrated a powerful force in attitudinal stability: the deep-rooted nature of attitudes. They usually are indiscernible to observation.

Since we must begin with the presentation of true facts, what type of communication is most likely to cause change? From the above example, it is clear that information to which a student actively responds is probably the most effective method of bringing about change. This is particularly true if the group situation can be utilized and a student brought to make a change himself. This has the dual aspect of self-change and harmony with the group (King and Janis, 1956).

That self-involvement in the change of attitudes can be potent is seen in a study by Janis and King (1954). Male college students were divided into two groups, one of which played an active role in presenting a certain view, while the other group was passive; it read and listened. Opinion scores were obtained before and after the experiment. The results showed that the active participants were more influenced by the communications than the passive members. The authors also conclude that the active members were undoubtedly impressed by their own performance, and that they experienced feelings of pleasure at their accomplishments.

We may presume, then, that attitudes are best changed by a combination of information, persuasion, activity, and group pressure. One final, cautionary word is necessary before we leave this subject. Formerly, it was thought that an appeal for attitude change should be charged with emotion. Studies such as those by Weiss and Lieberman (1959) and Lewan and Stotland (1961) indicate that there is no significant relationship between change and the emotional nature of the communication. Summarizing these, and other similar studies, Moscovici (1963) remarks that nothing conclusive has been established about the emotional content of the communication.

The Affective Taxonomy

The authors of the *Affective Taxonomy* view attitude as a behavioral reaction that extends, in their classification, from willingness to respond to conceptualization of a value. That is, at the lowest level the student desires to make a voluntary choice, begins to derive satisfaction from his behavior, commences to respond consistently to the object with which the attitude is associated, seeks it out, is committed to it and wishes to develop it further, and, finally, he sees the relationship of it to the values he holds, or those that he is acquiring.

There certainly is no conflict between this tracing of attitudinal range and intensity and the above presentation of the development of attitudes. Once the attitude is acquired, observation enables us to place the individual's reactions in the suggested categories. It would appear that the *Taxonomy* may serve as an invaluable guide in attitude change. If we can place an attitude in a given category, added knowledge about the perspectives of this category will definitely aid persons such as teachers or counsellors in attempts to modify attitudes.

Learning and Attitudes

Any analysis of attitudes is intimately bound to the learning process. Attitudes are acquired by deliberate intent or by the process of conditioning. Either an individual seeks a cause for his attitudes or he assimilates them from his environment. Frequently, teachers may be a source of attitudes, by example, or by instruction. More often, the teacher's task is that of modifying attitudes.

Although learning affects attitudes, attitudes similarly influence learning. Attitudes that have been learned in the past, often exercise control over future learning. Youngsters who have older brothers and sisters in school commonly acquire an attitude of liking, or displeasure, for school because of the comments, fears, joys, and so forth of the older children. Often, students who have difficulty with one teacher in a school find that this attitude spreads into other classes, and all their marks suffer. Learning and attitudes travel a two-way street and teachers are well advised to look both ways.

APPRECIATIONS

A question often asked by educators concerns the lasting effects of learning. Is the time, effort, and expense which education requires worth the effort? No instructor attempts to answer such a question by insisting that factual knowledge is retained for many years after school. It is to be hoped, though, that students maintain an interest in, and a favorable attitude toward, those goals and ideals which the school strives to inculcate.

Since forced interests and questionable attitudes are not among the conditions of positive transfer that we previously discussed, it is apparent that an appreciation of the inherent worth of such ideas is a necessary provision for sustained activity in intellectual pursuits. This, then, brings us to an examination of appreciation.

The *Dictionary of Education* (Good, 1959, p. 34) states that appreciation is an emotionally fringed awareness of the worth, value, or significance of anything. This definition implies that appreciation has both an emotional and intellectual component. The dual nature of appreciation could be one reason why most authors and investigators have avoided inclusion of this topic in their analysis of learning. Admittedly, it is difficult to specify the conditions which produce it, the variables that affect it, and the manner in which it disposes an individual's behavioral pattern.

This omission seems a regrettable lapse by educators. The school is committed to desirable interests, favorable attitudes, and deserving values, but, unless students develop an appreciation for the worth or significance of something, these other affective objectives will remain unattainable. For without this recognition of value and emotional inflection, students will fail to respond voluntarily, that is, without coercion by some authority such as the school.

The Affective Taxonomy

This statement of affective objectives is one of the very few attempts to scrutinize the meaning of appreciation and to weigh its educational significance. For these authors, appreciation, at its lowest level, is seen when an individual is capable of distinguishing a particular stimulus from other surrounding stimuli. Then he begins to respond on a rather tentative basis, which is closely followed by a more voluntary commitment.

Next, the individual begins to experience definite feelings of satisfaction from his response. Finally, there is a consistency of response to something considered worthy and a tendency to pursue it for this worth which the individual has ascribed to it. In the language of the *Taxonomy,* appreciation may manifest itself as controlled or selected attention, acquiescence in responding, willingness to respond, satisfaction in response, acceptance of a value, and, last, preference for a value.

If we now relate the definition which is given in the *Dictionary of Education* to these affective categories of appreciation, it is clear that Krathwohl *et al.* have specified the degrees of appreciation which are found in the above definition, that is, they endeavor to locate on their continuum just where appreciation as an awareness begins, approximately the point at which emotion appears, and, ultimately, its adoption into a person's value system. The authors of the *Taxonomy* (1964, p. 36) state that appreciation does not include the lowest levels of the taxonomy, nor the highest.

Learning and Appreciation

Bossing (1952, p. 216) remarks that an appreciation is an emotional disposition to choose those values in life conceived to be of greatest ultimate significance to the individual and society. He postulates a dual classification of appreciation: aesthetic and ethical-social. Each of these needs a distinct educational technique to further its development.

Defining aesthetic appreciation as a satisfaction derived from the beautiful in a situation (1952, p. 217), Bossing stresses the teacher's belief in that which he wishes others to enjoy. Teachers should present classroom experiences that encourage students to seek more knowledge and understanding and, hopefully, enable them to derive genuine enjoyment from this activity.

Bossing (1952, p. 218) characterizes ethical-social appreciation as satisfaction resulting from recognition of the social and moral qualities of goodness and truth present in a given situation. To aid students in achieving such goals the teacher should evidence his own appreciation of the inherent worth of any suitable object or event. And, again, he should urge active pupil participation.

Throughout his analysis of appreciation, Bossing stresses the roles of both emotion and intellect, which are components of any type of appreciation regardless of the classification used. Watkins (1958) likewise admits the importance of the development of appreciation in the classroom and flatly states that all motivation is a matter of appreciation (p. 152). And he also urges that appropriate learning experiences be selected which will entail active student participation and which will result in satisfaction for the learner.

From this brief discussion of the nature and educational significance of appreciation, the reader undoubtedly realizes that there is a strong need for research in this subject. Can we clarify the meaning of appreciation? What are the variables that influence its progress? What is its relation to motivation? How can learning foster appreciation, and how does appreciation affect the learning process? What should be the role of the school in its development? It is these questions that research must answer, thus supplying the empirical evidence which teachers can utilize in more effective means of inspiring student appreciation of worthy goals.

VALUES

Individuals will remain committed to what they determine is important, that is, what holds worth for them. If we consider value from this perspective, it becomes evident that a value signifies an interest in, an attitude toward, and an appreciation of something. It is impossible to isolate any one of these categories and study it as a distinct and unique entity. There is an interaction of which the reader should be conscious, and which helps to explain the variability of intensity which each affective characteristic manifests. The more a person is interested in, appreciates, and is favorably disposed toward an object, the more a person values it.

A person's value system, then, is a powerful force in directing and guiding that person throughout life. As an aid in understanding the meaning of value systems, the value-types of Edward Spranger (1928) have been widely used, and, in fact, Dukes (1955) states that recent value study is based almost exclusively upon Spranger's work. He identifies six types of values which exercise various influences upon a person's life:

1. The theoretical. The determination of truth is of paramount importance to such a person. This type of individual is guided mainly by his cognitive processes throughout life.
2. The aesthetic. For this person, beauty and harmony are of greatest worth. The artistic aspects of life exercise the most potent appeal for this type.
3. The economic. Here the material and the useful are most decisive. This is the "practical" man.
4. The social. Human relations are crucial to this value-type. He is characterized by friendliness and a positive attitude toward others.
5. The political. This type of person values power, and control, above all else.
6. The religious. This kind of person tries to organize life's experiences into meaningful wholes. He wishes to combine all his values into a purposeful way of life.

Any person is stimulated by more than one kind of value. A value system is a composite of all six types with one, two, or even three types predominating. The advantages of Spranger's classification is that it furnishes a basis for analysis and is a possible explanation for the integration of personality. A value is a uniquely personal behavioral reaction.

Recall what was said about the other affective categories that we have mentioned: an interest *in,* an appreciation *of,* and an attitude *toward.* Each of these is "outer" directed, whereas a value, by definition, is "inner" directed. What is the importance to me; what is the worth to me? The importance of guiding students toward meritorious values should never be neglected by teachers. It is too necessary for the individual and for society. This is far from a purely theoretical statement. Individuals and nations rise and fall according to their value selection. If an individual is devoted to purely materialistic goals (the economic person), other elements of personality suffer, and distortion of the behavioral pattern too often leads to an unhealthy, unhappy life. Exactly the same is true of nations, but it is the individual who will determine his nation's values. Education has no more important, or practical, function.

Still, more knowledge is needed about values, as with all the affective categories. Berelson and Steiner (1964, pp. 484–488) present a fine summary of class values, from which they infer:

1. Formal education becomes more desirable as the class becomes higher.
2. The middle class values achievement and prestige more than the lower class.
3. There is more conformity to the values of society among the middle class than either the upper or lower classes.
4. The lower class tends toward the extreme type of person (dominated by a single value, as we observed in the discussion of Spranger's types). For example, they are characterized by fervent religion or a rabid political position.

Our knowledge of value systems is still in its infancy. Dukes (1955) attributes the lack of progress in research about values to a tendency to confine psychology to empirical facts. Knowledge of values has resulted from such techniques as measuring the values of groups and relating the results to other data about group members; study of the origin and development of values within the individual; and, finally, by studying the influence of values upon cognitive processes.

In summarizing the results of investigating values by these methods, Dukes concludes that there is a more scientific basis for accepting such facts as individual differences in values. Men and women differ noticeably; those of various faiths and occupations also differ.

Home and family are most important in the development of an individual's social values, but there is no general agreement about the time of appearance of value systems.

He states that values have been studied at many points along the age continuum and only a few significant factors in value formation and reorganization have been isolated. Most of the research has been "suggestive" (Dukes, 1955, p. 40); therefore it is best to state that value can function as an organizer in cognition.

The Affective Taxonomy

In his discussion of values, McDonald (1959) declares that, although a distinction is made between attitudes and values, the difference is uncertain. He maintains that the psychological processes of acquisition are identical for both, and that the terms may be used interchangeably. The authors of the *Taxonomy* appear to agree with this position. The reader, then, is referred to the section under Attitudes, which presents the view of the authors of the *Taxonomy*.

Krathwohl *et al.* (1964, p. 36) believe that attitudes and values evince the same range and they give this account:

Similarly when we examined the range of interpretations, given to the terms "attitude" and "value" in educational objectives, we found they ranged from situations where the student was expected to display a particular behavior, especially with a certain amount of emotion (enthusiasm, warmth, or even disgust, if appropriate), to situations in which he might go out of his way to display the value or to communicate to others about it. Thus the lines in Figure 1 for these terms extend from 2.2 "Willingness to respond" to 4.1 "Conceptualization of a value."

Learning and Values

There is a growing recognition that value is a term that can no longer be excluded from the vocabulary of American education. There was, is, and will be staunch opposition from adherents to a strictly disciplinary educational context toward accepting values as a legitimate concern of the school. Unquestionably, such arguments are raised by those who are unfamiliar with the method of incorporating values into instruction.

Allport (1961), long a devoted investigator of man's value system, has endeavored to outline a procedure which teachers could fruitfully adopt. Admitting the problems which youth faces and concerned with the American value predicament (materialism), he nevertheless feels that the school can function effectively in the development of the individual value system.

It is not a simple task. Frequently, the instructor must combat values that have been indoctrinated in the home. If society places a premium upon production and consumption, teachers and schools usually reflect these values. Not always, however. And where a teacher or a school wishes to engage in the attempt to aid youngsters construct worthy value systems, what can they do and how can they do it?

First, he suggests that teachers begin with what the student has and then try to focus attention upon the value-attributes of the content. Other value-attributes should be drawn from the body of Judeo-Christian ethics, from the essentials of human relationships, and from man's intellectual curiosity, among others.

The "how" of value instruction poses a major obstacle. Allport refrains from including value study in a curriculum, both from a practical and theoretical viewpoint. Practical, because it could never be accomplished in American society; theoretical, because the subject of values is too difficult for the curriculum builders. Rather, he urges education for values when teachers teach what they believe, regardless of the subject. This, of necessity, dictates incidental teaching.

And yet, incidental or not, these are the experiences that are most vividly recalled by the student in later years. Why? The child is usually impressed by enthusiasm and warmth, and he himself becomes ego-involved. Students do not merely imitate; they are excited to self-discovery.

Particularly interesting to teachers and future teachers is a criticism which Allport makes of courses in educational psychology. In the analysis of the learning process, instructors emphasize what is extraneous to the subject matter: marks, rewards, and so forth. Then, as the student leaves school and these extraneous props are withdrawn, intellectual curiosity collapses. He recommends that teachers link intellectual curiosity to independence from the first days of instruction so that the individual eventually may educate himself. If this becomes a goal of instruction, gradually students acquire values and the values themselves serve as an inducement to continual intellectual exploration.

Garrison, Kingston, and McDonald (1964, p. 305) agree with this conclusion when they state:

Children need to live and grow in an environment which fosters the development of sound values as a basis for their actions. The modern school, emphasizing the development of the whole child, is concerned with his spiritual development. Moreover, the child is exposed to a variety of values from many sources in the environment of the home, school, church, and neighborhood. Some of these are wholesome; others are less wholesome and sometimes unwholesome, depending partially, upon the interpretation given to them. The teacher has the responsibility of accepting the value patterns which the child brings to school and guiding him in the attainment of those values cherished and decreed as worthwhile by the society of which the individual and the school is an integral part.

CONCLUSION

In this chapter, a strong plea was made for the incorporation of affective objectives into educational thought. That the chore is not simple is attested to by the many problems which were called to the reader's attention. Since cognitive achievement does not insure affective achievement and since conditions change so rapidly in today's society, the products of our schools should possess desirable and relatively stable, affective reactions.

There is an interaction between interests, attitudes, appreciations, and values that can aid or hinder learning, and continue or cease to function as a stimulus to adult intellectual curiosity. As recognition and acceptance of affective objectives grow, our need for knowledge likewise grows. Thus far, research shows an encouraging trend toward empirical verification of tangible changes which affective toning has upon the learning process.

A study by Page (1958) was conducted with seventy-four secondary school teachers and 2,139 unknowing students in their regular classes. An objective test was administered as part of the regular instructional procedure. After the papers were scored and graded, they were distributed into three groups. One group had no comment upon their papers; a second group had whatever comments the teacher normally would make; the third group received uniform comments, all of which were encouraging.

After the next test, it was found that both sets of students who had *some* comments on the first test did better than those who received no comment. Those whose papers the teachers had freely commented upon did better than those who received uniform, encouraging comments, but the difference was not significant. Page concludes that when the teacher makes the effort to comment upon student papers, it causes some change in attention or attitude, or something that causes learning to improve.

If teachers bring these affective characteristics to bear upon learning, both the teachers' and the pupils' task becomes easier, more enjoyable, and more lasting. Perhaps we can visualize the interaction of both domains as shown in Figure 10-1.

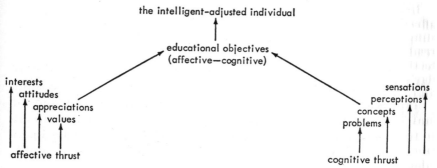

FIGURE 10-1. *Learning and the Affective Domain*

CHAPTER XI

Emotional Behavior and Learning

INTRODUCTION

It is apparent to everyone that learning has a considerable role in emotional and affective behavior. Most of our likes and dislikes, for example, are acquired. All students of elementary psychology know that fear of snakes and mice is not necessarily native. Many if not most of our fears are the results of experience. Clinical psychologists and psychiatrists place much emphasis upon the role of experience in the development of disturbances of personality. Thus, learned emotional reactions are of great importance in the development of personality.

So it is easy to see why many investigators have concerned themselves with the role of learning in the development of emotionally disturbed behavior. A problem which is perhaps equally important, but one which has received much less attention, is that of the role of emotional behavior in learning. We shall have occasion to examine these questions briefly in the course of this chapter, as well as some questions about behavior under conflict. Fundamentally, then, this chapter is concerned with the interaction between emotion and learning (Deese, 1952, p. 302).

MAN'S REACTIONS to his environment will determine his success or failure as he matures and as he learns, that is, as he adjusts to his surroundings and strives for mastery of his personal world. The pattern of his emotional responses weighs heavily in the struggle for happiness and achievement in his career and life. And, as Deese indicates in the opening paragraph, investigators have long realized the value that a reasoned, calm analysis of emotional situations has for an individual's mental health. Only recently, however, has the function of the emotions in the learning process assumed a place of importance in the psychological literature.

The influence of the emotions upon learning is not restricted to times of stress, for example, the taking of an examination or the fear of failure. It also applies, as we shall see later in the chapter, to man's physiological functions. If anything is amiss in the autonomic nervous system, learning is affected.

To admit the importance of the emotions is one thing; to explain our meager knowledge of its action is another. One of the basic questions that remains unanswered is just what is meant by emotion. There is little agreement among psychologists on a definition of emotions. For example, Mouly (1960) refers to emotion as some kind of stirring-up in the organism. He continues by stating that this is not perfectly clear, but at least it denotes action by the total organism.

Hilgard (1962) feels that defining an emotion as a stirred-up state is inadequate because it leaves emotion indistinguishable from other stirred-up states which result from completely different causes. He gives the example of chopping wood as the occasion of a stirred-up state of the body. Hilgard bases his reasoning upon the pleasantness or unpleasantness of experience which we refer to as affective tone. There is a wide range from less intense to more intense in our emotional reactions. Thus, Hilgard refuses to define "emotion" but concerns himself with an analysis of emotional states. By this he means the condition of the organism as it reacts in an affective manner, regardless of whether it is moderate or fierce.

Deese (1952) is skeptical of all attempts to define emotion. He calls our present efforts to explain the effects of emotion "primitive" and states that no one has solved the problem of definition. How, then, can we evaluate the relationship between learning and emotion? If psychologists can produce emotion under controlled conditions, which they can, it is still impossible to appraise the significance of their findings since what else other than emotion is produced remains unanswered.

Still, this in no way negates our need to understand as much as possible about emotional behavior because there is a definite link between it and learning. Anything that so permeates all aspects of an individual's life deserves the time and efforts of behavioral scientists. To those engaged in the task of aiding in the development of wholesome personalities, it is especially meaningful.

It is interesting to reflect upon the interaction of the ingredients of the learning process. In Chapter I we discussed them separately as the characteristics of learning, and we stressed the central role that some obstacle to a goal assumes. If there is no obstacle, there is no learning because the person will rely upon previously established response patterns. An obstacle to a desired goal arouses emotion, such as frustration, anger, perhaps even fear. The tension and energy it excites permits us to engage in the search for solution which results in the modification of behavior which we designate as learning.

Some authors are reluctant to limit their discussion of learning and the emotions to the influence of one upon the other since this implies a dichotomy which these authors regard as artificial. For example, Anderson (1942) states that this separation of the two is acceptable only if we realize that it is a human being who is reacting, and he is reacting as a unified whole. Emotional behavior and the learning process then become mere categories which facilitate our description of one unique process, that of adjustment.

Even as we argue for the admission of the emotions in any examination of the learning process, the results of both psychological and physiological experimentation support the relevancy of emotions to learning. Berlyne (1964, p. 129) comments on this encouraging trend when he states:

Psychological techniques used in conjunction with physiological techniques are bringing into focus one important fact that could hardly have been discovered by other forms of investigation. This is that affective processes have a special role in helping a new form of learned behavior to establish itself. In a surprisingly varied range of experimental situations, there is evidence of their participation during the early phase of the learning process and their subsequent disappearance when the learned response has become firmly implanted.

According to Berlyne, then, there is some affective reaction that expedites the learning process. This is a new avenue of research into learning, and one that promises to be most fruitful.

There appears to be fundamental agreement among theorists that our emotions refuse to be eliminated from any portion of our experience. Can the intellectual life of man, therefore, be divorced from the emotional? From what we have suggested thus far, it is apparent that learning is both intellectual and emotional. And even this statement needs qualification because learning entails man's physical and his social nature, as well as his intellectual and emotional. For our purposes, it is sufficient to emphasize that there is an emotional component to the learning process.

Commins and Fagin (1954) summarize this reasoning when they state that man, encountering a problem, both thinks and feels, and that problems differ with regard to their intellectual and emotional content. Since the emotions do operate in learning, therefore, teachers should understand both the nature of emotions and the way in which they influence learning, and, in turn, are influenced by learning.

THE NATURE OF EMOTIONS

Several theories have been proposed to explain emotional behavior. Among the most famous of these is the James-Lange theory. Hilgard (1962, p. 623) defines the theory as follows:

James-Lange theory. A classical theory of emotion named for the two men who independently proposed it. The theory states that the stimulus first leads to motor responses, and then the awareness of these responses constitutes the experience of emotion.

Simply stated, this means that we are afraid because we run. We react to our bodily responses, which resulted from certain stimuli. The James-Lange theory attracted much attention because it is logical enough, once the initial, ostensible contradiction is accepted. If we analyze an experience that most of us have shared, the appeal of this theory is seen more clearly.

Imagine that you are driving down a main street, with several side streets leading into it, each with a stop sign. For some reason, another driver overlooks the stop sign and comes on the main street just as you approach. Most of us react in an identical manner: we jerk the wheel in an effort to swerve and avoid striking the other car, or we slam on the brakes and attempt to stop before there is a collision. Then, and only then, when the immediate crisis is averted, do we become aware of our emotional reaction. We have first responded physically, and now the weak feeling in the pit of the stomach, the consciousness of the pounding heart, and the hot, flushed feeling in the face become apparent. Note that this all develops *after* the bodily reaction to the exciting stimulus.

This explanation seems incomplete on closer scrutiny. Although we became cognizant of our emotional reaction after we responded, nevertheless, we had instantly perceived the stimulus situation (oncoming car) as threatening. It appears, therefore, that this theory omits part of the total emotional experience.

Cannon and Emergency Reactions

Cannon (1929) was among the first to show the inherent weakness of the James-Lange theory, and also to advance an account of emotional behavior which has guided modern, theoretical interpretations. Emotions disturb the routine of the body and, by so doing, quicken its pace and enable it to cope more effectively with emergencies. The emotions, then, encourage rapid physical responses which permit the organism to organize its behavior, and adjust to this novel encounter. Anderson (1942, pp. 336–337) summarizes this theory as follows:

The essential elements of this theoretical position are (1) the emergency situation which interferes with normal activities and throws the organism out of equilibrium; (2) the energization of the organism to a high degree and the mobilization of its resources in order to meet the emergency situation; (3) meeting the situation both as a result of the display of energy and range of activities called forth; and (4) a modification in the individual's pattern of reaction as a result of the experience.

Watson and Emotions

In Chapter VIII, Watson's classical Behaviorism was presented in our discussion of associationist learning theories. Watson's theory of emotions attracted much attention when it was first proposed because it refuted the hereditary theory of emotions. Watson believed that the infant at birth could experience three emotions: fear, rage, and love.

In his *Behaviorism* (1930, p. 120), he states:

I feel reasonably sure that there are three different forms of emotional response that can be called out at birth by three sets of stimuli. Don't misunderstand me if I call these responses "fear," "rage," and "love." Let me hasten to assure you that while I use the words fear, rage, and love, I want you to strip them of all their old connotations. Please look upon the reactions we designate by them just as you look upon breathing, heart beat, grasping, and other unlearned responses studied in the last chapter.

These emotions are not "feelings" as was formerly thought; they are bodily responses of a predominantly visceral nature. Unconditioned stimuli with unconditioned responses are the basis for acquiring the complicated patterns of behavior which we designate as the emotions.

Thus, these emotions are identical with other bodily reactions, both by nature and in their development. There is conditioning of stimulus and response, and, gradually, the number of stimuli eliciting the response is increased, and the response range is widened. To illustrate this phenomenon in the human, Watson describes the famous case of Albert B. When the infant boy, Albert, first saw a white rat, he manifested no fear. While his attention was on the rat, he was startled by a loud noise. After this, he showed fear of the rat or any furry object. The fear had transferred (Watson, *Behaviorism,* 1930, pp. 125–129).

From these three unlearned responses, the human organism builds complicated emotional patterns by the process of conditioning. In all emotional reactions, visceral and glandular features are most prominent. Heidbreder (1933, p. 249) concludes that the complicated emotional responses of the human result from learning:

The original fear-responses themselves—starting, crying, withdrawing—may become greatly modified by the substitution of their reactions through conditioning. But however wide the ramifications, however intricate the connections, the complex emotional pattern is a product of learning or conditioning.

Watson's conclusions were unable to stand the test of time and experimentation. Observation of emotional responses is an unreliable method because different observers report different emotional causes for certain kinds of behavior (Sherman, 1927). Fear, rage, and love as three distinct, inherited emotions seem unlikely according to the classic work of Bridges (1930).

Today, the search for more satisfactory explanations of emotional behavior is rooted in the physiology of the body. What happens within the individual when a stimulus is identified as threatening? What causes the affective tone of the experience? Do the emotions operate at the subconscious level?

The Physiological Basis of Emotions

Modern inquiries into emotional behavior have an objectivity of technique that was unavailable to the theorists mentioned above. Instruments are readily attainable which measure a subject's skin resistance to electricity. Resistance decreases as perspiration increases. This is called the galvanic skin response (GSR) and reliably reports emotional changes in subjects. X-rays are used to ascertain any changes in the stomach and intestine. The more familiar norms are heartbeat, blood pressure, and the like, and, when the results of all these measurements are joined, a fairly accurate assessment can be made of the body's involvement in emotional behavior.

These quantifications reflect the swift and intense modifications which are occurring within the body. Among these we may mention:

1. The rate of heartbeat quickens and the blood pressure mounts. More oxygen is needed, and it is used more quickly. The circulatory system must speedily furnish and remove materials. This is unquestionably the most significant among the adaptive mechanisms. If we consider the functions of blood and body fluids, their prominence in emotional behavior is obvious. Best and Taylor (1944, pp. 18–19) list some of them as follows:

a. Respiratory. Oxygen is taken from the lungs to the tissues; carbon dioxide is removed from the tissues to the lungs.
b. Nutritive. Nutritive materials are taken from the alimentary canal to the tissues.
c. Excretory. The waste products of metabolism are removed.
d. Protective and regulative. The blood and other body fluids carry chemicals which aid the body at time of infection or injury.

There are other functions, most important of which for a physiological understanding of the emotions is the blood's service in carrying the hormones of the endocrine system to the tissues.

2. Secretions of adrenalin are released into the circulatory system.

3. The pupils of the eyes dilate.

4. Digestion is affected. The familiar loss of appetite is present.

5. Since more oxygen is required, the rate of respiration quickens.

These are some of the physiological changes that occur during emotional behavior. Now the question might be asked: what specifically causes these changes in the human body? In Chapter II, brief mention was made of the autonomic nervous system with its control of man's involuntary acts. Recall that there are two divisions of the autonomic nervous system, the sympathetic and the parasympathetic, each of which is frequently antagonistic in its action on any organ. Where one excites, the other usually inhibits. The chief exception to this is the adrenal gland, which is linked only with the sympathetic division and is excitatory in nature.

Present knowledge of the action of the sympathetic and parasympathetic divisions of the autonomic nervous system seems to suggest that a positive-negative factor is associated with this division. Olds, Travis, and Schwing (1960) state that reward effects result from stimulation of that section of the brain which controls parasympathetic action. Schneirla (1959) makes the statement that, in the animal kingdom, a weak stimulus causes parasympathetic action and approach movements, while stronger stimuli cause sympathetic action and withdrawal movements.

Usually, the sympathetic division is dominant in the more intense emotional reactions, while the parasympathetic predominates in milder emotional states. The central nervous system also acts during emotional responses. It causes actions such as frowning, laughing, and muscular tension by its control of the skeletal muscles. As Hilgard (1962, p. 163) concludes:

What we do know with assurance is that intense emotions involve profound changes throughout the body, which are regulated in a complex way by the central nervous system, by both divisions of the autonomic system, and by the endocrine glands.

Research continues to add to our knowledge of emotional be-havior. There is increased speculation today that man possesses a regulator of his emotional responses. This is commonly referred to as the reticular arousal system, or the reticular activating system. It is a mass of neurons which reaches from the top of the spinal cord into the thalamus and hypothalamus. It appears that all avenues of communication pass through the reticular system, both receptor and effector.

There also appears to be evidence that the reticular activating system has a selective kind of effect on the action of muscles and glands. This is extremely important in emotional behavior, espe-cially for the key role of the endocrine glands. The master endo-crine gland is, of course, the pituitary, and it is controlled by the brain, specifically, the hypothalamus. Sensory nerves "report" to the hypothalamus, which then sends "orders" to the pituitary. The re-ticular activating system seems to control a wide range of bodily muscular and glandular responses (Woolridge, 1963). Glickman (1960) has shown that stimulation of various points of the reticular system causes approach and withdrawal behavior. Thus, it appears to be responsible for an orientation reaction which is based upon the selective nature of the reticular arousal system.

New and promising information about the physiological founda-tion of emotion will steadily add to our knowledge about the emo-tional state itself. This is an excellent example of the benefits which accrue from an interdisciplinary approach to psychological prob-lems. From our knowledge of the contribution of the body to emo-tional states, it is possible now to reassemble the segments of "emotion" and examine it again as a whole.

The Three Faces of Emotion

When we inspect an emotion, we see that, psychologically, it is one event composed of three discernible parts:

1. The first, and perhaps most important, element in emotional behavior is the feeling which the individual experiences. This may range from pleasant to unpleasant, from attention to rejection (Schlosberg, 1954). It is interesting to note that formerly (recall the work of the early behaviorists) emotion as feeling was a sus-picious concept because it could not be observed and measured.

Only the overt characteristics deserved the term "emotion." The appearances of an emotional reaction can be induced (such as quickened breath and accelerated heartbeat), but the subject is unable to arouse any impression of pleasantness or unpleasantness. It is highly unlikely that this experience could be designated "emotional."

2. The second element also is not easily discernible; this is the visceral. We have discussed this rather extensively in the preceding section, so it will only be briefly mentioned here. The changes in blood pressure, pulse rate, and so forth are included in this category.

3. The last element is that of skeletal behavior. Here the person expresses his emotion by some kind of physical reaction. If the emotion is happiness, the person may laugh. If it is anger, he may clench his fists and strike somebody or something. If it is fear, he may run.

As we have observed, some psychologists thought emotions could only apply to the overt characteristics of the specific type of behavior. Conversely, others have stated that only the feeling that attends these visceral and skeletal reactions is the true emotion.

Actually, it seems much more logical to view emotions as the entire system of reactions: skeletal, visceral, and feeling. Once a stimulus situation is perceived as emotional, the nervous system sends impulses to the endocrine system, which releases its hormones into the bloodstream to be carried to the tissues. Then the visceral changes begin to occur, followed by a skeletal reaction. Throughout the experience, the individual is sustaining definite feeling. To reject any part of the total reaction would leave the emotional state incomplete and unfit for classification as an emotion.

THE DEVELOPMENT OF EMOTIONS

Of all the attempts to trace the origin and development of emotions, none has made a more lasting impact than that of Bridges (1930, 1932). Daily observations of the emotional behavior of sixty-two infants led her to the conclusion that there are three main kinds of change in their emotional development. The initial responses following birth are undifferentiated and are made to diffuse situations. Gradually, more specific reactions occur to more specific stimuli, and the process of differentiation begins. While this is happening, the method of specific emotional response is undergoing modification. Bridges gives the example of anger expressed by an eighteen-month-old differing from that expressed by a ten-month-old child.

Excitement and Distress

The children in her study had an age range of under one month to two years. From her observation of the infants under one month, she feels that there is no basis for postulating the three intact emotions of fear, rage, and love. Rather, the child manifests an indefinite type of agitation or excitement upon the appearance of any intense stimuli. This prompted Bridges to hypothesize that excitement probably is the original emotion.

Since excitement is common to all infants, and since it usually is a response to feelings of unpleasantness, Bridges is uncertain if the expression of distress which infants display is a native emotion, or if it is a form of differentiation from excitement. Because kicking and crying, however, bring relief from uncomfortable circumstances, they quickly become associated with disagreeable stimuli. Bridges, therefore, theorizes that distress is differentiated from excitement almost directly after birth because the two emotions are observable in a three-week-old infant.

Delight

Delight, as a distinct emotional reaction, makes its appearance much later than distress. After the source of discomfort is removed, or upon patting a one-month-old infant, there is little reaction other than passivity. This certainly cannot be classified as emotional. By three months, Bridges felt that the children in her study were evincing the emotion of delight rather than mere excitement or repose.

Delight is discriminated from sheer excitement by such characteristics as the lack of tension in the muscles, smiles, and squeals which are totally different from the anger screams. From three months, the child demonstrates delight in an increasingly differentiated fashion. These expressions of pleasure slowly transfer to individuals, and, with some youngsters, affection for one nurse rather than another was evident by the age of six months. Affection for individuals seems, however, most frequently, to emerge between twelve and twenty-four months.

Affection, then, has its origin in the delight of being fondled, patted, and so forth. It transfers to familiar individuals initially, and then to playmates.

Continued Differentiation

After the child passes the age of three months, when delight is clearly distinguished, other definite emotional responses begin to materialize rapidly. Fear, disgust, and anger all were clearly seen during the three- to six-month period.

All of these succeeding emotional states are added to the original display of excitement and, later, to distress and delight. As new emotions appear, they are attached to the previous emotions; they do not eliminate them. A person's emotional capacity becomes the total of these identified emotions.

Between six and twelve months, the child evidences elation and affection, and, from twelve to twenty-four months, affection is differentiated into affection for adults and affection for children, joy is differentiated from delight, and jealousy is differentiated from distress.

When we reflect upon Bridges' findings, it seems that, throughout life, the state of excitement is the thread of emotional continuity. From this main trunk of emotion, man commences to form distinct types of excitement, first distress, soon followed by delight. From the distress branch, fear, anger, disgust, and, finally, jealousy separate into clear, well-defined emotional states. From the delight branch, elation, affection (for adults and for children), and, finally, joy emanates. The age at which the various emotions appear is not rigid and inflexible. As in all aspects of growth and development, it is a highly individual transformation.

The Pace of Differentiation

When we inspect Bridge's theory, it is clear that, in tracing the development of the various emotions, there is a sharp dichotomy between the pleasant and the unpleasant. This is the familiar continuum which most psychologists accept as basic for analysis. As the child matures, the differentiation which we discussed, and which occurred so swiftly, begins to slacken.

By the time the youngster enters school his ability both to express and to control his emotions should be adequate to insure the necessary social adjustment. Refinement in development, expression, and control now slows considerably. Different stimuli are forcing the youth to adjust his emotional responses. This is the great tool of differentiation as the child ages.

He begins to specify what objects, people, and events bring him pleasure. He commences to select the pleasant stimuli in his environment by a more rational processs. Similarly, when confronted by an unpleasant situation, the child learns to organize his behavior and to ascertain if he has adequate responses to master the problem; if not, the child tries to determine how they can be attained.

The Pattern of Development

It is in the person's response to the entire range of emotional experiences, pleasant to unpleasant, that we see the place of learning. If the emotion overwhelms the individual, behavior becomes quickly disorganized; if controlled, it becomes a powerful motivating agent. Also, the learning process acts on the emotions and, to a great extent, aids the individual in the struggle to gain ascendancy over the emotions.

Formal learning and maturation are not the only factors that shape the emotions. Another major agent in the emotional development of a youth is his social environment. How stable are the adults who represent authority for him? Are the home conditions conducive to sound emotional growth?

Although the degree to which a child's emotional responses are influenced by the members of his immediate environment demands classification as a part of the learning process, nevertheless it deserves separate study. This is a kind of emotional learning by imitation which is not initiated by the school and not directed at specific objectives. It is an incidental, but vigorous, force in the growth and development of any youngster. As such, it cannot be overlooked in any discussion of the dynamics of emotion.

Certainly, a youngster's physical condition will have much to do with the pattern of his emotional development. If anything is physically amiss, there is the constant danger that frustration and anger may cause a warped personality. Acceptance of self in the adjustment to the environment is a potent factor for healthy emotional growth.

Another contributing agent to the emotional development of the human being is the culture itself. It often determines what emotions an individual can express. For example, the American male is never expected to cry. This is far from true in many other cultures. How this suppression affects the emotional development of American men is difficult to say, but it surely does affect them in some way.

Society expects the maturing person to inhibit his emotions; to control them so that they do not become a source of embarrassment to himself, or others. Where is the line to be drawn between healthy suppression and healthy expression? With our present knowledge, the behavioral scientists have left the decision mostly to the individual, as long as, either way, he does not interfere with others.

The school has aided most individuals in the development of unique but socially acceptable patterns of expression.

THE EMOTIONS AND LEARNING

How has learning functioned in the process of development and adjustment just mentioned? Of its importance in emotional development, there can be little doubt. From our comments, we see that maturation and learning are vital for an individual's emotional health. When we speak of schools, the imitation of adults and the demands of culture, we are referring to the impact that the learning process has on emotional behavior.

While differentiation is occurring, the learning process accompanies it and begins to cause significant modifications. The child learns to specify emotions, and also learns what reaction is suitable for a particular situation. He also learns to discriminate among stimuli, and to assess them more realistically. For example, stimuli which once resulted in an intense fear reaction now assume a more neutral, or indifferent, classification. The child has *learned* which stimuli are actually threatening, or actually pleasant.

Conditioning

Conditioning is an effective instrument in emotional learning. Often the emotion that is attached to a particular stimulus shifts to the neutral stimuli that are present at the time of the emotional reaction. A person, who is attending the theatre when a fire starts, frequently transfers the fear that was aroused on that occasion to other similar situations, such as a church or hall. Of course, this is a negative reaction, and we are more concerned here with the positive aspects of learning upon the emotions.

The individual, particularly the child, and occasionally the adult, usually is unaware of the process just described. When the person does not know the cause of his feeling, he cannot understand why he feels the way he does. This is the frightening part of emotional behavior, and it is commonly the source of the disorganization of behavior.

The Conscious Reaction

Learning should aid in the identification and comprehension of the origin of our emotional states. Anderson (1942) draws a close parallel between emotion and learning. Recall his description of the essential elements of an emotional reaction: the emergency situation, energization of the organism, meeting the situation, and modification of the reaction pattern.

If we compare the emotional reaction to learning, we can interchange a problem for the emergency situation; for mobilizing resources, we can interchange the range of trial-and-error behavior; and for the modification of the reaction pattern, we can interchange learning. The resulting modification of behavior reduces the drive within the person because he has achieved his goal, that is, he has eliminated or reduced the intensity of the emotion.

Again, we note the characteristics which accompany learning. A motivated individual is driven toward a goal by an emotion. An obstacle is present since the person is unsure of an immediate, accurate response. His perception of the environmental stimuli informs him that the situation is threatening, frustrating, or pleasant.

Because of his perception, he now decides upon a specific response pattern. If successful, the internal tension or the exciting nature of the emotion decreases. If unsuccessful, he must reevaluate his perception of the stimuli and again modify his response pattern.

At this stage, there is a significant difference between emotional learning and other forms of learning. If an individual is frustrated by some type of cognitive problem, discouragement may cause him to abandon his attempt at solution. Or, his objectives may exert a sufficiently strong force to compel him to try again.

Consider the consequences of an unsuccessful reaction to threatening stimuli. Will the individual attempt to reorganize his behavior to combat a fearful situation? If he is reacting on the conscious level, he may try again. This is the goal of learning, that is, to enable the person, consciously, to continue his efforts to discover both the cause of the emotion and a suitable response pattern.

Unfortunately, very often panic is the result of an unsuccessful response. This is true under a variety of conditions and need not be confined to the more spectacular examples, such as fire, accidents, and so forth. A student, faced with an important examination, is unable to answer the first few questions. Instead of omitting these questions for the present, he frequently spends a disproportionate amount of time on them, and the remaining questions are neglected. Or, he is thrown into such a state of confusion that the entire examination suffers.

Youngsters, however, can learn to react rationally under emotional circumstances. Many occasions arise in a classroom where a thoughtful teacher can contribute much to emotional development. Some children, for example, have a genuine fear of thunderstorms. If a teacher takes the time to correlate a lesson in science or geography with actual storm conditions, frightened children start to learn what causes thunderstoms, the relative safety that comes from adequate provision, and what they can do while the storm continues. If they learn this in school, it will transfer to home and other locations.

Similarly, the adolescent soon learns to control his anger, and he then expresses it in such a way that it will actually benefit him. As he matures, he discovers that the uncontrollable rages and temper tantrums are distasteful to everyone. He learns from his own observations, from imitation, and from direct instruction by adults and teachers how he can control these outbursts, and how he can utilize these intense emotions. So the teenager no longer cries out in rage or strikes in anger. Instead, he uses the energy to better himself, to strive harder in competition, and to control this emotion and achieve healthy adjustment.

Emotional control can be acquired. The characteristics of both emotional reactions and learning are sufficiently similar to warrant instruction, incidental though it must be, in the achievement of emotional control. Since learning acts on the emotions, the question may be asked: do the emotions affect learning?

LEARNING AND THE EMOTIONS

Undoubtedly, when stimuli are perceived as emotional, they will influence the learning process. If the emotion is so intense that behavior becomes confused, the emotion dominates learning and disrupts a logical response sequence. Occasionally, however, controlled emotion is a needed stimulus to learning. As we shall see, the exciting emotions, unless strictly controlled, are a barrier to the organization of behavior, while less intense states, both pleasant and unpleasant, may be a necessary prod to action.

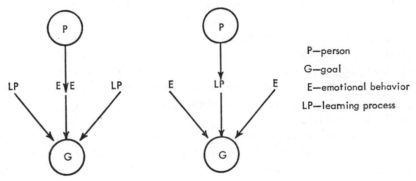

P—person
G—goal
E—emotional behavior
LP—learning process

FIGURE 11-1. *Learning and the Emotions: An Interactive Process*

For example, the pleasure that is associated with certain tasks, because of previous success, is a spur to learning that particular task. Fear of failure, if restrained, often will provide an added urge to succeed. It is the intensity of the emotion as well as its control which determine its positive or negative character for learning.

We see, then, that the emotions act on learning, as the learning process acted on emotional behavior. It is well to reinforce this idea because, again, we have analyzed a whole into parts for better understanding. What we are depicting here is an interactive process which can be illustrated as shown in Figure 11-1. In the figure it is evident that, while the emotion is affecting learning, the person is learning how to control and use his emotions.

Man's emotions are not distinct from man. What *arouses* the person is thought of as extrinsic, but his perception and reaction are intrinsic, and highly personal. Consequently, the person *uses* the emotion for better or worse. It serves a purpose; to the individual, it is an adaptive reaction. From lack of knowledge, a tense situation may cause a person to think only of running away. Another, more experienced person may reflect, determine what is producing the threat, and either remove or avoid it. The emotion, man's modification of it, that is, control, and use of the emotion all are part of a unitary process. It is *man's* fear; not an external fear pressing upon man.

Physiology, Learning, and the Emotions

There is substantial evidence that the emotions are active in the early phases of any kind of learning (Berlyne, 1964). Again, we note the need to study emotional behavior as a whole; it cannot be removed from any aspect of man's behavioral pattern. Wynne and Solomon (1955) carried out experiments with dogs which had their autonomic nervous systems impaired. They were then unable to learn avoidance responses, but they retained those responses previously acquired.

More sophisticated techniques are yielding much the same results with humans. Obrist (1950) found the galvanic skin response to be most evident when subjects were in the initial stage of learning nonsense syllables.

Among the more interesting findings are those of Walker (1962) and Kleinsmith and Kaplan (1963). While testing the recall of paired-associate verbal material, they discovered that immediate recall was less for the pairs which caused the most intense galvanic skin responses. After a time lapse, however, these were recalled more successfully than the others. The investigators concluded that there was interference during the immediate recall of the pairs which produced the more intense GSR. A strong emotional reaction appears to hinder immediate recall during the initial phases of the learning process, but, once learning is complete, it appears to aid learning and recall over a longer period of time.

Specific Emotions and Learning

Although an extended discussion of man's emotions is beyond the scope of this section, the nature of certain of the more obvious emotions, and their place in the learning process, deserves comment. From our discussion, it should be clear that the child and the adult express similar emotions. It is only the extent and quality of the emotional reaction that differ. A child lacks the experience to judge realistically the arousing properties of a stimulus. Thus, he is much more easily aroused.

The implications for learning are both positive and negative. Since children are readily stimulated, it is a fairly simple task to develop in young children an enthusiasm for school and its work. But, the dangers of emotional arousal are as real as the rewards are promising. The risk of nonpromotion can be meaningless to a youngster, whereas denial of a privilege because of a misdemeanor may cause an intense disturbance in the same child. At the secondary level, a "loss of face" before one's friends is far more damaging than a low academic mark that could, conceivably, jeopardize future college entrance.

Also, a child may demonstrate his emotions more freely than an adult, and thus rid himself of them quite rapidly. The school should capitalize on this and distract the youngster from a negative emotional experience; otherwise, the learning process will be crippled for the day. The boy who has just had a fight in the yard, if allowed to brood, will hardly be receptive for social studies or science.

All boys who found themselves in a situation where the boy just mentioned decided to fight will not react in the same fashion. Teachers should recollect that there are considerable differences among students of the same age, grade, or sex. Not only is there a difference among the various children, but there is also a difference in the same child at different times. On one occasion, a test failure may cause withdrawal; on another occasion, it may make the youngster belligerent; on yet another, fear may begin to build in the child. Understanding children, and recognizing the true emotion for what it is, permit the teacher to remove the emotional stimulus or apply it, if necessary, and thus proceed with the teacher-learning task. Some of the more common emotions as well as their educational overtones are explored here.

Affection

The average child is friendly and has approach reactions directed to persons, things, or events which are associated with pleasant experiences. His affective attitude depends upon his treatment by others in his environment. His need for affection in infancy is linked with his parents. Later it transfers outside the home to his peers.

The human being needs a feeling of security (recall Maslow's hierarchy of motives). If the need for affection is satisfied, a child gradually begins to offer his own affection to others. Love, respect, and companionship, if found in the home, result in a healthy attitude toward a person's associates, including classmates and teachers. Jersild (1963) states that, at the elementary school level, children manifest their need for affection in their wish to be accepted by their peers, and by the manner in which they describe the kind qualities of their teachers.

If a child feels unwanted in school, his motivation will be negligible; without motivation, there will be little, if any, learning. As we have insisted throughout this book, a motivated individual is the prime requisite for learning. The opposite also holds true. By capitalizing on the affectionate side of man's nature, the school is able to aid learning by the student's desire to please his parents and teachers, and remain with his friends. This is equally true for secondary, as well as elementary, school pupils. Perhaps it must be more subtle with teenagers, nonetheless it is as effective.

Anger

The range of emotional reaction from resentment to rage is usually designated as anger. Anger in some occasions is a healthy reaction for the normal human being. If someone unjustly attacks him or his family, anger is an indication of a rational, normal individual. It is the manner in which anger is expressed that reflects a person's control of his emotions.

Jersild (1963) mentions that the expression of anger eventually involves the child in a dual struggle: with others and with himself. The chief causes of a child's anger are frustration and thwarting.

The very young child (birth to about four years) reacts angrily in explosive, aggressive behavior of a general kind. After four years, the youngster's anger begins to be directed at the specific object or person whom he feels to be responsible for his difficulty (Goodenough, 1931).

Temper tantrums, which some primary grade teachers know only too well, begin to decrease as a youngster's wrath is directed at particular causes, that is, from three to four years of age. Occasionally, they briefly reappear at the age of seven or eight. It is interesting to note that, during these developmental changes, verbal behavior is substituted for the more overt, physical expressions of the person's drives.

Learning is prevailing upon the emotions in such a way that not only is the child's method of expressing his anger changing, but the stimulus conditions which produce the anger are also changing. The manner in which those in authority respond to a youngster's display of anger will largely determine the way in which this emotion influences the person's response pattern.

If parents accept a child's abilities and limitations, they will not expect him to perform tasks or to achieve far beyond his ability. Such a sensible appraisal of a child's talents enables both the child and parent to remove many potentially frustrating encounters. Unfortunately, this is easier said then done. Parents often find it impossible to judge objectively their children's capacities.

Parents also should be consistent in their treatment of children. If parents exert harsh authority one day and then allow the use of the car the next day for the same offense, both actions are highly unlikely to produce desirable behavior. When children realize what they can and cannot do and what the consequences will be if they explode, uncertainty is removed, and a fairly steady pattern of behavior will be the result.

Much the same is true of the school and a child's learning. Teachers should react in an identical manner as parents. That is, they should judge students fairly, expect consistent behavior, and they themselves should respond to violations in a consistent manner.

Children bring their emotions, and their ways of expressing them, to the classroom. If they are undisciplined in their responses, the learning process will be seriously jeopardized. There is nothing that dissipates energy as rapidly as anger. Motivation disappears, the goal is obscured, perception of desirable environmental stimuli is distorted, and the response pattern, which was intended to achieve an educational objective, is shattered. The characteristics of the learning process fade, and learning fails.

As the child matures and learns what is thought to be acceptable behavior, he likewise learns to suppress the explosive side of anger. This does not mean that anger disappears. Jersild (1963, p. 292) quotes Harry Stark Sullivan as saying that it is easier to swallow anger than to digest it. Quite the opposite is frequently true. A person may adopt an entirely different expression to hide his anger, that is, a smiling face may conceal seething anger. That is why it is so difficult to judge an emotion from its overt expression. Teachers would do well to be skeptical of surface appearances and to seek constantly the causes of emotion. If a student responds to an emotional situation in a totally unexpected manner, a teacher should be on his guard for possible future trouble.

Finally, a statement by Jersild (1963), pp. 295–296) summarizes an ideal reaction to an emotional outburst:

It is difficult to deal wisely with an angry child because a display of anger is likely to arouse anger in the person against whom it is directed. Few parents or teachers are so robust that they are immune to this tendency, and it is helpful to recognize this and not feel guilty about it. However, when an episode of anger is over and feelings have calmed down, it is possible for an adult to try to look at the child's anger from a larger point of view: What can be learned from it? Why was the child so angry? What touched him off? Why are his feelings so raw and sensitive on the issue that aroused him? Was he perhaps striving anxiously to protect his pride? What weakness might the anger-provoking circumstance threaten to expose? What might this flare-up of anger reveal concerning the expectations he places on himself or on others? What long-standing grievance might he be harboring?

Fear

As with the other emotions that we have discussed, a moderate amount of fear is a welcome ingredient in an individual's adjustment to his environment. To know when to be afraid is a sign of an intelligent person. The overwhelming fear which panics and disrupts behavior, however, too often persists from childhood into adult life. Persons who are terrified of height, of crowds, or by thunder and lightning are examples of the lasting effects of some fears which have their roots in childhood.

Emotional states which arise from feelings of insecurity are not dependent upon age—they can occur at any age. A person needs to feel confident in his relations with others and in his reaction to daily, challenging situations. Otherwise, there is a real danger that such a person will retreat from the ordinary relationships of normal life and, eventually, lose contact with reality.

Because children's emotions are aroused very simply, both by real and imaginary fears, they must quickly learn to differentiate between what is to be feared and what is to be ignored. This is the task of learning. Studies by Jersild and Holmes (1935, 1935) showed that there is radical change in children's fears at different ages. The child under six or seven fears loud noises, falling, strangers, darkness, and so forth. These fears gradually diminish and another set of fears becomes active.

Angelino, Dollins, and Mech (1956) report that youngsters nine to eighteen show a marked increase in educational fears and fears related to social relations. Children of this age are concerned about the consequences of school failure. In today's society, where the necessity and value of a college education are impressed upon youngsters from early childhood, school-related fears are becoming more plentiful. This is also associated with an alarming increase in the percentage of college students who are subject to emotional disturbances because of parental and societal pressure to be admitted to college, to achieve at a high level (perhaps an unrealistic level), and to graduate, preferably with honors. An even more subtle type of educational pressure is begining to appear: in an age of specialization, the college gradually is experiencing keen competition for admission to prestigious graduate schools.

Not only educational fears, but several other fears, continue into adult life. From his studies, Jersild (1963, p. 265) states that among the fears which persist into the later years are fear of animals, bodily harm, the unknown, and being alone. When we add these to the adult's newly acquired list of fears (illness, death, job security, and so forth), we realize that the normal human being carries a heavy load of fears.

The school, then, must help youngsters to control their fears and make certain that fear does not disturb the learning process. We have indicated how learning aids in the achievement of emotional control, and it should now be apparent that fear can totally remove the child from any commitment to learning. When fear overwhelms the individual, it dominates him, in mind and body. We traced the physiological reaction to intense emotion. The intellectual reaction is no less obvious. When fear controls, the individual is unable to think of anything else.

Sometimes it is difficult to eliminate the fears which youngsters bring to school, but they must be extinguished if there is to be successful academic achievement. Teachers should determine the cause of a child's fear, and then bring the child to an understanding of the situation from which the fear arises. This implies providing children with the needed information, in a manner which they can interpret. Usually a child cannot be talked out of fear. Examples of desirable behavior by others, under similar conditions, is an effective method. This, coupled with successful achievement and enjoyable activity, has positive tension-reducing value. Whatever method is adopted, teachers must recognize and help youngsters to overcome the fears which can very easily destroy learning.

CONCLUSION

In this chapter, an effort was made to emphasize the importance of the emotions to the learning process. The emotions can either aid learning or disrupt the process. The difficulty of defining emotion was discussed, as was the problem of attributing a specific emotion to a specific cause. Finally, the interaction of the emotions and learning was analyzed.

What can the school do to help children develop into emotionally healthy adults? First, teachers must be aware that youngsters bring their emotions into the classroom. Second, there can be no neglect of emotional behavior, since, unfortunately, it not only may block learning for the individual, but it may also interrupt the learning process for an entire class. Teachers must ascertain the exact cause of the emotion and help students to recognize and assess emotional stimuli realistically. Third, the classroom atmosphere must be such that success is possible and conditions are conducive for learning to act on, and help control, the emotions. Finally, teachers must accept the positive side of emotional behavior and try to utilize it to facilitate learning.

It is not the function of the school to strip students of their emotional reactions. Rather, it should be the school's purpose to assist students to accept the emotions which they have, to regulate and use their emotions, and to express them in such a way that the emotions benefit both the individual and society.

CHAPTER XII

Classroom Atmosphere and Learning

INTRODUCTION

THE TEACHER slowly paced back and forth across the front of the room as he talked to the class. In the rear of the room, a boy slowly eased his books toward the edge of his desk. As the teacher turned to emphasize a point, the boy gave the books a final nudge. The loud clatter startled everyone and interrupted the class discussion. The teacher stopped his pacing; the boy mumbled something and bent to retrieve the books. As the teacher resumed the lesson, the boy again dropped his books. At this, some of the class laughed; others glanced at the teacher. What would he do?

Probably there is no teacher who, at some time in his career, has not experienced such problems and recognized their seriousness. So much depends on the teacher's reaction to disciplinary problems, but two items seem worthy of special attention. First, a teacher's career may be at stake because, if he is unable to control a class, both discouragement and failure will drive him from the profession. This is harsh, but it is reality. A teacher will have a feeling of dread every time he enters a classroom. Students sense this doubt and anxiety and are quick to capitalize on it. Rather than face such a feeling each morning, many potentially fine teachers decide to seek employment elsewhere. There are many possible reasons for such happenings, and foremost among them is the lack of preparation most prospective teachers receive. Encountering such a difficult environment, many sincere teachers blame themselves and flee from the classroom. Ironically, the fault is not theirs. Much of the blame rests on the teacher-training institution that prepared them. They were not equipped to handle the troublesome, delinquency-prone youngsters whom they encounter.

The second noteworthy item of a teacher's reaction to disciplinary problems centers on the learning process. Everything for which the school stands is threatened by an unhealthy classroom atmosphere. How much learning results when the classroom discipline is either too rigid or too lax? If a teacher consistently frightens, intimidates, and bullies students, little learning occurs. Creativity and inquiry are stifled. Students are unwilling to risk ridicule and abuse. Unfortunately, in too many classrooms, it is the teacher who is abused and bullied, and, again, little learning results.

The classroom environment contains the ingredients which either encourage or discourage learning. Courses and texts in the psychology of learning have an obligation to stress that academic stimuli, motivation, goal achievement, and the like, are useless if an atmosphere conducive to learning is lacking. And much depends on the teacher—his use of authority, his response to crises, and, in general, his manipulation of the materials and personnel in his room.

For example, consider the illustration with which this chapter began. Should the teacher ignore the incident and thereby encourage similar difficulties? Should he send the offender to the principal for discipline and thereby indirectly inform the remainder of the class that he is incapable of controlling them? Should he react immediately to the disturbance and attempt to handle it himself in his own classroom?

Many readers might question the last alternative because it momentarily disrupts the class; it makes them tense and will undoubtedly result in negligible learning for the duration of the period. Granted; this is an accurate statement with which few would disagree. However, it is far better to lose one period by a display of firmness than to lose an entire year, perhaps even a career.

Most teachers with experience will develop a fairly decisive manner of responding to routine disciplinary problems. What disturbs many new and unexperienced teachers, is that many of today's disciplinary cases are *not* routine; they represent a reaction against society that cannot be designated as "growing up" or "letting off steam." These are the problems for which many teachers are unprepared and for which they themselves have no reaction pattern. There is a type of youngster who responds to no appeal, who disregards discipline, who just wants to get out of that school, and who is willing to try almost anything to achieve this goal.

Can learning progress when the classroom atmosphere is filled with such feeling? Hardly. But, if teachers know at least something about this increasing phenomenon, they are able to react so that the offender receives guidance (or is removed from the class, which might be necessary), and some learning results until the problem is resolved. If teachers realize that they are not alone with such a class and that there are many others undergoing identical trials, they may feel reassured. Also, if they are familiar with the background and nature of such maladjustments, they may be able to initiate remedial action in sufficient time to help the student and to prevent classroom disorders which are so disastrous to the learning process. Teachers should realize that experienced, as well as inexperienced, teachers face such troubles and that such incidents happen in wealthy, as well as poor, communities. A teacher will be greatly helped if he knows something about delinquency, its symptoms and causes, in school and out.

THE PROBLEM

Delinquency has assumed the proportion of a national problem. There is a steadily increasing number of delinquents appearing before our courts. The Bureau of Census predicts that in the 1960's the population will be such that the United States will have fifty per cent more boys and girls in the ten to seventeen years of age group than in 1955. Therefore, it is readily seen why figures predicting delinquency in the 1960's assume astonishing dimensions.

The shocking part of these figures is that they represent only a fraction of the actual delinquents, because these are the boys and girls who have been apprehended and whose cases have been adjudicated. What of the others, who either have not been apprehended, who are treated by private agencies, or who are shielded from the law? As Kvaraceus (1954) points out, because only a small portion of children who engage in delinquent behavior are actually brought to court, delinquents who get into court can hardly be taken as representative of delinquents in general.

The majority of boys and girls appearing before juvenile court are between fifteen and seventeen years of age. Table 12-1 will show the wide range of delinquent behavior exhibited by America's delinquents. Boys (and girls) guilty of such deeds are not the average disciplinary case, but these youngsters do appear in school until apprehension and confinement.

TABLE 12-1

1963 JUVENILE ARREST STATISTICS (abridged) [a]

Under 18

Murder	477
Negligent manslaughter	199
Robbery	9,963
Assault	9,473
Burglary	85,151
Larceny	160,089
Auto theft	54,417

[a] Federal Bureau of Investigation, *Uniform Crime Reports for the United States.* Annual Bulletin (Washington: Government Printing Office, 1963), p. 108.

What is being done to combat this growing menace to society? Nation, state, county, city, town, and private organizations are banding together for a coordinated attack on the problem. There are two distinct aspects to this attack:

1. There is an increase in the type of research that leads to a greater understanding and knowledge of the nature of delinquency.

2. More careful and comprehensive research studies are being carried forward concerning *prevention* of the delinquent act.

With regard to understanding the nature of delinquency, it is becoming increasingly clear that criminal or delinquent behavior cannot be explained by any one element. Criminal activity involving the child or adult involves a human being possessed of a free will and living in a society which is becoming increasingly more complex. A study of the causation of delinquency reveals that economic, social, political, and moral factors underly misbehavior.

Therefore, authorities investigating delinquency are agreed that its causes are multiple, complex, and interactive (Mihanovich, 1950, p. 35).

The youth of America are being brought up in the midst of new notions of happiness and new values. Prevalent today are changing attitudes of law and order, the results of which may be seen in any juvenile court. The influences acting upon a youngster during the formative years of ten to seventeen produce results which must be analyzed in each individual case. Nevertheless, such influences may be brought together into certain categories such as home, church, school, and community. While these categories encompass wide areas of human activity, a few specific examples will illustrate the manner in which they react and combine in the individual to cause or prevent delinquent behavior. Even though these factors may be considered causative, caution must be urged lest any one of them be considered as *the* cause of delinquency. Seldom, if ever, does a youngster become delinquent because of any one factor. Rather, delinquency is the result of a combination of forces.

Certain influences within each category do appear with remarkable frequency. Among these may be included:

1. Home Conditions. Divorce, desertion, separation, poor discipline, immorality, emotional disturbances, and criminality in the home.
2. Church. Lack of religion, nonattendance at religious services, no moral values, inadequate facilities, and untrained personnel on church staffs.
3. School. Poor teaching, lack of proper curriculum, poor guidance, lack of sufficient vocational training, inadequate facilities, and so forth.
4. Community. Lack of interest in the problems of youth, salacious literature, improper movies and television programs, poor court facilities for juvenile action, lack of proper recreational outlets, and scarcity of trained officers.

These are some of the causative forces at work in any one delinquent. These influences are external to the individual and act upon him. What of the youngster, his attitudes, thought patterns, and habits? It is also necessary to focus attention on the delinquent to ascertain if there are any pertinent individual characteristics that might be considered significant. Studies by the Gluecks (1952), Kvaraceus (1954), Mihanovich (1950), and Healy and Bronner (1936) have attempted to isolate these characteristics.

The personal characteristics most frequently observed are:

1. Intelligence. Formerly, mental deficiency seemed to be the chief cause of delinquency. More recently, however, intelligence of delinquents appears to be only slightly lower than nondelinquents; in certain intelligence tests, such as the Wechsler-Bellevue, delinquents frequently are superior in the nonverbal section. As a general conclusion, we may state that on the usual intelligence test delinquents' scores are lower on sections requiring some cultural achievement. This assumes special significance when the academic climate of our schools is considered. School failure may be causative as far as antisocial behavior is concerned.

2. Age at onset of initial delinquent behavior. Authorities are almost unanimous in agreement that signs of deviate behavior originate very early in life. Unfavorable home conditions are usually responsible for delinquents making a bad start. In analyzing the age of delinquents involved in their study, the Gluecks (1952, p. 12) state:

In addition to their record of official delinquencies, as determined by court appearances, arrests, convictions, and commitments, a study in retrospect of the first clear, true signs of the delinquents' social maladaption—stealing, truancy, etc.—reveals that nearly half of them showed evidences of maladaption before their eighth year, and another two-fifths before their eleventh year, making a total of 88% whose anti-social conduct was already unmistakable before puberty. The average age at the onset of their anti-social behavior proved to be 8.3 years, in contrast with the average age of 12.4 years at their first court appearance.

This finding is of great importance, particularly to schools, because it shows that delinquent tendencies appear at an early age. This is the age when preventive measures should be undertaken.

3. Personality. As a group, the delinquents exhibit less self-control than nondelinquents, are more impulsive, and tend to act out their emotional conflicts. As a group, they are more restless, active, and defiant of authority. Therefore, these personality traits and emotional tendencies frequently make it difficult for this type of youth to adjust to society's concept of law and order.

4. Interests. The interests and activities of the delinquents tend to be more adventurous and harmful than nondelinquents. Sullen-

ger (1936, p. 46) states that fifty-five per cent of the delinquents studied found trouble while seeking recreation. Delinquents prefer to spend their free time on street corners, pool rooms, and arcades, rather than at home or at playgrounds or other places of supervised activity. A favorite form of recreation among delinquents is attendance at the movies, particularly those movies with criminal or adventure themes. Another important consideration is today's means of transportation. The city boy or girl seeking excitement merely goes to the subway, or a car, and moves to another neighborhood or town in search of adventure. Not being known in this new environment, he is more prone to activities that lead to trouble.

5.   Physical Features. A decided change has been noted in the latest research on the physical characteristics of delinquents. The Gluecks' study shows that delinquent boys had sturdier, stronger bodies and were more muscular than the nondelinquents (1950, pp. 316–325). In a study conducted by Healy and Bronner, the delinquents were found to be in as good physical condition as average school children (1936, p. 56). Burt concluded in his study that most delinquents are normal rather than diseased (1933, p. 596). This is an interesting outcome since it was formerly believed that the delinquent was often physically defective. The correlation between physical endowment and delinquency has received inadequate attention in most studies. The significance of the present findings is vague, but there is a reversal of earlier views.

6.   Economic Factors. Unemployment and the resort to welfare agencies are typical of the majority of the families of delinquents. This cannot be a universal statement because delinquency knows no financial boundaries, but it may be safely stated that delinquents are more likely to come from needy homes. Behind the more apparent causes of delinquency in a home of this type, two very interesting facts are seen. The first is that mothers of delinquents more often work than do mothers of nondelinquents. Secondly, the work habits of fathers of delinquents were generally considered poor. It seems reasonable to expect a boy coming from such home conditions to be strongly attracted to ways of acquiring "easy money."

7.   School Life. As a group, delinquents possess very strong feelings toward school. They usually manifest negative attitudes, low performances, poor behavior, and repeated truancies. Failure appears to mark the delinquent's school experience. Delinquents seem

to misbehave consistently in the school from the age of eight. Such behavior is extremely meaningful since it is in school that the youth must make his first real adjustment to society outside his immediate home. For the antisocial school act, truancy is more widespread than any other violation. According to Reckless and Smith, truancy was a recurring element among the delinquents in their study (1932, p. 161). A history of truancy is so often noted among criminals that it is called the "kindergarten of crime."

The implications of the foregoing statements are far-reaching since alert teachers can detect the initial signs of delinquency. If the school is considered a "society within a society," the manner in which the child adjusts to this novel, externally imposed authority is indicative of the way in which he will adjust in the future to the laws and mores of a wider society.

Finally, remember that the causes of delinquency are multiple, complex, and interactive. These causes emerge frequently in certain categories, for example, home, church, school, and community. Also, as a result of a combination of these causes, the delinquent shows some definite deviant symptoms, such as restlessness, aggressiveness, negative attitude toward school, early manifestation of misbehavior, and so forth.

CAUSES OF DELINQUENCY

Although few believe that poor health, poor environment, low intelligence, or similar factors are the sole cause of delinquent behavior, nevertheless there is a disturbing tendency to accept either social or organic factors as the particular cause of the delinquent act. While sociological conditions may be said to be the primary cause in an individual case, there may be another instance where a youth's trouble is organic (psychological and psychiatric). Although this may be true for isolated cases, it is hardly suitable for a comprehensive theory of causation. It is difficult to accept either of these classifications as being a substantial improvement over the "particularistic" school. It has expanded the theory but hardly improved it. What is lacking is the interaction between the two. This is the bridge that must be crossed if there is ever to be an acceptable theory of delinquency and crime causation.

To admit that there is a void to be filled should not discourage attempts to bring additional knowledge to this phase of delinquency study. If continued research is not forthcoming, it is almost impossible to foresee any improvement in present attempts at delinquency prevention and control. This is tantamount to acceptance of increasing delinquency as a necessary evil in our society. If general principles are lacking, how can we know what behavior or activity is delinquent-prone? How can we determine methods of prevention unless we are acting in accordance with a theory of causation? What is needed is research intended to form a theoretical structure that will permit wide interpretation and usage.

The delinquent may be studied, measured, analyzed, and compared, but there is a disturbing lack of recognition of his humanity. As a human, he is different—he is "other." This otherness separates him from all other elements of the universe and at once makes him the most puzzling and frustrating object that science can study. Even as the psychologist's estimate of human nature determines his learning theory, the sociologist's or psychologist's view of the delinquent will decide his theory of delinquency. So, the theorists see the human responding to the pressure of the environment in a purely determined manner; or as a representative of the animal kingdom driven by singularly primitive urges; or as man, because of his uniqueness, needing an interpretation on a higher level.

Let us for a moment move from the theory of causation and consider some concrete examples that will make clear to the reader the difficulties involved in arriving at such a theory, and perhaps equally as important, the need for such a theory.

Probably no reader would deny that a youngster's delinquency may be caused by a physical, intellectual, emotional, familial, or environmental factor. For the sake of argument, let us agree that any one of the above, or any combination, could be causative. We may further subdivide them into "within" and "without" agents:

Within	*Without*
physical	home
intellectual	church
emotional	general community
	school

In a particular case, a teacher, club worker, or similar person discovers that a boy is emotionally disturbed by home conditions—perhaps constant quarreling between the mother and father. Thus, a combination of emotional (within) and home conditions (without) is driving this youngster toward a display of aggressive behavior that could culminate in delinquency. We can visualize it as illustrated in Figure 12-1.

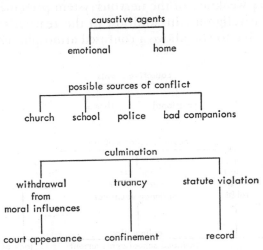

FIGURE 12-1. *Causative Agents: Negative*

While these are all negative aspects, nevertheless they represent only a fraction of the possible consequences. Undoubtedly, such a youth would wish to remove himself from his home environment. Consider the possible additional ramifications that may result: vagrancy, running away, loss of school time and lack of achievement, physical damage caused by malnutrition, drinking, and so forth. And to repeat, these are only some of the possible results.

Let us now examine more positive possibilities. Is there anything of a positive nature at work in such a youngster? Perhaps the material shown in Figure 12-2 could be influential.

Is this an oversimplification? Indeed it is! The home conditions can unquestionably be considered the cause of the youth's emotional troubles. What are these troubles? This would entail an involved report not needed or desired at this point. What must be considered important is which case more accurately represents such a disturbed youngster.

Who can say? Will all possible combinations of positive influences offset the negative, or vice-versa? Will the effect of bad companions and the conflict with authority in addition to the home conditions be decisive? Why may a brother or sister be able to withstand the onslaught of equally bad conditions and not be bothered? Was there any hereditary weakness of the nervous system present? Why did the help from the religious, in addition to the teacher's aid, give the needed incentive to rise above a confused atmosphere?

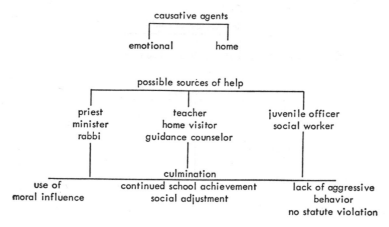

FIGURE 12-2. *Causative Agents: Positive*

How many combinations of relationships are possible—both positive and negative? Which is decisive? Why? Given the same conditions with a different youngster will the results be the same? These are the questions that must be faced; it is the answers to these questions that are lacking. How is it possible to place all such problems into a neatly packaged theory? A combination of methods must be employed. Sometimes it is the social in one instance and the organic in another; however, it is the individual who determines the approach. We cannot force the youngster to fit our idea of what the cause should be, but, again, it is the individual who determines the approach. Attempts at solution must consider these multiple and complex causes.

Should primacy be considered? No one should question the centrality of this concept of delinquency causation. But once again, primacy must be adequately understood in order that it may serve its purpose of explanation in an individual case. It is only when primacy is indiscriminately applied to all cases that it becomes self-defeating. The student allows his fascination for a particular theory or set of recurring factors to interfere with his objective assessment. Properly interpreted, however, the notion of primacy is valuable to the student of delinquency. Bloch and Flynn (1956, p. 74) state:

The subject of primacy is intriguing and difficult. Two things are involved: something that occurred in the past which may have been basic in producing a given problem, or something which is rooted in the personality now and which is the activating source of the disorder. Thus, in more technical terminology, primacy refers to either (1) the primary factor in a chronological causal sequence which may have been basic in contributing toward delinquency or (2) the basic syndrome, or combination of factors (personality, behavioral or environmental, considered separately or in clustered arrangements), which is significant in producing a problem of behavioral maladjustment or delinquency.

We must know the individual thoroughly and must understand the conditions surrounding him. Finally, we must make an effort to comprehend the underlying forces that have brought *this* individual to *this* situation. Figure 12-3 will help to clarify this statement.

FIGURE 12-3. *Figure and Ground*

Can Figure 12-3 be fully understood until the entire structure is completed? It was unintelligible until the face was completed. We must similarly examine the theories of causation. If one element is neglected, our analysis of cause and endeavor at prevention becomes one-sided and ineffective. A given factor may be the major determinant of delinquent behavior in a particular case. There must always be primacy but generalization of a factor is impossible. The search for primacy must include both the social and the organic.

Still, there are those who feel the search for cause is futile—that there is such a wide variety of delinquent behavior that any one explanation of cause is inadequate or even unreasonable. It seems as if there is an interesting parallel here that is often overlooked. The American school is doing a capable job of educating its youth. But it is doing this with no universally accepted theory of learning. In fact, the clash between theorists is frequent and sharp. The pages of psychological thought for these last several years are replete with the learning theories of Thorndike's Connectionism, Watson's Behaviorism, Classical Gestalt thought, plus its various interpretations, Hull's Behavioral System, and so forth. These theories are controversial and conflicting. However, as each theory contributes more knowledge about the learning process, the education within the school improves because of it.

The same should be true for delinquency theory. As the quest for causation continues, the added light it sheds will constantly improve present interpretations and procedures. We have not reached the terminal point—we have barely passed the starting line.

Thus, it behooves investigators into causation not to dismiss too quickly any theories that would bring welcome information to the theoretical frame of reference all are seeking. For example, learning is a process which results in the modification of behavior. Delinquency is modified behavior. Otherwise, we could not so designate it. Behavior is response to a stimulus or stimuli; psychologists usually think of behavior as all things that the human being does in thinking, feeling, acting, imagining, and so forth. How much of this behavior is learned; how much is instinctive? At least in behavior that can be categorized as learned—why was it learned? What were the learning conditions that resulted in this behavior? Learning certainly results in actions that are not improvements, and instead are maladjustments. Why? Could it be something in the learning process itself? Once again, a great deal depends upon the reader's view of the human being. Are his activities determined in some manner, or is he free to choose? The following question is intriguing: can analysis of the learning process also aid in the quest for delinquency causation?

Any definition of learning, irrespective of its psychological origin, implies the concept of change. But change results because of a tendency towards a greater good—goal achievement. What determines the greater good? Some psychologists would have us believe that a type of reflex action is instrumental; others merely use the term instinct; others say that man relies on habit in such a situation. Is such activity anything more than blind, unreasoning movement toward something (good or bad) which the individual thinks will satisfy his need? Does man not manifest a superiority to this type of activity? In other words, determinism is not the explanation of choice. If it were, there would be no difficulty in predicting man's behavior. By knowing the forces that act on man, we would also know man's reaction to these forces. All would agree that no such predictive device exists today—the complexity of man is not so simply expounded.

Therefore, any comparison of learning and delinquency must be made upon basic principles. The possibility that delinquency and crime may be better explained by learning cannot be overlooked since learning is behavioral modification and concerns itself with the acquisition of control over conduct. Such investigations could be a potentially fertile source of information about the cause of delinquency.

THE SCHOOLS

The relationship between the delinquent and the school is a vital adjustment for the youth, and one that is becoming ever more important in today's society. What can we expect of a boy or girl who is constantly exposed to strife, separation, bickering, drinking, and so forth? Teachers who have investigated the family background of a deviant youth sometimes marvel that the youngster is as good as he or she is.

More and more, the school is accepting functions once thought to be familial. Many teachers may question the advisability of such a trend—the duty of the school is to educate, not to raise a brood of children. But, if the father (or mother) is remiss in his duty, if the youngster has no one to whom he can turn—where will he go? The answer is obvious—to the street, to the corner, or to the penny arcade. The point is not being argued here that the school should adopt such a policy. The school *must* accept this responsibility; it has no choice. What teacher can turn away from a boy headed for trouble, and simply say, "That's not my worry"?

The best example that can be given to show the delinquent's need of help at school is the exhaustive study of the Gluecks (1952, pp. 69–80). The academic differences between the boys are striking. The importance of these differences is significant for, as they state (1952, p. 69):

Nevertheless, it is important to find out as much as possible about the school experiences of our two groups of boys; for, though schooling does not completely account for the structuring of character and the motivation of conduct, it can provide a sense of emotional satisfaction in the achievement of skills; it can arouse socially acceptable ambitions; it can place the pupil in contact with adults with whom he can identify and whom he can strive to emulate. On the other hand, it can leave scars in the psyche of the growing child which may well enhance the development of antisocial attitudes and defiance of all authority.

The importance of the school in its contact with youth is that it is the first test of his ability to adjust to a segment of society that represents authority with the ability to reward or punish. In their study of matched groups with regard to school, the Gluecks found that the delinquents were a year behind the nondelinquents in educational achievement. Why? Remember that all recent investigations had shown the delinquents and nondelinquents to be at about the same level of intelligence. The greater mobility of the delinquent seems to be one answer—not only correctional placement for the youth but mainly because of the family moving frequently. Thus, the youth encounters new situations, teachers, methods, and so forth, all of which contribute to his insecurity.

Slower progress through the grades and poorer scholarship all point toward greater antipathy of the delinquent for the school. Aside from intellectual inferiority, the delinquents stated they disliked school because it was not interesting, was too restrictive, and too routine.

What is extremely important about the delinquents' reactions to school is that nine in ten of the delinquents persistently and seriously misconducted themselves in class. The implications of this statement for delinquency prediction are staggering. Particularly, when it is noted that much of this school misbehavior occurred when the child was eight years or younger. Therefore, there is startling evidence that social adjustment, expressed in school misconduct, was faulty at an early age in the future delinquent. Mention must be made again of the school as a social institution, accepting new responsibilities. Can the school, today, avoid the liability that is so clearly thrust upon it?

Nevertheless, what can the schools do about the problem? The percentage of delinquents in any group is small; accordingly, we cannot shape our entire school program to them. But let any teacher answer this question—did not the presence of a norm violator greatly affect the quality of instruction offered—and did not the classroom atmosphere, rather than encourage learning, become tense and disturbed, and disrupt learning—did not the teacher change as a person while such a youth was in the classroom?

Unquestionably, the school must recognize and face the problem in a general sense and, at the same time, be prepared to adopt specific curricular changes.

First, what should be the general role of the school? Of the many institutions established to work with youth, undoubtedly, the one that contacts all youngsters in the community is the school. Schools have under their jurisdiction for many years each and every boy and girl in the community, and this single fact makes it very important in the battle against delinquency. Prediction, recognition, and rehabilitation (to a limited extent) all are possible for the school.

However, unless the administrator views the school as a factor in delinquency prevention, it becomes a "swinging door" for the youngster. The alert administrator has a twofold responsibility (J. F. Travers, 1962):

1. He must help warn the community about the dangers of teenage crime. This can be done by bringing his years of experience with the young, and his organizational ability to existing community youth services. If such services are nonexistent, then he must aid in their development. At this point, the administrator is probably questioning the time element. Where does a busy principal or superintendent find time for such activity? The answer is simple— he must. To think otherwise is short-sighted. This is one of the most important aspects of the school's prevention program. Isn't it much better to solve these problems before they reach the school?

2. There must be an extremely careful selection of teachers. Any district has its schools that house more than the average number of delinquency-prone youngsters. The teachers appointed to these

schools must be of special quality. They must desire to work with this type of youngster; they must be prepared for what they face; if possible, they should have had some previous experience working with this type of youngster, not necessarily teaching.

Too often, teachers are either forced to shift to another school, or are even lost to the profession because of their inability to cope with the unexpected.

Once teachers are assigned to such schools they must not be forgotten. A form of in-service training should be offered, if at all possible. Here, outside specialists should be brought into faculty meetings, and a common meeting ground of problems should be established. Also, where possible, the teachers should be encouraged to pursue graduate work in areas that would benefit themselves and their students, for example, sociology, delinquency, and abnormal psychology.

Ideally, it is hoped that in the not too distant future teacher-training institutions will enter the program. As undergraduates, certain students should be allowed to select electives that would give them theoretical preparation for their future work with the delinquency-prone—courses in abnormal psychology, educational sociology, guidance, delinquency, and criminology. Finally, a requirement should be that student-teaching be done in a school where there are many delinquency-prone youngsters. A student equipped in this manner will be prepared for future eventualities.

One last comment must be made about the significant position of the school in this battle. This is prediction. Much recent research has concentrated upon this vital element. Probably the best example of this work is the research of the Gluecks (1959, p. 118). In their investigation of 500 delinquents and 500 nondelinquents, they compared the two groups with respect to biological, psychological, psychiatric, socioeconomic, and cultural factors, and they attempted to isolate distinguishing characteristics between the two groups. From the several predictive devices they constructed, one, the social prediction table, has particular significance for the schools.

The social prediction scale is based upon five factors:

1. Discipline of boy by father
   Overstrict or erratic (72.5)
   Lax (59.8)
   Firm but kindly (9.3)

2. Supervision of boy by mother
   Unsuitable (83.2)
   Fair (57.5)
   Suitable (9.9)

3. Affection of father for boy
   Indifferent or hostile (75.9)
   Warm (33.8)

4. Affection of mother for boy
   Indifferent or hostile (86.2)
   Warm (43.1)

5. Cohesiveness of family
   Unintegrated (96.9)
   Some cohesion (61.3)
   Cohesive (20.6)

Each of the subdivisions is weighted for scoring purposes (the numerals in the parentheses are the percentages of delinquents found in each category during their study). The individual "scores" are summed, and, if a youngster has a total of less than 250, the prediction is made that the chances of delinquency are 16/100. For a total of over 250, the prediction is 79.1/100.

Although the values of such tables are easily seen, the inherent dangers are not. What is the result? The teacher and school could treat the youngster as a delinquent and he could soon live up to their dire belief. Would this boy become delinquent if there were no prediction tables? This is an interesting question. However, for the teacher, accurate prediction of delinquency-proneness could be a valuable tool in prevention.

Kvaraceus (1958, p. 17) also gives an interesting check list:

Delinquency Proneness Check List

Yes	No	Not Sure	
			1. Shows marked dislike for school.
			2. Resents school routine and restriction.
			3. Disinterested in school program.
			4. Is failing in a number of subjects.
			5. Has repeated one or more grades.
			6. Attends special class for retarded pupils.
			7. Has attended many different schools.

Delinquency Proneness Check List

Sure
Yes   No   Not

8. Intends to leave school as soon as the law allows.
9. Has only vague academic or vocational plans.
10. Has limited academic ability.
11. Is a child who seriously or persistently misbehaves.
12. Destroys school materials or property.
13. Is cruel and bullying on the playground.
14. Has temper tantrums in the classroom.
15. Wants to stop schooling at once.
16. Truants from school.
17. Does not participate in organized extra-curricular programs.
18. Feels he does not "belong" in the classroom.

So, the schools, if properly oriented and properly staffed, can function effectively in the fields of identification, treatment, and referral (J. F. Travers, 1960).

Moore (1961) summarizes the role and function of the school as follows:

1. There should be a close relationship between school and community.
2. School personnel and programs must be constantly evaluated for their effectiveness in combatting and improving undesirable behavior.
3. Better-trained personnel should be the school's goal.
4. Teachers should continue child-study to improve diagnosis and referral.
5. Guidance programs should be strengthened.
6. The case conference method should be adopted.
7. Flexible curriculum and teaching methods should be utilized by the school.
8. Marking, promotion, and the manner of discipline should be improved to avoid feelings of defeat and hostility.
9. There should be a close relationship between home and school.
10. The school must interpret its role in delinquency prevention to the school board and to the community in order to achieve maximum co-operation.

Consider the intellectual and emotional sides of the delinquent —he is capable of academic achievement but he hates school. If the school can offer one item that such boys (or girls) like, and do it successfully, the chances are great that drop-outs will dwindle and classroom problems ease. How can this one part of school life be discovered? Here the special facilities of the school should be thoroughly utilized. Can the guidance counselor help, or the psychologist or psychiatrist? Is there any person such a youth trusts? Only by obtaining as much information as possible, can clues be found that may aid the pupil. An obstacle then arises. How can this be worked into the curriculum? The only possible reply is flexibility. A curriculum should certainly not be flexible to the point of chaos. However, it is better to move a boy away from a given track to capitalize on his interest, aid his adjustment, and prevent one or two trouble makers from disrupting an entire class.

As capable as the school is, there are some cases that cannot be handled within the school setting. They are simply beyond help by the average teacher or guidance department. They must be referred to a special agency and removed from the classroom as quickly as possible. There should be no sense of failure about this. Rather, the teacher should feel a sense of achievement because an early, accurate prediction was made. This implies a thorough knowledge of the facilities available within the system.

Shulman (1961, p. 701) summarizes the unlimited possibilities for growth, given a dynamic learning situation when he says:

The classroom is a community possessing many dynamic potentialities for social growth. It is usually co-educational, and includes children of many different ethnic and racial backgrounds and sometimes of a wide socio-economic range, with differences in interests and experiences. Used both as a cultural deposit and resource and as a living group for social interaction, the classroom has importance in the handling of problem behavior, both as a group situation and as a setting for differential treatment approach to individuals.

CONCLUSION

During this decade the school will encounter a spreading number of unique disciplinary cases. These are not the normal kind which may be solved by the school alone, or by cooperation between home and school. The exceptional maladjustments which the delinquent or the delinquency-prone exhibit are increasing and, in many classrooms, are poisoning the educational milieu for effective learning.

Such problems are destroying teaching careers for those who are not forewarned, and they are also paralyzing classroom teaching and learning. If teachers are provided with basic knowledge about the situation—the nature and extent of delinquency—they will be better equipped to initiate remedial action in the early stages of delinquency, and they will be better able to carry on with the school's business, that is, learning.

If the reader recalls the characteristics of the learning process—motivation, obstacle, stimuli, perception, responses, and goal—he will understand that each characteristic is frustrated by a tense and disturbed learning environment. Desirable motivation is quickly lost when a classroom is constantly distracted and youngsters are wondering what will happen next. The obstacles to goal achievement are of such magnitude that the goal is obscure and lost in the turmoil of disorder. The individual's perception of environmental stimuli becomes so vague and confused that his reaction pattern becomes disorganized. He cannot focus upon the goal; finally, he becomes bewildered. He wonders what is the goal of this class?

The effect of poor classroom management upon the learning process cannot be exaggerated; if the conditions for learning are unfavorable, it is the rare student who truly learns. Thus, it is the teacher's duty to be ready for the multiplicity of crises that will inevitably face him. How he reacts to them will determine his success as a teacher, and his ability to facilitate the delicate process of learning.

Bibliography

Adams, Jack A. "The Relationship Between Certain Measures of Ability and the Acquisition of a Psychomotor Criterion Response." *Journal of General Psychology,* 1957, **56**, 121–134.

Adams, Jack A. "Motor Skills." *Annual Review of Psychology,* 1964, **15**, 181–202.

Ahmann, J. Stanley, and Glock, Marvin D. *Evaluating Pupil Growth.* (2nd ed.) Boston: Allyn and Bacon, 1963.

Allport, Gordon W. *Pattern and Growth in Personality.* New York: Holt, Rinehart and Winston, 1961.

Anastasi, Anne. *Differential Psychology.* New York: Macmillan, 1958.

Anderson, G. Lester, and Gates, Arthur I. "The General Nature of Learning," *The Forty-ninth Yearbook of the National Society for the Study of Education.* Part I. Chicago: University of Chicago Press, 1950.

Anderson, John E. "The Relation of Emotional Behavior to Learning," *The Forty-first Yearbook of the National Society for the Study of Education.* Part II. Bloomington, Ill.: Public School Publishing Company, 1942.

Angelino, H., Dollins, J., and Mech, E. V. "Trends in the Fears and Worries of School Children as Related to Socio-economic Status and Age." *Journal of Genetic Psychology,* 1956, **89**, 263–276.

Asimov, Isaac. *The Human Brain: Its Capacities and Functions.* Boston: Houghton Mifflin, 1964.

Ausubel, David P. "The Use of Advanced Organizers in the Learning and Retention of Meaningful Verbal Material." *Journal of Educational Psychology,* 1960, **51**, 267–272.

Ausubel, David P., and Blake, Elias, Jr. "Proactive Inhibition in the Forgetting of Meaningful School Material." *Journal of Educational Research,* 1958, **52**, 145–149.

Ausubel, David P., and Fitzgerald, Donald. "Meaningful Learning and Retention: Intrapersonal Cognitive Variables." *Review of Educational Research,* 1961, **31**, 500–510.

Baller, Warren R., and Charles, Don C. *The Psychology of Human Growth and Development.* New York: Holt, Rinehart and Winston, 1961.

Bayles, Ernest E. "The Idea of Learning as Development of Insight." *Educational Theory,* 1952, 2, 65–71.

Beilen, Harry. "Teachers' and Clinicians' Attitudes Toward the Behavior Problems of Children: A Reappraisal." *Child Development,* 1959, 30, 9–25.

Berelson, Bernard, and Steiner, Gary A. *Human Behavior: An Inventory of Scientific Findings.* New York: Harcourt, Brace, 1964.

Berlyne, Daniel E. "The Influence of Complexity and Novelty in Visual Figures on Orienting Responses." *Journal of Experimental Psychology,* 1958, 55, 289–296.

Berlyne, Daniel E. *Conflict, Arousal, and Curiosity.* New York: McGraw-Hill, 1960.

Berlyne, Daniel E. "Emotional Aspects of Learning." *Annual Review of Psychology,* 1964, 15, 115–142.

Best, Charles, and Taylor, Norman. *The Living Body.* New York: Henry Holt and Company, 1944.

Bigge, Morris L. *Learning Theories for Teachers.* New York: Harper and Row, 1964.

Bigge, Morris L., and Hunt, Maurice P. *Psychological Foundations of Education.* New York: Harper and Row, 1962.

Blair, Glenn M. "How Learning Theory is Related to Curriculum Organization." *Journal of Educational Psychology,* 1948, 39, 161–166.

Blair, Glenn Myers, Jones, R. Stewart, and Simpson, Ray H. *Educational Psychology.* (2nd ed.) New York: Macmillan, 1962.

Bloch, Herbert A., and Flynn, Frank T. *Delinquency: The Juvenile Offender in America Today.* New York: Harper and Brothers, 1956.

Bloom, Benjamin S. (ed.) *Taxonomy of Educational Objectives, Handbook I: Cognitive Domain.* New York: David McKay, 1956.

Bloom, Benjamin S., and Broder, Lois J. "Problem-Solving Processes of College Students." *Supplementary Educational Monographs,* No. 73, 1–31. Chicago: University of Chicago Press, 1950.

Boehm, George A. W. "Can People Be Taught Like Pigeons?" *Fortune,* 1960, 62, 176–179, 259–266.

Book, William F. "The Psychology of Skill." University of Montana Publications in Psychology, Bulletin, No. 53, *Psychological Series No. 1,* 1908, 7–100.

Boring, Edwin G. *A History of Experimental Psychology.* (2nd ed.) New York: Appleton-Century-Crofts, 1950.

Bossing, Nelson L. *Teaching in Secondary Schools.* Boston: Houghton Mifflin, 1952.

Braun, John R. (Ed.) *Contemporary Research in Learning.* Princeton, N.J.: D. Van Nostrand, 1963.

Bridges, Katherine, M. B. "A Genetic Theory of Emotions." *Journal of Genetic Psychology,* 1930, 37, 514–527.

Bridges, Katherine, M. B. "Emotional Development in Early Infancy." *Child Development,* 1932, 3, 324–334.

Brown, W. P. "Conceptions of Perceptual Defence." *British Journal of Psychology, Monograph Supplement,* No. 35, 1961, 107 pp.

Brubacher, John S. *A History of the Problems of Education.* New York: McGraw-Hill, 1947.

Bruner, Jerome S. *Contemporary Approaches to Cognition.* Cambridge: Harvard University Press, 1957.

Bruner, Jerome S. *The Process of Education.* Cambridge.: Harvard University Press, 1960.

Bruner, Jerome S. "The Act of Discovery." *Harvard Educational Review,* 1961, 31, 21–32.

Bruner, Jerome S., Goodnow, Jacqueline, J., and Austin, George A. *A Study of Thinking.* New York: John Wiley, 1956.

Bugelski, B. R. *The Psychology of Learning.* New York: Henry Holt and Company, 1956.

Bugelski, B. R. *The Psychology of Learning Applied to Teaching.* Indianapolis: Bobbs-Merrill, 1964.

Buros, Oscar K. (Ed.). *Fifth Mental Measurements Yearbook.* Highland Park, N.J.: Gryphon Press, 1959.

Burt, Cyril L. *The Young Delinquent.* New York: Appleton-Century, 1933.

Buswell, Guy. "Educational Theory and the Psychology of Learning." *Journal of Educational Psychology,* 1956, 47, 175–184.

Cannon, W. B. *Bodily Changes in Pain, Hunger, Fear, and Rage.* (rev. ed.) New York: Appleton and Company, 1929.

Carmichael, Leonard (Ed.). *Manual of Child Psychology.* (2nd ed.) New York: John Wiley, 1954.

Chase, R. A., Harvey, S., Standfast, S., Rapin, I., and Sutton, S. "Studies on Sensory Feedback: I. Effect of Delayed Auditory Feedback on Speech and Keytapping." *Quarterly Journal of Experimental Psychology,* 1961, 13, 141–152.

Chase, R. A., Rapin, I., Gilden, L., Sutton, S., and Guilfoyle, C. "Studies on Sensory Feedback: II. Sensory Feedback Influences on Keytapping Motor Tasks." *Quarterly Journal of Experimental Psychology,* 1961, 13, 153–167.

Commins, W. D., and Fagin, Barry. *Principles of Educational Psychology.* (2nd ed.) New York: Ronald Press, 1954.

Conant, James Bryant. *The Education of American Teachers.* New York: McGraw-Hill, 1963.

Cronbach, Lee J. *Essentials of Psychological Testing.* (2nd ed.) New York: Harper and Row, 1960.

Cronbach, Lee J. *Educational Psychology.* (2nd ed.) New York: Harcourt, Brace, 1963.

Crowder, Norman A. "Automatic Tutoring by Means of Intrinsic Programming." In Galanter, E. (Ed.) *Automatic Teaching: The State of the Art.* New York: John Wiley, 1959.

Davis, R. "The Role of 'Attention' in the Psychological Refractory Period." *Quarterly Journal of Experimental Psychology,* 1959, 11, 211–220.

Davis, R. "Choice Reaction Times and the Theory of Intermittency in Human Performance." *Quarterly Journal of Experimental Psychology*, 1962, **14**, 157–166.

Deese, James. *The Psychology of Learning*. New York: McGraw-Hill, 1952.

De Rivera, J. "Some Conditions Governing the Use of the Cue-Producing Response as an Explanatory Device." *Journal of Experimental Psychology*, 1959, **57**, 299–304.

Dewey, John. *How We Think*. Boston: D. C. Heath, 1910.

Dukes, W. F. "Psychological Studies of Values." *Psychological Bulletin*, 1955, **52**, 24–50.

Duncker, Karl. "On Problem Solving," *Psychological Monographs*, 1945, No. 5, **58**, 1–14.

Ebel, Robert L. "Measurement and the Teacher." *Educational Leadership*, 1962, **20**, 20–24.

Estes, W., Koch, S., MacCorquodale, D., Meehl, P., Mueller C., Schoenfeld, W. and Verplanck W. *Modern Learning Theory*. New York: Appleton-Century-Crofts, 1954.

Feldhusen, John F., and Klausmeier, Herbert J. "Anxiety, Intelligence, and Achievement in Children of Low, Average, and High Intelligence." *Child Development*, 1962, **33**, 403–409.

Findley, Warren G. "Purposes of School Testing Programs and Their Efficient Development." *The Sixty-second Yearbook of the National Society for the Study of Education*. Part II. Chicago: University of Chicago Press, 1963.

Fiske, D. W., and Maddi, S. R. *Functions of Varied Experience*. Homewood, Ill.: Dorsey, 1961.

Flavell, John H. *The Developmental Psychology of Jean Piaget*. Princeton, N.J.: D. Van Nostrand, 1963.

Fleishman, E. A. "Testing for psychomotor abilities by means of apparatus tests." *Psychological Bulletin*, 1953, **50**, 241–262.

Fleishman, E. A., and Parker, J. F., Jr. "Factors in the Retention and Relearning of Perceptual-motor Skill." *Journal of Experimental Psychology*, 1962, **64**, 215–226.

Fuller, John L. *Motivation: A Biological Perspective*. New York: Random House, 1962.

Furst, Edward J. *Constructing Evaluation Instruments*. New York: Longmans, Green, 1958.

Gage, N. L. (Ed.). *Handbook of Research on Teaching*. Chicago: Rand McNally, 1963.

Garrison, Karl C., Kingston, Albert J., and McDonald, Arthur S. *Educational Psychology*. (2nd ed.) New York: Appleton-Century-Crofts, 1964.

Gerberich, J. Raymond. *Specimen Objective Test Items*. New York: Longmans, Green, 1956.

Gerberich, J. Raymond, Greene, Harry A., and Jorgensen, Albert N. *Measurement and Evaluation in the Modern School*. New York: David McKay, 1962.

Getzels, J. W. "Creative Thinking, Problem Solving, and Instruction," *The Sixty-third Yearbook of the National Society for the Study of Education*. Part I. Chicago: University of Chicago Press, 1964.

Getzels, J. W., and Jackson, P. W. *Creativity and Intelligence: Exploration with Gifted Students.* New York: John Wiley, 1962.

Ghiselin, Brewster (Ed.). *The Creative Process.* New York: New American Library, 1955.

Glickman, S. E. "Reinforcing Properties of Arousal." *Journal of Comparative and Physiological Psychology,* 1960, **53**, 68.

Glueck, Sheldon, and Glueck, Eleanor. *Unraveling Juvenile Delinquency.* New York: The Commonwealth Fund, 1950.

Glueck, Sheldon, and Glueck, Eleanor. *Delinquents in the Making.* New York: Harper and Brothers, 1952.

Glueck, Sheldon, and Glueck, Eleanor. *Predicting Delinquency and Crime.* Cambridge: Harvard University Press, 1959.

Good, Carter V. *Introduction to Educational Research.* New York: Appleton-Century-Crofts, 1959.

Good, Carter V. (Ed.). *Dictionary of Education.* New York: McGraw-Hill, 1959.

Goodenough, F. L., "Anger In Young Children," *Institute of Child Welfare Monograph Series, No. 9.* Minneapolis: University of Minnesota Press, 1931.

Guilford, J. P. "A System of the Psychomotor Abilities." *American Journal of Psychology,* 1958, **71**, 164–174.

Guilford, J. P. "Three Faces of Intellect." *American Psychologist,* 1959, **14**, 469–479.

Guthrie, E. R. "Conditioning: A Theory of Learning in Terms of Stimulus, Response and Association," *The Forty-first Yearbook of the National Society for the Study of Education.* Part II. Bloomington, Ill.: Public School Publishing Company, 1942.

Guthrie, E. R. *The Psychology of Learning.* (rev. ed.) New York: Harper and Brothers, 1952.

Harlow, Harry F. "The Formation of Learning Sets." *Psychological Review,* 1949, **56**, 51–65.

Harlow, Harry F. "Performance of Catarrhine Monkeys on a Series of Discrimination Reversal Problems." *Journal of Comparative Physiological Psychology,* 1950, **43**, 231–239.

Harlow, Harry F. "Mice, Monkeys, Men, and Motives." *Psychological Review,* 1953, **60**, 23–32.

Harlow, Harry F. "Motivation as a Factor in the Acquisition of New Responses." In Brown, J. S., *et al. Current Theory and Research in Motivation.* Lincoln, Nebraska: University of Nebraska Press, 1953.

Harlow, Harry F., Harlow, Margaret K., and Meyer, Donald R. "Learning Motivated by a Manipulation Drive." *Journal of Experimental Psychology,* 1950, **40**, 228–234.

Harris, Chester W. (Ed.) *Encyclopedia of Educational Research.* (3rd ed.) New York: Macmillan, 1960.

Harrison, J. S. "Psychological Refractoriness and the Latency Time of Two Consecutive Motor Responses." *Research Quarterly of the American Association of Health, Physical Education and Recreation,* 1960, **31**, 590–600.

Hartmann, G. W. "The Field Theory of Learning and Its Educational Consequences," *The Forty-first Yearbook of the National Society for the Study of Education*. Part II. Bloomington, Ill.: Public School Publishing Company, 1942.

Healy, William, and Bronner, Augusta. *New Light on Delinquency, and Its Treatment*. New Haven: Yale University Press, 1936.

Hebb, D. O. "Studies of the Organization of Behavior: I. Behavior of the Rat in a Field Orientation." *Journal of Comparative Psychology*, 1938, **25**, 333–352.

Hebb, D. O. *The Organization of Behavior*. New York: John Wiley, 1949.

Hebb, D. O. "The Motivating Effects of Exteroceptive Stimulation." *American Psychologist*, 1958, **13**, 109–113.

Heffernan, Helen. "Evaluation—More Than Testing." *National Education Association Journal*, 1958, **47**, 227–229.

Heidbreder, Edna. *Seven Psychologies*. New York: Appleton-Century, 1933.

Heidbreder, Edna, Bensley, Mary L., and Ivy, Margaret. "The Attainment of Concepts: IV. Regularities and Levels." *Journal of Psychology*, 1948, **25**, 229–329.

Hermanowicz, Henry J. "Problem Solving as Teaching Method." *Educational Leadership*, 1961, 18, 229–306.

Heron, Woodburn. "Cognitive and Physiological Effects of Perceptual Isolation." In Solomon, Philip, *et al.* (Eds.), *Sensory Deprivation*. Cambridge: Harvard University Press, 1961.

Hilgard, Ernest R. *Theories of Learning*. New York: Appleton-Century-Crofts, 1956.

Hilgard, Ernest R. *Introduction to Psychology*. (3rd ed.) New York: Harcourt, Brace, 1962.

Hilgard, Ernest R. "The Place of Gestalt Psychology and Field Theories in Contemporary Learning Theory," *The Sixty-third Yearbook of the National Society for the Study of Education*. Part I. Chicago: University of Chicago Press, 1964.

Hill, Winfred. "Contemporary Developments Within Stimulus-Response Learning Theory," *The Sixty-third Yearbook of the National Society for the Study of Education*. Part I. Chicago: University of Chicago Press, 1964.

Himmelweit, Hilde T. "Social Status and Secondary Education Since the 1944 Act: Some Data for London." In Glass, David V. (Ed.), *Social Mobility in Britain*. New York: Free Press, 1954.

Hull, C. L. "Conditioning: Outline of a Systematic Theory of Learning," *The Forty-first Yearbook of the National Society for the Study of Education*. Part II. Bloomington, Ill.: Public School Publishing Company, 1942.

Hull, C. L. *Principles of Behavior: An Introduction to Behavior Theory*. New York: Appleton-Century-Crofts, 1943.

Hull, C. L. *Essentials of Behavior*. New Haven: Yale University Press, 1951.

Hull, C. L. *A Behavior System*. New Haven: Yale University Press, 1952.

Humphreys, Lloyd G. "Transfer of Training in General Education." *Journal of General Education*, 1951, **5**, 210–216.

Hunt, J. McVey. *Intelligence and Experience*. New York: Ronald Press, 1961.

Inhelder, B., and Piaget, Jean. *The Growth of Logical Thinking from Childhood to Adolescence*. New York: Basic Books, 1958.

Jacob, Philip E. *Changing Values in College*. New York: Harper and Brothers, 1957.

James, William. *The Principles of Psychology*. New York: Henry Holt and Company, 1890.

Janis, I. L., and King, B. T. "The Influence of Role Playing on Opinion Change." *Journal of Abnormal and Social Psychology*, 1954, **49**, 211–218.

Jersild, Arthur T. *Child Psychology*. (5th ed.) Englewood Cliffs, N.J.: Prentice-Hall, 1963.

Jersild, A. T., and Holmes, F. B. "Children's Fears," *Child Development Monographs*, No. 20. New York: Teachers College, Columbia University, 1935.

Jersild, A. T., and Holmes, F. B. "Methods of Overcoming Children's Fears." *Journal of Psychology*, 1935, **1**, 282–283.

Judd, Charles H. "The Relation of Special Training to General Intelligence." *Educational Review*, 1908, **36**, 28–42.

Katz, D. *Gestalt Psychology, Its Nature and Significance*. New York: Ronald Press, 1950.

Katz, D., and Stotland, E. "A Preliminary Statement to a Theory of Attitude Structure and Change." In Koch, S. (Ed.), *Psychology: A Study of a Science*, Vol. III: *Formulations of the Person and the Social Context*. New York: McGraw-Hill, 1959.

Kearney, N. C. *Elementary School Objectives*. New York: Russell Sage Foundation, 1953.

Kelly, William A. *Educational Psychology*. (4th ed.) Milwaukee: The Bruce Publishing Co., 1956.

Kersh, B. Y. "The Motivating Effect of Learning by Directed Discovery." *Journal of Educational Psychology*, 1962, **53**, 93–100.

King, Bert T. and Janis, Irving L. "Comparison of the Effectiveness of Improvised Versus Non-improvised Role-playing in Producing Opinion Changes." *Human Relations*, 1956, **9**, 177–186.

Kingsley, Howard L. and Garry, Ralph. *The Nature and Conditions of Learning*. (2nd ed.) Englewood Cliffs, N.J.: Prentice Hall, 1957.

Klausmeier, Herbert. *Learning and Human Abilities: Educational Psychology*. New York: Harper and Brothers, 1961.

Kleinsmith, L. J., and Kaplan, S. "Paired-associate Learning as a Function of Arousal and Interpolated Interval." *Journal of Experimental Psychology*, 1963, **65**, 190–193.

Koffka, Kurt. *Principles of Gestalt Psychology*. New York: Harcourt, Brace, 1935.

Köhler, Wolfgang. *Gestalt Psychology*. (rev. ed.) New York: Liveright, 1947.

Köhler, Wolfgang. "Gestalt Psychology Today." *American Psychologist*, 1959, **14**, 727–734.

Kolesnik, Walter B. *Educational Psychology*. New York: McGraw-Hill, 1963.

Kragh, U. "Subliminal Gradation in the Visual Field." *Scandinavian Journal of Psychology*, 1962, **3**, 165–170.

Krathwohl, David R., Bloom, Benjamin S., and Masia, Bertram B. *Taxonomy of Educational Objectives, Handbook II: Affective Domain*. New York: David McKay, 1964.

Krech, David, and Crutchfield, Richard. *Elements of Psychology*. New York: Alfred A. Knopf, 1958.

Kubzansky, Philip E., and Leiderman, P. Herbert. "Sensory Deprivation: An Overview." In Solomon, Philip, *et al.* (Eds.), *Sensory Deprivation*. Cambridge: Harvard University Press, 1961.

Kvaraceus, William C. *Juvenile Delinquency and the Schools*. New York: The World Book Co., 1945.

Kvaraceus, William C. *The Community and the Delinquent*. New York: The World Book Co., 1954.

Kvaraceus, William C. *Juvenile Delinquency*. Washington: National Education Association, 1958.

Lane, Robert E. *Political Life: Why People Get Involved in Politics*. New York: Free Press, 1959.

Lashley, K. S. *Brain Mechanisms and Intelligence*. Chicago: University of Chicago Press, 1929.

Leeper, Robert. "Cognitive Processes." In Stevens, S. S. (Ed.), *Handbook of Experimental Psychology*. New York: John Wiley, 1951.

Lewan, P. C., and Stotland, E. "The Effects of Prior Information on Susceptibility to an Emotional Appeal." *Journal of Abnormal and Social Psychology*, 1961, **63**, 636–638.

Lewin, Kurt. *A Dynamic Theory of Personality*. Translated by Adams, Donald K., and Zener, Karl E. New York: McGraw-Hill, 1935.

Lewin, Kurt. *Principles of Topological Psychology*. Translated by Heider, F., and Heider, G. M. New York: McGraw-Hill, 1936.

Lewin, Kurt. "Field Theory and Learning," *The Forty-first Yearbook of the National Society for the Study of Education*. Part II. Bloomington, Ill.: Public School Press, 1942.

Lewin, Kurt. "Forces Behind Food Habits and Methods of Change." *National Research Council Bulletin*, 1943, No. 108, 35–65.

Lindquist, E. F. (Ed.) *Educational Measurement*. Washington, D.C.: American Council on Education, 1951.

Longwell, Sarah G. "Progressive Change in Simple Action: A Study of Learning." *American Journal of Psychology*, 1938, **51**, 261–282.

Lumsdaine, Arthur A. "Instruments and Media of Instruction." In Gage, N. L. (Ed.) *Handbook of Research on Teaching*. Chicago: Rand McNally, 1963.

Maccoby, Eleanor E. "Developmental Psychology." *Annual Review of Psychology*, 1964, **15**, 203–250.

Maslow, A. H. "A Theory of Human Motivation." *Psychological Review*, 1943, **50**, 370–396.

Maslow, A. H. *Motivation and Personality*. New York: Harper and Brothers, 1954.

Mayer, Martin. *The Schools*. New York: Harper and Brothers, 1961.

McCarthy, Dorothea. "The Language Development of the Preschool Child." *Institute of Child Welfare Monograph Series*, No. 4. Minneapolis: University of Minnesota Press, 1930.

McClelland, David C. *Studies In Motivation*. New York: Appleton-Century-Crofts, 1955.

McDonald, Frederick J. *Educational Psychology*. San Francisco: Wadsworth Publishing Co., 1959.

McDonald, Frederick J. "The Influence of Learning Theories on Education (1900–1950)," *The Sixty-third Yearbook of the National Society for the Study of Education*. Part I. Chicago: University of Chicago Press, 1964.

McGeoch, John A., and Irion, Arthur L. *The Psychology of Human Learning*. (rev. ed.) New York: Longmans, Green, 1952.

Mihanovich, Clement S. *Principles of Juvenile Delinquency*. Milwaukee: Bruce Publishing Co., 1950.

Miller, K. M., and Biggs, J. B. "Attitude Change Through Undirected Group Discussion." *Journal of Educational Psychology*, 1958, 49, 224–228.

Miller, Neal E., and Dollard, John. *Social Learning and Imitation*. New Haven: Yale University Press, 1941.

Moore, Bernice M. "The Schools and The Problems of Juvenile Delinquency: Research Studies and Findings." *Crime and Delinquency*, 1961, 7, 201–212.

Moscovici, Serge. "Attitudes and Opinions." *Annual Review of Psychology*, 1963, 14, 231–260.

Mouly, George J. *Psychology for Effective Teaching*. New York: Holt, Rinehart and Winston, 1960.

Mowrer, O. H. *Learning Theory and Behavior*. New York: John Wiley, 1960.

Mowrer, O. H. *Learning Theory and the Symbolic Process*. New York: John Wiley, 1960.

Murray, Henry A. *Explorations in Personality*. New York: Oxford University Press, 1938.

Obrist, W. D. "Skin Resistance and Electroencephalographic Changes Associated with Learning." (Doctoral Thesis, Northwestern University, Evanston, Illinois, 1950).

Olds, J., Travis, R. P., and Schwing, R. C. "Topographic Organization of Hypothalamic Self-stimulation Functions." *Journal of Comparative and Physiological Psychology*, 1960, 53, 23–32.

Overton, Richard K. *Thought and Action: A Physiological Approach*. New York: Random House, 1959.

Page, Ellis B. "Teacher Comments and Student Performance: A Seventy-four Classroom Experiment in School Motivation." *Journal of Educational Psychology*, 1958, 49, 173–181.

Pavlov, I. P. *Conditioned Reflexes*. London: Oxford University Press, 1927.

Peck, Robert F., and Havighurst, Robert, J. *The Psychology of Character Development*. New York: John Wiley, 1960.

Pepinsky, Harold, and Borow, Henry. "Research Frontier." *Journal of Counseling Psychology*, 1961, 7, 272–277.

Piaget, Jean. *The Psychology of Intelligence*. London: Routledge and Kegan, Paul, 1950.

Piaget, Jean. *The Origins of Intelligence in Children*. New York: International Universities Press, 1952.

Plutchik, Robert. *The Emotions: Facts, Theories, and a New Model*. New York: Random House, 1962.

Pressey, Sidney L. "A Simple Apparatus Which Gives Tests and Scores—and Teaches," *School and Society*, 1926, **23**, 373–376.

Pressey, Sidney L. "Development and Appraisal of Devices Providing Immediate Automatic Scoring of Objective Tests and Concomitant Instruction," *Journal of Psychology*, 1950, **29**, 417–447.

Ragsdale, C. E. "How Children Learn the Motor Types of Activities," *The Forty-ninth Yearbook of the National Society for the Study of Education*. Part I. Chicago: University of Chicago Press, 1950.

Rapp, Albert. "The Experimental Background of the Problems of Learning." *Classical Journal*, 1945, **40**, 467–480.

Rasmussen, E. A., and Archer, E. J. "Concept Identification as a Function of Language Pretraining and Task Complexity." *Journal of Experimental Psychology*, 1961, **61**, 437–441.

Reckless, Walter, and Smith, Mapheus. *Juveline Delinquency*. New York: McGraw-Hill, 1932.

Redl, Fritz, and Wineman, David. *Children Who Hate*. New York: Free Press, 1951.

Rhine, R. J. "A Concept-formation Approach to Attitude Acquisition." *Psychological Review*, 1958, **65**, 362–370.

Ross, C. C., and Stanley, Julian C. *Measurement in Today's Schools*. (3rd ed.) Englewood Cliffs, N.J.: Prentice-Hall, 1954.

Ruch, G. M. *The Objective or New-Type Examination*. Chicago: Scott, Foresman, 1929.

Russell, David. *Children's Thinking*. Boston: Ginn, 1956.

Sandiford, Peter. "Connectionism: Its Origin and Major Features," *The Forty-first Yearbook of the National Society for the Study of Education*. Part II. Bloomington, Ill.: Public School Publishing Company, 1942.

Sarason, Irwin G. "Test Anxiety, General Anxiety, and Intellectual Performance." *Journal of Consulting Psychology*, 1957, **21**, 485–490.

Sawry, James M., and Telford, Charles W. *Educational Psychology*. (2nd ed.) Boston: Allyn and Bacon, 1964.

Schlosberg, H. "Three Dimensions of Emotion." *Psychological Review*, 1954, **61**, 81–88.

Schneirla, T. C. "An Evolutionary and Developmental Theory of Biphasic Processes Underlying Approach and Withdrawal." In Jones, M. R. (Ed.), *Nebraska Symposium on Motivation*. Lincoln, Nebraska: University of Nebraska Press, 1959.

Sears, Pauline S., and Hilgard, Ernest R. "The Teacher's Role in the Motivation of the Learner," *The Sixty-third Yearbook of the National Society for the Study of Education*. Part I. Chicago: University of Chicago Press, 1964.

Sherif, M., and Hovland, C. I. *Social Judgment*. New Haven: Yale University Press, 1961.

Sherman, M. "The Differentiation of Emotional Responses in Infants: I. Judgments of Emotional Response from Motion Picture Views and from Actual Observation." *Journal of Comparative Psychology*, 1927, **7**, 265–384.

Shore, E., and Sechrest, L. "Concept Attainment as a Function of Number of Positive Instances Presented." *Journal of Educational Psychology*, 1961, **52**, 303–307.

Shulman, Harry Manuel. *Juvenile Delinquency in American Society*. New York: Harper and Brothers, 1961.

Skinner, B. F. The Behavior of Organisms: *An Experimental Analysis*. New York: Appleton-Century-Crofts, 1938.

Skinner, B. F. *Walden Two*. New York: Macmillan, 1948.

Skinner, B. F. *Science and Human Behavior*. New York: Macmillan, 1953.

Skinner, B. F. "The Science of Learning and the Art of Teaching." *Harvard Educational Review*, 1954, **25**, 86–97.

Skinner, B. F. *Verbal Behavior*. New York: Appleton-Century-Crofts, 1957.

Sloane, William. "The Lincoln-Oseretsky Motor Development Scale." *Genetic Psychology Monographs*, 1955, **51**, 183–252.

Smedslund, Jan. "Educational Psychology." *Annual Review of Psychology*, 1964, **15**, 251–276.

Smith, Louis M., and Hudgins, Bryce. *Educational Psychology: An Application of Social and Behavioral Theory*. New York: Alfred A. Knopf, 1964.

Smith, P. C., and Smith, O. W. "Veridical Perceptions of Cylindricality: A Problem of Depth Discrimination and Object Identification." *Journal of Experimental Psychology*, 1961, **62**, 145–152.

Solomon, Philip (Ed.). *Sensory Deprivation*. Cambridge: Harvard University Press, 1961.

Spence, Kenneth W. *Behavior Theory and Conditioning*. New Haven: Yale University Press, 1956.

Spranger, Edward. *Types of Men*. Translated by Pigons, P. J. W. (5th ed.) Halle: Neumeyer, 1928.

Stalnaker, John M. "The Essay Type of Examination." In Lindquist, E. F. (Ed.), *Educational Measurement*. Washington, D.C.: American Council on Education, 1951.

Stanley, Julian C. *Measurement in Today's Schools*. (4th. ed.) Englewood Cliffs, N.J.: Prentice-Hall, 1964.

Stendler, Celia B. *Readings in Child Behavior and Development*. (2nd ed.) New York: Harcourt, Brace, 1964.

Stevens, S. S. (Ed.). *Handbook of Experimental Psychology*. New York: John Wiley, 1951.

Strong, E. K., Jr. "Satisfactions and Interests." *American Psychologist*, 1958, **13**, 449–456.

Suchman, J. Richard. "Inquiry Training in the Elementary School." *Science Teacher*, 1960, **27**, 42–47.

Suchman, J. Richard, and Aschner, Mary Jane. "Perceptual and Cognitive Development." *Review of Educational Research*, 1961, **31**, 451–462.

Sullenger, Earl. *Social Determinants in Juvenile Delinquency*. New York: John Wiley, 1936.

Symonds, Percival M. "Classroom Discipline." *Teachers College Record*, 1949, **51**, 147–158.

Thompson, R. and Malin, C. F. "The Effect of Neocortical Lesions on Retention of a Successive Brightness Discrimination in Rats." *Journal of Comparative Physiological Psychology*, 1961, **54**, 326–328.

Thompson R., and Massopust, L. C. "The Effect of Subcortical Lesions on Retention of a Brightness Discrimination in Rats." *Journal of Comparative Physiological Psychology*, 1960, **54**, 488–496.

Thorndike, Edward Lee. *The Psychology of Learning*. Vol. II. New York: Teachers College, Columbia University, 1913.

Thorndike, Edward Lee. *The Fundamentals of Learning*. New York: Teachers College, Columbia University, 1932.

Thorndike, Edward Lee, and Woodworth, R. S. "The Influence of Improvement in One Mental Function Upon the Efficiency of Other Functions." *Psychological Review*, 1901, 8, 247–261, 384–395, 553–564.

Thorndike, Robert L., and Hagen, Elizabeth. *Measurement and Evaluation in Psychology and Education*. New York: John Wiley, 1955.

Thorpe, L. P., and Schmuller, A. M. *Contemporary Theories of Learning with Applications to Education and Psychology*. New York: Ronald Press, 1954.

Time Magazine, Inc. (March 24, 1961), No. 13, **77**, 38.

Torrance, E. Paul. "Explorations in Creative Thinking." *Education*, 1960, 81, 216–220.

Torrance, E. Paul. *Guiding Creative Talent*. Englewood Cliffs, N.J.: Prentice-Hall, 1962.

Townsend, Edward, and Burke, Paul. *Learning for Teachers*. New York: Macmillan, 1962.

Travers, John F. "Schools and Delinquency." *Education*, 1960, 80, 364–368.

Travers, John F. "A Critical Problem of the School: Delinquency." *The Clearing House*, 1962, **36**, 337–342.

Travers, John F. "The Last Defense." *Education*, 1963, **83**, 440-42.

Travers, John F., and Davis, Russell G. "A Study of Religious Motivation and Delinquency." *The Journal of Educational Sociology*, 1961, **34**, 205–220.

Travers, John F., and Davis, Russell G. "Etude du mobile religieux et de la delinquence." *Social Compass*, 1961, **4**, 327–345.

Travers, Robert M. W. *How to Make Achievement Tests*. New York: The Odyssey Press, 1950.

Travers, Robert M. W. *Educational Measurement*. New York: Macmillan, 1955.

Travers, Robert M. W. *Essentials of Learning*. New York: Macmillan, 1963.

Tyler, Ralph. *Basic Principles of Curriculum and Instruction*. Chicago: University of Chicago Press, 1950.

Tyler, Ralph. "Educational Measurement: A Broad Perspective." *The National Elementary Principal*, September, 1961, 8–13.

Vinacke, William E. *The Psychology of Thinking*. New York: McGraw-Hill, 1952.

Walker, E. I. "Memory Storage as a Function of Arousal and Time." (Presented at American Association of the Advancement of Science Meeting, Philadelphia, 1962.)

Watkins, Ralph K. *Techniques of Secondary School Teaching*. New York: Ronald Press, 1958.

Watson, John B. *Behaviorism.* (rev. ed.) New York: W. W. Norton, 1930.

Weidmann, Charles C. "Written Examination Procedures." *Phi Delta Kappan,* 1933, **16**, 78–83.

Weidmann, Charles C. "Review of Essay Test Studies." *Journal of Higher Education,* 1941, **12**, 41–44.

Weiss, W., and Lieberman, B. "The Effects of Emotional Language on the Induction and Change of Opinions." *Journal of Social Psychology,* 1959, **50**, 129–141.

Welford, A. T. "Evidence of a Single-channel Decision Mechanism Limiting Performance in a Serial Reaction Task." *Quarterly Journal of Experimental Psychology,* 1959, **11**, 193–210.

Wertheimer, Max. *Productive Thinking.* (rev. ed.) New York: Harper and Brothers, 1959.

Westie, F. R., and DeFleur, M. L. "Autonomic Responses and Their Relationship to Race Attitudes." *Journal of Abnormal and Social Psychology,* 1959, **58**, 340–347.

Wiener, Morton. "Word Frequency or Motivation in Perceptual Defense." *Journal of Abnormal and Social Psychology,* 1955, **51**, 214–218.

Witkin, H. A., Dyk, R. B., Faterson, H. F., Goodenough, D. R., and Karp, S. A. *Psychological Differentiation.* New York: John Wiley, 1962.

Wolman, Benjamin. *Contemporary Theories and Systems in Psychology.* New York: Harper and Brothers, 1960.

Woodruff, Asahel, D. *The Psychology of Teaching.* (2nd ed.) New York: Longmans, Green, 1948.

Woodworth, R. S. *Contemporary Schools of Psychology.* New York: Ronald Press, 1948.

Woolridge, Dean E. *The Machinery of the Brain.* New York: McGraw-Hill, 1963.

Wrightstone, J. Wayne. "Tests and What They Test." *National Education Association Journal,* 1958, **47**, 221–223.

Wundt, Wilhelm. *Physiological Psychology.* (5th ed.) New York: Macmillan, 1910.

Wynne, L. C., and Solomon, R. L. "Traumatic Avoidance Learning: Acquisition and Extinction in Dogs Deprived of Normal Peripheral Autonomic Function." *Genetic Psychology Monographs,* 1955, **52**, 241–284.

Zigler, E. "A Measure in Search of a Theory?" *Contemporary Psychology,* 1963, **8**, 133–135.

Index